THOMAS PAINE
Liberator

Romney Pinx.   Wright Sculp.

THOMAS PAINE.

Courtesy of Mr. Morton Pennypacker

THOMAS PAINE
Liberator

By

FRANK SMITH

With a frontispiece

FREDERICK A. STOKES COMPANY
NEW YORK   MCMXXXVIII

Printed in the United States of America

CONTENTS

THOMAS PAINE

Liberator

CHAPTER I

One of the Swinish Multitude

OF ALL the men who fought in the revolutionary movement of the eighteenth century, none deserves a larger and more lasting place in the democratic tradition than Thomas Paine. He was one of the greatest idealists in the history of man's struggle for a better world. There is a legend that Franklin once said, "Where liberty is, there is my country," and Paine replied, "Where liberty is not, there is my country." Wherever the cause of liberty was to be served, he served it by heroic pamphlets and heroic deeds. He blazed the path of independence for America, headed the revolutionary forces in England, and championed the French Revolution before the world. On two continents this tall, gaunt, strong-featured man, with his devastating attacks on privilege and injustice, was hailed as a Messiah by the embattled millions whose aspirations he expressed.

During his lifetime his courageous and inexhaustible idealism brought upon him powerful enemies, who made his life a hazardous and unenviable one. They set mobs upon him in the streets, burned him in effigy, and connived at his imprisonment for almost a year in the shadow of the guillotine. He weathered it all as part of the fight and died as he had lived, believing in the dignity of common men and the sacredness of struggle in their behalf. Since his death in 1809 he has had other enemies, who have sought to tarnish his memory and by implication the things for which he stood.

I

They have appealed to bigotry and prejudice by distorting as fiendish doctrine the simple message of his pamphlet, *The Age of Reason,* which voices faith in one God and pleads for universal freedom of worship. The vilifications of a century are condensed in Theodore Roosevelt's ignoble jibe at Paine—"the filthy little atheist."

Even to the millions who have daily benefited from his labors for democracy and who believe in his ideals, he is "the eagle that is forgotten." Americans who would be ashamed to admit ignorance about Washington and Jefferson know little or nothing about Paine, whose pamphlets are the best expression of what these men fought for.

"Where Facts are sufficient," Paine has said, "Arguments are useless." The plain historic facts provide his claim to the grateful recognition of the democratic peoples.

The western world of two hundred years ago, in which Thomas Paine was born, lay under the dead hand of the privilege of birth. The details varied from country to country, but the essential pattern was the same. Out of the feudal past had come the divinely ordained categories—king, nobles, clergy, bourgeoisie, artisans, peasants. The anointed king stood apart, a servant of God. The nobles and the upper clergy recruited from their ranks formed the privileged orders. They owned the land and freely enjoyed the pleasures of life, having no burdens beyond a theoretical responsibility to their inferiors. The other ninety-five percent of the population were socially lumped together as the unprivileged order—in Burke's view, "the swinish multitude." They did the work and paid the rents and tithes and taxes.

By the middle of the eighteenth century the privileged orders had become a gigantic parasitism, especially in the advanced countries like England and France. Many a resourceful tradesman, proud of making his own way in spite of governmental restrictions, came to resent the fact that political power and economic privilege belonged to the worthless descendants of cutthroats and court lackeys. Many a hard-hit artisan and peasant were inclined to blame their misery on the social arrangement. In England, after the deposition of James II in 1688, the landed aristocracy combined with subservient monarchs imported from Holland or Hanover to consolidate a régime of privilege over the people. In France, however, an autocratic Bourbon ruled, and jealous aristocrats gave ear to philosophers and reformers whose message would ultimately sweep out the king and the aristocrats too. The Englishmen Newton and Locke had achieved an intellectual revolution by discovering a systematic and unmysterious universe whose laws could be ascertained by human reason. Their French disciples—Montesquieu, Voltaire, Diderot, Rousseau, and others—turned the light of rationalism upon the whole range of social problems. In generalized treatises and witty parables they exposed the rottenness of an unreasonable and oppressive society and elaborated utopias of social freedom for all men. Life and thought were pointing to a new order of things.

The old régime did not yield peacefully. It had to be overthrown. A cycle of revolutions began with the revolt of the American subjects of British aristocracy in 1776 and reached a climax in the warfare of republican France against aristocratic Europe. In this revolutionary atmosphere philosophic refinements were not directly serviceable. Men who could barely read the letters of Liberty, Fraternity, Equality, rushed into the conflict for a better world. Propaganda had to be simple, clear-cut, unfalteringly optimistic, attuned to the dynamic impulses of common men. In the person of Thomas Paine the ferment of the times cast up the supreme propagandist of the epoch. In Paine's explosive personality the concepts of the philosophers were transformed into the spiritual ammunition of marching armies. What Madame de Staël said about Rousseau applies a thousandfold more properly to Paine: he originated nothing, he inflamed everything. Paine's pamphlets, particularly *Common Sense* and *The Rights of Man,* embody the fighting idealism of the revolutionary period in America and Europe.

For his rôle as a world-revolutionist Paine had a thirty-seven-year training in the England of George II and George III. A mere nobody, unconscious of his historic destiny, he left little record of these formative years.

He was born on January 29, 1737, the son of a stay-maker in Thetford, a village in Norfolk. His father was a Quaker; his mother, Frances Cocke, was a member of the Church of England, and he and his sister Margaret were baptized in the Established Church. Of his mother Paine has nothing to say; common tradition reported her to be "of sour temper." The son has left some tender tributes, however, to his Quaker father.

Paine's formal education was slight. Up to the age of thirteen he attended the Free Grammar School, a charity school at Thetford. Beyond that he was essentially self-taught.

But a thoughtful boy could find the true lessons of Thetford outside the classroom, in the injustice of pillory and gibbet, and in the corruption of farcical "elections" at the Guildhall, where the thirty-one voters of Thetford periodically sold two seats in the House of Commons to the highest bidder. Further, the ancient capital of East Anglia gave

4

silent reminders that no social arrangement was inviolable. The boy Paine might climb the hundred feet up Castle Hill, the highest earthwork in East Anglia, there to speculate perhaps on its origin with the shadowy Britons or on the Norman fortress which had once stood there. He might poke through the ruins of the great Cluniac Abbey, or gaze at the desolate nunnery which had begun to fall apart in the very year of his birth. Everywhere the dumb tokens of a vanished power, teaching the transitoriness of institutions. Men had made and unmade them at will to suit their needs. They could do so again.

To these daily hints to radicalism came the reenforcement of First Day at the Quaker meeting-house. Quakerism was built on the dignity of the common man. The inspired cobbler Fox had preached that all men were equal before the one God, to Whom alone should be given all honors and all titles. Here was a democratic creed, and a creed for democracy.

And Quakerism blended democracy with a social purpose, a fervid humanitarianism in harmony with the divine plan, "God's unspeakable love to the world." The Quakers were foremost in ameliorating the lot of the poor, the oppressed, the enslaved, and even dumb animals.

Yet there was an obstacle in Quakerism, an obstacle that might paralyze the energies of a radical in a revolutionary age—political passivity. Barclay's dictum, "It is not lawful for Christians to resist evil or to war or fight in any case," meant in effect to English Quakers a complete divorce from political action. Through bitter experience with a hostile society and in the maelstrom of revolution, Paine was finally to bid farewell to the proud quietism of the Quakers.

At thirteen he became apprenticed to his father in the

5

business of making stays. It was not a satisfactory arrangement. The boy was restless. At the grammar school he had listened eagerly to lurid stories of life on a man-of-war, as told by his master, the Reverend William Knowles. And he had picked up a natural history of Virginia and had dreamed of that remote country beyond the seas, with its wild forests and wilder men. He ran away. At sixteen, he tells us, "I began to be the carver of my own fortune." Paine went on board the privateer *Terrible,* but was taken off by "the affectionate and moral remonstrances" of his distracted father. Tearful embraces, repentance, resolves—and then, after a few more months, final escape from Thetford on the privateer *King of Prussia.*

The appetite for naval adventure was quickly surfeited. Paine was soon a derelict roaming through the haunts of the homeless in London; and later a journeyman maker of stays with a Mr. Morris in Hanover Street. In spare hours he attended the lectures of the celebrated Martin and Ferguson at the Royal Society. Here came the new revelation of science dispensed by the disciples of Newton. God Himself, Paine learned, was a Great Mechanic who had in the inconceivable past created a world machine and set it in motion by immutable laws. And there was no secret in the universe to which man could not penetrate with the divine gift of human reason.

In 1758 Paine was making stays in Dover; a year later, in Sandwich. Here he married a servant-girl named Mary Lambert. With the burdens of life doubled, he followed the trail of work from one town to another. In 1760 his wife died. Staymaking now began to appear more and more irksome and uncertain. A few months of study, and Paine qualified as an officer of the excise. At twenty-five he began

6

the new career of measuring beer barrels and chasing smugglers.

The life of an excise collector was not an enviable one. The pay was poor, the work unpopular. The age was notorious for heavy drinking, when every pub flaunted the boast that it could make all comers drunk for a penny, dead drunk for twopence. The bartenders and their customers looked with no love on the suspicious agent who came snooping into cellar and attic and behind partitions; especially when the rich, who brewed their own beer, were exempt from the tax.

Officer Paine did not seek martyrdom for the glory of King George. He became lax in riding the rounds, and fell into the common practise of making entries for goods and establishments which he had not inspected. In 1765 he was discharged.

Another unhappy bout with staymaking, in Norfolk and Leicestershire. In desperation he now turned to teaching English at twenty-five pounds a year (half his excise salary) in a Mr. Noble's academy in Goodman's Fields, London. Teaching palled. Paine thought of seeking ordination in the Church of England, but he lacked the necessary Latin training. Outside the Established Church, the Methodists welcomed lay preachers in the saving of souls. In the spiritual confusion that accompanies economic misery, Paine engaged in occasional preaching in the open fields about London. Here he found other lay preachers—tailors, housepainters, coal-heavers—by the magic of homely, vivid, emotional language swinging their common auditors out of mundane troubles into spiritual ecstasies. As the gaunt schoolmaster addressed the hurly-burly crowds, he could not help learning some fundamental truths about the workings or human nature—truths that would stand him in good stead when his pamphlets would play upon the passions of unseen millions in behalf of secular freedom.

Paine had applied for reinstatement in the excise in the summer of 1766. His letter to the Board contains only five sentences, but it is a monument of his bleak straits and spiritual abjectness. He reminds the Board that "No complaint of the least dishonesty or intemperance ever appeared against me." And always the same refrain: "in humble obedience," "humbly beg," "I humbly hope," "I humbly presume," "I am, your honour's most dutiful humble servant." The testimony of Thetford Meeting-house is drowned in the cruel necessity of cringing and scraping to the "Honourable Sirs." Paine was reinstated, and in February, 1768, resumed his excise duties in Lewes, Sussex, where he was to live and work for six years.

He took a room in Lewes with a Quaker tobacconist named Samuel Ollive. In July, 1769, Ollive died, leaving a widow and a daughter Elizabeth. Two years later Paine married Elizabeth, ten years his junior. Now came the problem of maintaining this household of three on the proceeds of the tobacco shop and the excise. Life began to pinch more acutely than ever.

The shop could not be improved. The new tobacconist had no talent for driving the petty bargains of retail business. But perhaps the Government would increase the wages in the excise. He would appeal to the big-wigs—not for charity, but for his due. The wages of the excise officers had been fixed over a hundred years before. Should they continue at this figure forever, in the face of a constantly increasing currency and rising prices? Instruments of oppression, the excisemen were themselves the victims of a pro-

8

gressive oppression. In this common plight the need was for united action. Paine began his public career in the winter of 1772-1773 as a labor organizer. He rounded up the excisemen and wrote their plea to parliament, *The Case of the Officers of Excise.*

"Humbly addressed to the members of both houses of parliament," the petition is an anxious and labored document in human misery. The form is excessively careful, with separate sections on the low salary, the menace of corruption, and the high qualifications of the officers, interspersed with appropriate quotations from the Bible and Shakespeare. Glints of the later Paine flash out: "Where Facts are sufficient, Arguments are useless," "The most effectual Method to keep Men honest is to enable them to live so," "There is a powerful Rhetorick in Necessity." Otherwise the petition speaks for a submissive group who had no resort beyond the bent back of supplication.

Paine came up to London to distribute some of the four thousand copies printed by his fellow excisemen. His simple faith in the Government was doomed to disappointment. There was no profit for the landed gentry and their parliamentary representatives in the plea of the moneyless collectors of revenue. The petition and the lobbyist were contemptuously rejected.

Frustrated, chagrined, embittered, Officer Paine returned to Lewes. The business of the tobacco shop went from bad to worse, and he had to flee into hiding to avoid indefinite confinement in debtors' prison. His Majesty's Government, catching at any pretext against the trouble-maker, now discharged him again, April 8, 1774. Soon his creditors were placarding Lewes: "To be sold by auction, on Thursday the 14th of April, and following day, all the household furniture, stock in trade and other effects of Thomas Pain, grocer and tobacconist, near the West Gate, in Lewes: Also a horse, tobacco and snuff mill, with all the utensils for cutting tobacco and grinding off snuff; and two unopened crates of cream-coloured stone ware." On top of these difficulties, his wife separated from him in June.

This marital rift is the great unsolved enigma in Paine's personal history. Not that it is necessary to search for mysterious reasons behind Mrs. Paine's dissatisfaction. Here was a husband who failed consistently to bring home enough daily bread; who dashed off to London to fight for the excisemen and left his own business to ruin; who could not manage a small shop, and talked grandly about the needs of humankind. But Paine's stony silence about his domestic affairs has lent countenance to the rumor that his wife left him because he was impotent. Some support for this rumor may lie in the fact that, in an open free-living society, surprisingly few charges of sexual immorality in Paine's later life are made, and that none can be substantiated. His phenomenal revolutionary energy itself might be interpreted as the expression of such impotence. In the absence of conclusive evidence, however, this whole matter must remain one of mere speculation.

At the age of thirty-seven Thomas Paine was at the rockbottom of English society. He had no job, no money, no property, no wife, no children—no fortune and no hostages to fortune. He could turn anywhere, and do as he pleased.

Dark, brooding days—and a swift resolve. He would go to America, the new world, the vast land of opportunity, the El Dorado of his boyhood dreams. Paine returned to London and pushed himself into the notice of the colonial agent, Benjamin Franklin, for a letter of introduction. Franklin looked the applicant over and liked him. Perhaps the talents of this vigorous talker and amateur scientist might be of some use in America. Franklin wrote a few lines introducing Paine to his son-in-law Richard Bache in Philadelphia: "The bearer Mr. Thomas Paine is very well recommended to me as an ingenious worthy young man. He goes to Pennsylvania with a view of settling there. I request you to give him your best advice and countenance, as he is quite a stranger there. If you can put him in a way of obtaining employment as a clerk, or assistant tutor in a school, or assistant surveyor, of all of which I think him very capable, so that he may procure a subsistence at least, till he can make acquaintance and obtain a knowledge of the country, you will do well, and much oblige your affectionate father."

Confident that a letter from the great Franklin was an open-sesame to America, Paine scraped together enough money for a ticket as cabin passenger on the *London Packet,* under Captain Cooke. He did not come to these shores as the lowliest immigrant, for the stifling hold contained a hundred and twenty indentured servants, willing to sell themselves into temporary servitude for the passage and ultimate freedom in the colonies. For nine weeks the *Packet* bounced its human freight over the Atlantic. A "putrid fever," breaking out among the indentured servants, quickly infested the whole ship. Five bodies were thrown overboard, and no more than five persons were free of the disease. Paine was severely stricken. "I had very little hopes that the Capt. or myself would live to see America." Paine had not been reticent about himself. When the *Packet* landed in Philadelphia, November 30, 1774, those who were able to leave without assistance told the curious throng at the wharves that back in the ship, too sick to get up, was a fellow bearing a letter from Franklin. On this an enterprising physician, Dr. Kearsley, sent up two men with a chaise, and the heavily swathed, half-dead fellow was carried down. So Thomas Paine began his American adventure.

CHAPTER II

AMERICANIZATION

PAINE had to stay indoors for six weeks to recover from the voyage. In mid-January of 1775 he stepped forth to meet America.

Before him unfolded Penn's snow-covered "great town" set amid the forest at the juncture of the Schuylkill and the Delaware. Philadelphia was the largest, richest, most refined, most urbane of colonial towns. The wide, straight, regular streets bore the singular names adopted by the founder in his aversion to "man worship"—High, Broad, First, Second, Pine, Spruce. And on these streets moved the daily pageant of American life—New England merchants, New York patroons, Virginia aristocrats, Quakers rich and poor, blanketed redskins, black men in chains.

To Paine, Philadelphia symbolized the rich possibilities of America. Though the homes of the mechanic and the merchant were not on the same pattern, he could not see the extreme contrasts that had made the British cities a tragic setting. Any enterprising man, regardless of his origin, could hack out a decent and respectable livelihood. Somewhere in this brave new world would surely be a good berth for the new immigrant.

Paine presented his letter to Bache, through whom he got small tutoring jobs in private families. In a few days he was approached by a local publisher and bookseller, the Scotchman Robert Aitken, to edit a projected monthly, *The*

Pennsylvania Magazine. This was something new, but Paine promptly accepted.

He took his editorship seriously and made a great success of *The Pennsylvania Magazine*. With the second number the subscriptions jumped from six hundred to fifteen hundred. At the subscription price of one shilling per month, and with an editor whose salary did not average more than fifty pounds a year, Aitken could begin to feel that he had struck a pretty good thing. .

No more attractive specimen of the monthly periodical has come down to us from eighteenth-century America. Besides Paine's contributions, successive issues contained literary sketches by Francis Hopkinson, philosophical essays by President Witherspoon of Princeton College, copious extracts from rare books and periodicals printed in the mother country—the whole decorated with engravings and garnished with "Select Poetry."

In the early issues Paine's own articles, contributed under various pseudonyms, dealt largely with practical science—*A Mathematical Question Proposed, Description of a New Electrical Machine, Useful and Entertaining Hints*. He also wrote moralizing essays—*Anecdotes of Alexander the Great* and *Reflections on the Life and Death of Lord Clive*. The same motif runs through both essays: How futile is the glory of kings! How are the mighty fallen!

There is an absence in these numbers of any articles dealing with the political problem. In the growing revolutionary struggle between the colonies and the mother country, the publisher Aitken was attempting the neutral stratagem of pleasing all sides by pleasing none. Nor did the editor wish to upset the apple-cart of his own newly found economic security. In the first issue he rejects a con-

14

tribution by Amicus as politically dangerous. And in February: "As it is our design to keep a peaceable path, we cannot admit R. S.'s and M. S.'s political pieces." In his letter to Franklin, March 4, 1775, Paine discusses the causes of "putrid fever," the magazine, his personal success, and Franklin's relatives in America, but completely ignores politics. The measure of his political interest is found in his heavy verses *On the Death of General Wolfe,* written in Lewes, which he now published in the March magazine:

> In a mouldering cave where the wretched retreat,
>   Britannia sat wasted with care;
> She mourned for her Wolfe, and exclaim'd against fate
>   And gave herself up to despair.

Not a line is added about new and stronger reasons for Britannia to waste with care, or about a greater than Wolfe appearing in the form of Colonel Washington.

At the beginning of 1775 the colonists themselves did not look forward to a radically new order of things. For more than a hundred years, immature, disunited, and afraid of the neighboring French, they had submitted to the selfish regulations of the British aristocracy. The colonial manufacture of hats, cloth, and wrought iron had been repressed; foreign goods in competition with the British had to pay heavy import taxes in the colonies; colonial sugar, tobacco, cotton, and furs could be exported only to England; import and export trade could move only in British or colonial ships.

But when the end of the French and Indian Wars, in 1763, removed the French danger, a thriving country came into conflict with a foreign overlordship burdened by debts and determined on enforcing and elaborating the profitable old arrangements. At first the colonists had sent passionate but respectful protests against the policy that regulated and restrained every detail of their economic life in the interest of English industry. Legalistic spokesmen had rummaged through charters and statutes, to prove in ponderous black and white that British liberties were being violated by Parliament and the ministry. Otis, Dickinson, and others had drawn hair-splitting distinctions between external and internal regulation, between direct and indirect taxation; and they had yearned for the good old days under "the glorious line of Brunswick."

Protests failing, shots were fired, East India tea dumped into the ocean; but few of the most zealous patriots looked beyond some kind of ultimate reconciliation. Even when the Intolerable Acts of 1774 clamped down upon Massachusetts, only a small minority in the other scattered colonies took the alarm. A conservative Continental Congress gathered at Philadelphia in September and adjourned in October after composing petitions and reluctantly forming a general economic boycott against the oppressor. When Paine landed in Philadelphia a month later, the controversy had simmered down to group discussions on street corners and in taverns.

After all, the conflict with England was in the first instance a merchants' affair, and rubbed most severely at the revenue gates and in shops and warehouses. It seemed to Paine, as he says in *Crisis VII,* "a kind of law-suit, in which I supposed the parties would find a way either to decide or settle it." But, glaring in the light of common day, stood a more atrocious abomination—chattel slavery. Across the street from Aitken's book store, in an open shed fronting the London Coffee House, was the chief slave market in Philadelphia. To a local paper, the *Journal* of March 5, Paine sent off a vehement protest against "our traders in men." He indignantly asks the colonists "with what consistency, or decency they complain so loudly of attempts to enslave them, while they hold so many hundred thousands in slavery; and annually enslave many thousands more, without any pretence of authority, or claim upon them?" The article is naïvely encumbered with the authority of "a succession of eminent men," and bears throughout evidences of the widely read anti-slavery pamphlets by Anthony Bénézet and Dr. Rush. Still, it was original enough to be annoying to extreme patriots.

Paine, however, was not destined to be a voice crying in the eighteenth-century American wilderness in behalf of the black man. The sweep of events hurled him into the colonial struggle, and everything else was forgotten.

Respectable neutrality in America came to a sudden dramatic end. In the late afternoon of April 24, a breathless rider jumped off his horse at the City Tavern in Philadelphia. He came from Trenton, and bore shocking news of a bloody skirmish with His Majesty's troops at Lexington on the 19th. A dream lay dead on that blood-stained Massachusetts field—the dream of peaceful and dignified reunion. England had thrown down the gage of battle: Submit or Perish! Philadelphia swung into the fight. On the morning of the 25th, without a formal summons, eight thousand persons massed at the State House and flung defiance at England by resolving upon an armed association in defense of their "property, liberty, and lives." Even the local Tories were shaken, and many young Quakers bound themselves to learn the arts of war. Soon the commons west of the city were covered in the early morning and late

17

afternoon with marching and counter-marching Associators, flashing before the excited spectators their gaudy new uniforms and large cartouch boxes painted LIBERTY. It was all spectacular, volcanic, inspiring.

What could a man do? Paine had not come to America to wage war. He was not habituated to think in terms of violence and bloodshed. It was grievous to have the country set on fire about his ears almost the moment he got into it and found a good job. But under the passionate influence of Lexington he threw in his lot with the Americans. Dating his conversion from this time, Paine says in *Common Sense:* "No man was a warmer wisher for a reconciliation than myself, before the fatal nineteenth of April 1775, but the moment the event of that day was made known, I rejected the hardened, sullen-tempered Pharaoh of England for ever; and disdain the wretch, that with the pretended title of FATHER OF HIS PEOPLE can unfeelingly hear of their slaughter, and composedly sleep with their blood upon his soul."

The pulsating course of events now strengthened Paine's emotional acceptance of the colonial cause. On May 5, Franklin came home from a last futile effort at His Majesty's Court, took command of the Pennsylvania party of action, and began with diplomatic indirectness to turn America toward the vision of independence. On the 10th, a militant Continental Congress convened at Philadelphia and proclaimed to the world that the Americans had taken up arms for the protection of their property and would lay them down "when Hostilities shall cease on the Part of the Aggressors, and all Danger of their being renewed shall be removed, and not before." To the May issue of *The Pennsylvania Magazine* Paine contributed *Reflections on*

18

Titles, a furious tirade against the arrogance of a privileged caste. It is the ancient Quaker testimony against worldly honors, imbued with a new positive social direction. "When I reflect on the pompous titles bestowed on unworthy men, I feel an indignity that instructs me to despise the absurdity. The *Honourable* plunderer of his country, or the *Right Honourable* murderer of mankind, creates such a contrast of ideas as to exhibit a monster rather than a man. Virtue is inflamed at the violation, and sober reason calls it nonsense."

Rapidly the City of Brotherly Love was being transformed into the headquarters of a nation at war. Troops drilled, Congress organized for a military campaign, Washington stepped forward. "The clergy here," exults John Adams, "thunder and lighten every Sabbath." In the life-and-death struggle now pending for liberty, the Quaker tenet of non-resistance came to appear to Paine more and more anachronistic, insincere, anti-social—a sophistical cover of Toryism. In *The Pennsylvania Magazine* for July, writing as A Lover of Peace, Paine expresses the sentiments of so many other Quakers whom the grim necessities of the hour were driving out of absolute pacifism. If all men were peace-loving Quakers, he argues, there would be no war; but "We live not in a world of angels." What is the true Christian duty before "the portrait of a parent red with the blood of her children"—a parent that has just begun her devouring career? "I am thus far a Quaker, that I would gladly agree with all the world to lay aside the use of arms, and settle matters by negotiation; but unless the whole will, the matter ends, and I take up my musket and thank heaven he has put it in my power."

Now America rushed past the inexorable mile-posts of

19

revolution—Bunker Hill, Ticonderoga, Crown Point, sea-fighting off the New England coast. With every new event the fighting morale of the capital city strengthened. Feeding on the militancy of the Continental Congress, communing with Franklin and the Philadelphia radicals, Paine began to regard *The Pennsylvania Magazine* as a trivial and absurd undertaking. By midsummer Aitken and Paine had parted company. Some "literary gentlemen" recommended that Paine attempt a periodical of his own, but he was not interested. He was here, there, everywhere, testing the colonial pulse in Philadelphia, thrilling to brawls, mass meetings, the carting of obstreperous Tories through the streets. To the local press he wrote urging a national association to manufacture saltpeter, indispensable ingredient of gunpowder. In October news came to Philadelphia that King George had rejected the last petition of the colonies. What should America do now? It was a fateful moment, and for Paine a fateful signal. He set about the labor of the next two months, the writing of a nation-wide argument for absolute independence—*Common Sense*. For himself, he had a few shillings in his pockets, and Providence would take care of the rest.

CHAPTER III

Common Sense

BEFORE *Common Sense* the Americans did not look upon their struggle as a war for independence. Even the bloody trail of 1775 had not been seen as leading to a complete separation. Washington, Jefferson, and John Adams still clung to the shaky hope of reconciliation, and at the opening of 1776 the Continental Congress was firmly committed against independence.

Excepting Franklin, the American leaders had kept their eyes closed to the distressing prospect of a free country. Once the British yoke was thrown off, what unity could be achieved from the American hodgepodge of nationalities, religions, and occupations? How could the stage-coach and the ferry-boat bring together the scattered communities buried in the almost trackless forest and among the treacherous rivers of a country a thousand miles long? Tories conjured up nightmares of the general confusion, civil wars, and Cromwellian despotism that would spring from this revolt against the powers appointed by God. The possibilities of independence were too ominous even for the Whigs to speculate about.

But the logic of events was bound to bring into vogue a more adventurous kind of thinking. After 1775 no other program but independence was reasonable. For nearly a year the Americans had been fighting on the battlefield against the imperial enemy, which thought to subdue these upstarts as ruthlessly as Clive had subdued the natives of India. Talk of reconciliation grew empty and ironic while the air swelled with the shots, the curses and groans of grappling armies. Actually, reconciliation would no longer do. America must find an objective more commensurate with her sacrifices. She was using the revolutionary method of violence, she must make the revolutionary demand for freedom. Congress was already exercising the basic functions of a sovereign power—waging war, making contracts, negotiating with foreign countries. And yet, excepting furtive suggestions in newspapers and private letters, the revolutionary appeal had not been made.

America needed a new epoch-making voice. She needed a revolutionist who could demonstrate that independence was the only sound solution, the only one worth fighting for; who could cut the cords of prejudice that still bound many Americans to an imaginary ideal British system; who was not limited by the habits of a lifetime to one province, but could stress the unifying grievances and common energies of the whole people; who could speak to the potential fighters, the farmers and mechanics, in their own plain language; who could stir thousands to the high daring of treason by the passion with which he flung his own life into the gamble for independence. In short, America needed Thomas Paine and *Common Sense*.

The Spirit of '76 found its first vital utterance on the 9th of January with the appearance of *Common Sense*. It had been difficult to find a printer, but through the mediation of Dr. Rush one Robert Bell had accepted the pamphlet. Although *Common Sense* appeared anonymously, it was an appalling enterprise, for this writer proclaimed an extreme position in extreme terms. One year of American

22

life had wrought a miracle. The wandering Quaker, the Royal Society student, the rejected exciseman, the Philadelphia editor—all had merged and risen into the supreme agitator of the revolutionary age.

The leading ideas of *Common Sense* are three: the English system is corrupt, despotic, and contemptible; reconciliation with such a system is a foolish and delusive recompense for American suffering; America should be and can become an independent republic. These ideas are conveyed with logic, with sentiment, with homely vigor, with impassioned eloquence, until they lodge in the reader's heart with all the uncritical certainty of fighting slogans.

The rationalistic basis of *Common Sense* was not original with Paine. He found ready to hand an intellectual system with which to sublimate the struggle for living needs. The colonial lawyers, while emphasizing the rights of British subjects under the British constitution, had also mentioned a broader principle—the natural rights of humanity. This latter argument was the only one suitable to the revolutionary phase. Natural rights formed the theoretical justification of the eighteenth-century warfare against privileged aristocracy, as common to that age as the concept of the class struggle during the subsequent epoch of capitalism. The notion of a pre-social state and pre-social rights, which had figured in speculation as far back as Aristotle, precisely met the philosophic requirements of the war for liberation against arbitrary despotism. In the religio-political upheavals of the seventeenth century, natural rights had been mixed with Biblical sanctions, as in Milton's *Tenure of Kings and Magistrates;* while a secular theory was reasserted after the revolution of 1688 in the classic formulation of Locke's *Second Treatise on Government.* In *Common Sense* Paine

grasped both handles, the religious and the purely natural—
"the authority of scripture" and "the equal rights of nature."
In this way he won assent to independence from the devout
and the sophisticated—the simple Protestant farmer and the
intellectual deist.

Not by the mere strength of ideas did Paine achieve mastery over his readers. He had looked into their very souls,
and he knew their deeper nature as men and Americans. No
propagandist has ever played upon the heart-strings of humanity with more consummate skill than the author of
Common Sense. He stirred the elemental devotion to home
and family: "Bring the doctrine of reconciliation to the
touchstone of nature, and then tell me whether you can
hereafter love, honour, and faithfully serve the power that
hath carried fire and sword into your land? . . . But if you
say, you can still pass the violations over, then I ask, hath
your house been burnt? Hath your property been destroyed
before your face? Are your wife and children destitute of
a bed to lie on, or bread to live on? Have you lost a parent
or a child by their hands, and yourself the ruined and
wretched survivor? If you have not, then are you not a
judge of those who have. But if you have, and can still
shake hands with the murderers, then are you unworthy
the name of husband, father, friend, or lover, and whatever
may be your rank or title in life, you have the heart of a
coward, and the spirit of a sycophant." He attuned himself
to the religious prejudices of the intensely Protestant Americans: "That the Almighty hath here [The Book of Samuel]
entered his protest against monarchical government is true,
or the Scripture is false. And a man hath good reason to
believe that there is as much kingcraft as priestcraft in
withholding the Scripture from the public in popish coun-

tries. For monarchy in every instance is the popery of government." Bluntly he sounded the economic interest: "I challenge the warmest advocate for reconciliation to show a single advantage that this continent can reap by being connected with Great Britain. I repeat the challenge; not a single advantage is derived. Our corn will fetch its price in any market in Europe, and our imported goods must be paid for, buy them where we will." He expanded with patriotic American pride: "There is something absurd, in supposing a Continent to be perpetually governed by an island. In no instance hath nature made the satellite larger than its primary planet; and as England and America, with respect to each other, reverse the common order of nature, it is evident that they belong to different systems. England to Europe: America to itself."

Over the whole argument glows the unwavering light of a supreme idealism, of a sublime certainty that the American struggle is no petty wrangle but an epochal stand against the forces of darkness and an overture to the earthly paradise. The sentences beat like the martial drums of a high dedication. "O! ye that love mankind! Ye that dare oppose not only the tyranny but the tyrant, stand forth! Every spot of the Old World is overrun with oppression. Freedom hath been hunted round the Globe. Asia and Africa have long expelled her. Europe regards her like a stranger, and England hath given her warning to depart. O! receive the fugitive, and prepare in time an asylum for mankind. . . . We have it in our power to begin the world over again. A situation, similar to the present, hath not happened since the days of Noah until now. The birthday of a new world is at hand, and a race of men, perhaps as numerous as all Europe contains, are to receive their portion of freedom from the events of a few months. The reflection is awful, and in this point of view, how trifling, how ridiculous, do the little paltry cavilings of a few weak or interested men appear, when weighed against the business of a world." *Common Sense* created a new level of American idealism, which six months later went into the Declaration of Independence.

Many learned critics, of that time and since, have spread their talents in pointing out the foibles of Thomas Paine in *Common Sense*. They have scoffed at his superficial theory of The State (the superficiality of Hobbes, Locke, Spinoza, Rousseau), at his swift summary of the British Constitution as "the remains of Monarchical tyranny," "the remains of Aristocratical tyranny," and "new Republican materials." They have felt superior to his "demagogic" appeal to the passions and prejudices of the American audience. They have been disturbed by the uncomplimentary labels which he fastened for all time on George III—"crowned ruffian," "Pharaoh," "the Royal Brute." They have found fault with his grammar. But all these arm-chair profundities are completely beside the issue. *Common Sense* is not a philosophic treatise, it is a revolutionary act. The only pertinent inquiry is, What did it accomplish?

Common Sense scrambled up the old alignments and made new ones necessary. Hitherto it had been possible to be a moderate Whig or an extreme Whig, a moderate Tory or an extreme Tory, or to hover on the wide borderline of indecision. Such distinctions had no pertinence after the 9th of January. The pamphlet was reprinted far and wide, advertised and posted in clubs and taverns, proclaimed from the pulpits, debated in the provincial assemblies. It has been estimated that over a hundred thousand copies were sold;

in other words, the whole reading public was reached. Modern mass propaganda had begun, and America proceeded to divide into opposing camps—for and against independence.

To consider in detail this wide-spread influence of *Common Sense* (or of any subsequent Paine pamphlet) would involve an endless cataloguing. Here we can only illustrate the force of the wind by its action on a few straws. To the American generals in the field, the simple reasonableness of *Common Sense* carried conviction. On the 22nd of January, Gates wrote to Charles Lee: "There is a pamphlet come by Irwin from Philadelphia, entitled *Common Sense*—it is an excellent performance." On the 24th, Lee relayed to Washington: "Have you seen the pamphlet—*Common Sense*? I never saw such a masterly, irresistible performance. It will, if I mistake not, in concurrence with the transcendent folly and wickedness of the ministry, give the coup-de-grâce to Great Britain. In short, I own myself convinced, by the arguments, of the necessity of separation." And on the 31st, Washington was declaring to the Pennsylvania leader, Joseph Reed: "A few more of such flaming arguments as were exhibited at Falmouth and Norfolk [the burning of towns by British troops], added to the sound doctrine and unanswerable reasoning contained in the pamphlet 'Common Sense,' will not leave numbers at a loss to decide upon the propriety of separation." In the *Pennsylvania Evening Post* of February 13, a letter from Maryland exclaims: "If you know the author of *Common Sense* tell him he has done wonders and worked miracles, made Tories Whigs, and washed Blackamores white. He has made a great number of converts here." In the Adams circle in Boston, James Bowdoin urged the independence idea, taking his weapons from Paine's battery: "I would refer the objector to that excellent Pamphlet entitled *Common Sense;* which, if he is not influenced by private interest and attachment, will probably disciple him to the author's doctrine, that an Independence of Great Britain has now become absolutely necessary to the well-being of the Colonies." In New York objectors to independence were more sternly "discipled." There a printer, Samuel Loudon, having advertised a reply to *Common Sense,* was promptly visited by a mob who seized the whole impression and the manuscript and carried them off to the commons for a bonfire. The next day every printer in town received a note from The Committee of Tarring and Feathering, which promised "death and destruction, ruin and perdition" if he should "print or suffer to be printed anything against the rights and liberties of America, or in favor of our inveterate foes, the King, Ministry, and Parliament of Great Britain."

Further testimony to the great effect of *Common Sense* has been left unwillingly by the British adherents in America. Reporting in March to the Colonial Secretary Germain, Governor Franklin of New Jersey—an illegitimate son of Benjamin Franklin—derided the prospect of independence, but added: "It must be allowed that the minds of a great number of the people have been much changed in that respect since the publication of a most inflammatory pamphlet in which that horrid measure is strongly and artfully recommended." A Philadelphia Tory merchant, Edward Shippen, complained to his brother-in-law on the 19th of January: "A Book called Common Sense, wrote in favor of a total separation from England, seems to gain ground with the common people; it is artfully wrote, yet might be easily refuted. This idea of an Independence, tho' some time ago abhorred, may possibly by degrees become so familiar as to

28

be cherished." Nicholas Cresswell, a British immigrant traveling through Virginia, notes in his diary on the 19th of January: "A pamphlet called 'Commonsense' makes a great noise. One of the vilest things that ever was published to the world. Full of false representations, lies, calumny, and treason, whose principles are to subvert all Kingly Governments and erect an Independent Republic. I believe the writer to be some Yankey Presbyterian, Member of the Congress. The sentiments are adopted by a great number of people who are indebted to Great Britain."

So Thomas Paine became overnight, through the transparent anonymity of *Common Sense,* the most conspicuous advocate of extreme measures in the Colonies.

For the next two or three weeks he was busy getting out new editions with supplementary material. In February he left Philadelphia for New York, where an army under General Charles Lee was putting up fortifications against an imminent attack by Clinton's troops. Paine carried with him letters of introduction to Lee from Dr. Rush, Franklin, and John Adams. On the 25th the General reported to Dr. Rush: "Your Mr. Payne din'd with me yesterday, I am much oblig'd to you for the introduction—He has genius in his eyes—his conversation has much life—I hope he will continue cramming down the throats of squeamish mortals his wholesome truths."

The British menace to New York proved to be a false alarm, and Paine returned to Philadelphia to resume the literary fight against "squeamish mortals." The advocates of reconciliation had found many voices, and Congress was being regaled by the most vehement forensics that preceded the Declaration of Independence. The newspapers—the *Post, Ledger, Journal, Gazette*—bounded into a busy circulation

29

purveying the rival arguments. The air was heavy with Patriot and Loyalist brickbats—"pigeon-hearted wretches," "puling, pusillanimous cowards," "libations at the altar of Royal despotism"; "principles equally inconsistent with learned and common sense," "total perversion of the understanding," "maniacum delirium."

In Pennsylvania, as in the Colonies generally, the conflict over national independence was complicated by a struggle for democracy within the province. The wealthy Quakers and Anglicans of the eastern counties opposed not only national independence, but also democratic reform of the provincial Assembly, for whose members most of the adult males in Philadelphia and half of the western frontiersmen had no vote, and in which the three eastern counties had twice as large a representation as the eight western counties. The oligarchical Assembly steadily instructed its delegates in Congress to resist any propositions leading to the twin evils, independence and a reform in the provincial government. To this alliance of local and royal despotism, popular committees of discontented mechanics and farmers retorted by clamorous pressure for independence from the King and the King's charter.

In *Common Sense* Paine had taken a passing blow at the undemocratic Pennsylvania system. He now enlisted his national reputation with the Pennsylvania radicals, thus advancing them and the national movement which needed their support. He met with a company of embittered storekeepers, schoolmasters, scientists, apostate Quakers—Daniel Roberdeau, James Cannon, Dr. Rush, David Rittenhouse, Timothy Matlack, Christopher Marshall. In taverns and private homes, amid copious draughts of coffee and more inspiring beverages (avoiding the detested tea), these leaders

30

organized for provincial democracy and national independence.

The chief writing Tory to be vanquished in Philadelphia
was the Reverend William Smith. A year before he had
been the most militant preacher, solemnly assuring the local
troops who crowded into his church, "The cause of *virtue*
and *freedom* is the CAUSE of GOD upon earth." In April of
1776, in a series of newspaper letters under the signature
Cato *To the People of Pennsylvania,* the Reverend Mr.
Smith defined God's cause more precisely as *"reconciliation*
with Great Britain, upon *constitutional principles."* And
Thomas Paine, who had listened with troubled spirit to
the pulpit-pounding for blood in 1775, now took up the
cudgels for independence against the clerical advocate of
compromise.

In his first three letters Cato defended "our chartered
constitution" and the Assembly from the lawless popular
committees and described the differences with Great Britain
as merely a lovers' quarrel. In his fourth letter he struck
out sneeringly at the author of *Common Sense.* Paine now
made his first rejoinder, signing as The Forester, a shrewd
identification of himself with the democratic frontier. He
flays Cato for "absurdity, confusion, contradiction, and the
most notorious and wilful falsehoods." The struggle can
no longer be considered in terms of "reconciliation" and
"constitutional principles" as a dispute with the ministry
for British rights. These are "silly and water-gruel defini-
tions," an "attempt to catch lions in a mousetrap." Not the
royally chartered Assembly but the people of Pennsylvania
are the true source of power. They must unite with the
other colonies in a common fight for independence, against
reunion with the corrupt British system.

31

Under Paine's attack Smith returned more vigorously to the debate. He riddled the scriptural argument against monarchy and warned against invasions by foreign powers. These were strong points, and in quieter days might have been more effective. The British army in America, however, had forced the issue, and The Forester could overwhelm Cato by tremendous phrases. To Smith's protest against "interested writers, and strangers intermedling in our affairs," Paine grandly replied, "A freeman, Cato, is a stranger nowhere—a slave, everywhere." Reconciliation would produce an "endless and chequered round of blood and treacherous peace." "God hath made a world and Kings have robbed him of it"; yet this "cold and creeping Tory" would strengthen the hand of "a Royal Savage."

In desperation Smith clutched at any means to discredit the protagonist of revolution. In his eighth letter he accused Paine of being an *agent provocateur,* sent here by the British administration itself in order to lead the unwary "into untried regions, full of tremendous precipices and quagmires treacherous to the foot." Paine would have let this sinister charge go unnoticed, but "those gentlemen whose acquaintance I am honored with" advised otherwise. The Forester sent a brief note to the local press on the 30th of April, declaring: "The person supposed by some, and known by others, to be the author of Common Sense, and The Forester's Letters, came a cabin passenger in Jeremiah Warder's ship, the *London Packet,* last Christmas twelvemonth, bringing with him two unsealed letters of introduction from Dr. Franklin to his friends here, in which he says, 'I recommend the bearer hereof, Mr. ——, as a worthy, ingenious, &c.'" Smith's most envenomed arrow had missed its mark.

32

Cato intended "two or three letters more" in favor of the British system and the Pennsylvania charter, but that was not to be tolerated. The period of free speech was closing in Philadelphia. Militant members of Congress, like John Adams and Richard Henry Lee, now standing out firmly for independence, expressed their displeasure at the turn-coat or rather stand-still Smith. And the Pennsylvania government which he defended was hopelessly crumbling under popular attack. Threatened by a call for an illegal provincial conference, to revise the Pennsylvania charter and to declare for national independence, the Assembly compromised in March by permitting the election of seventeen additional members (four from Philadelphia, thirteen from the frontier counties), to be held on the 1st of May. The radicals won twelve of the frontier seats, but only one in Philadelphia. Still controlling a majority in the Assembly, the eastern oligarchy stood firm against national independence and further changes in the provincial government. It was a decision for suicide. The impatient Continental Congress and the rebellious mechanics of Philadelphia, seeing that only revolution could move this mountain, joined hands for a revolutionary assault. On the 10th of May Congress recommended to the colonies generally "to adopt such government as shall, in the opinion of the majority of the people, best conduce to the happiness and safety of their constituents in particular, and of America in general." A mass meeting of Philadelphia radicals came together on the morning of the 20th under the chairmanship of the hot-blooded merchant Daniel Roberdeau. They proclaimed the aristocratic Assembly bankrupt, and declared for a provincial convention that would really express

33

"the opinion of the majority of the people." The frightened Assembly now tried to save its own life by rescinding the instructions against independence, but such negative compliance could hardly appease the awakened workers and farmers. They would be free from the Assembly itself. On the tide of national independence the old charter government and its undemocratic foundation were swept into oblivion.

Pennsylvania was dramatizing for Congress the general course of sentiment in America. The revolutionary party had jumped into power. To the ominous news that thousands of Hessian mercenaries were coming over the sea to supplement the British troops under Howe, an emboldened Congress rejoined by the Declaration of Independence.

The relation of *Common Sense* and *The Forester Letters* to the Declaration of Independence is a matter of historic perspective. Obviously, the American revolution was produced by profound economic causes working on millions of people. Individuals could only hinder or hasten the inevitable rupture between the diverse interests of America's phenomenal growth and British mercantilism. While others may have seen the unconscious trend to independence, Paine alone had the heroism to proclaim and stimulate the movement from its hazardous beginning. By a systematic approach to the colonial mind, *Common Sense* opened a new cycle of political thinking in America. In six months the logic of events made independence the general American creed, and it was Jefferson's merit to give classic phrasing to that accomplished fact. In the familiar path blazed by Paine, Jefferson appealed broadly to the rights granted by "nature and nature's God," and hurled America's in-

34

dictment at the crowned head of the British constitution. It was no mere verbal coincidence when Jefferson later described his rôle as formulating "the common sense of the matter." The common sense of Paine had become the common sense of America.

CHAPTER IV

The Times That Try Men's Souls

IN AUGUST of 1776 Paine left his Pennsylvania friends at the making of a democratic State constitution, and joined the Associators as volunteer secretary to the merchant-soldier General Roberdeau. They were stationed in New Jersey at Amboy, dangerously close to the British troops on Staten Island. As the lookouts reported ships coming in twenty and thirty at a time and pouring out smartly dressed companies to join Howe, the raw Pennsylvania militia could not help feeling jittery. They deserted in groups. Roberdeau's secretary went among the men, handing out copies of *Common Sense,* enforcing the General's plea to fight "for your honor's sake" against "an army of sixpenny soldiers." When the Associators were withdrawn to Pennsylvania in September, Paine moved up the Jersey coast to Fort Lee and became a volunteer aide-de-camp to General Greene.

Meanwhile, the main army under Washington was having a very bad time of it. Military experts had pointed out to Washington the impossibility of defending New York with a chaotic rabble of 20,000 against Howe's 35,000 trained troops. But some show of resistance was necessary to keep up the morale of the Colonies. In August the Americans were severely beaten by the British in the Battle of Long Island, the Hessians romping through a slaughter of the prisoners. In September Howe marched leisurely into New

York, as Washington fled northwards with the disorganized remnants of his army. Washington groaned, "I am wearied to death with the retrograde motion of things." In November Fort Washington fell, and the female British camp-followers skipped along the line of march of the 3,000 prisoners, hooting "Which is Washington? Which is Washington?"

The loss of Fort Washington made Fort Lee across the Hudson untenable. On the 20th of November, as the enemy approached unexpectedly after a rainy night, Greene's men ran off, leaving baggage and hot breakfasts for the intruders. "The rebels fled like scared rabbits," sneered a British officer, and added, "They have left some poor pork, a few greasy proclamations, and some of that scoundrel Common Sense man's letters, which we can read at our leisure, now that we have got one of the 'impregnable redoubts' of Mr. Washington to quarter in."

There were many "darkest" moments in the Revolution; none darker than these last months of 1776. The Americans retreated in panic across New Jersey and the Delaware. American enlistments were expiring daily, and men were going home with their arms and equipment. Philadelphia, the capital city, was in a turmoil of anxiety. The sidewalks were piled high with household goods; heavily laden carriages careened through the streets; men changed their politics as the enemy drew near. Congress scrambled to Baltimore. The printing presses were still. Who dared to proclaim independence now, when the British flag would be waving over the State House in a few hours? In the midst of the terror-stricken city Paine poured his full energies into a cry to battle, the first *Crisis* paper.

The beginning of *Crisis I* is the most dynamic and memorable of all revolutionary utterances. "These are the times that try men's souls. The summer soldier and the sunshine patriot will, in this crisis, shrink from the service of their country; but he that stands it *now,* deserves the love and thanks of man and woman. Tyranny, like hell, is not easily conquered; yet we have this consolation with us, that the harder the conflict, the more glorious the triumph."

Every word counts, every phrase is calculated to make the decent reader ashamed of holding back from the greatest cause that ever summoned men to battle. "I call not upon a few, but upon all: not on *this* State or *that* State, but on *every* State: up and help us; lay your shoulders to the wheel; better have too much force than too little, when so great an object is at stake. Let it be told to the future world, that in the depth of winter, when nothing but hope and virtue could survive, that the city and the country, alarmed at one common danger, came forth to meet and to repulse it. Say not that thousands are gone, turn out your tens of thousands; throw not the burden of the day upon Providence, but *'show your faith by your works,'* that God may bless you. It matters not where you live, or what rank of life you hold, the evil or the blessing will reach you all. The far and near, the home counties and the back, the rich and the poor, will suffer or rejoice alike. The heart that feels not now, is dead: the blood of his children will curse his cowardice, who shrinks back at a time when a little might have saved the whole, and made *them* happy. I love the man that can smile in trouble, that can gather strength from distress, and grow brave by reflection. 'Tis the business of little minds to shrink; but he whose heart is firm, and whose conscience approves his conduct, will pursue his principles unto death. My own line of reasoning is to myself as straight and clear as a ray of light. Not all the treasures of the world, so far as I believe, could have induced me to support an offensive war, for I think it murder; but if a thief breaks into my house, burns and destroys my property, and kills or threatens to kill me, or those that are in it, and to 'bind me in all cases whatsoever' to his absolute will, am I to suffer it? What signifies it to me, whether he who does it is a king or a common man; my countryman or not my countryman; whether it be done by an individual villain, or an army of them? If we reason to the root of things we shall find no difference; neither can any just cause be assigned why we should punish in the one case and pardon in the other. Let them call me rebel, and welcome, I feel no concern from it; but I should suffer the misery of devils, were I to make a whore of my soul by swearing allegiance to one whose character is that of a sottish, stupid, stubborn, worthless, brutish man."

The doctrine of *Common Sense* and of the Declaration of Independence was reenforced throughout the nation by these pulsating words, with their vibrant overtones of recent experiences in camp and battlefield. At Washington's order the inspiriting pamphlet was read aloud to every corporal's guard in the army. The summer tatters of the soldiers were transformed into a glorious winter uniform. Napoleon has said that an army travels on its stomach. The American army in December of 1776 traveled on its newly invigorated heart.

On Christmas Eve, Washington made his famous crossing over the ice-clogged Delaware, captured the drunken Hessians in Trenton on the morrow, and completed a series of brilliant maneuvers by routing the British cantonment at Princeton. Howe was now ready to call it quits for the

39

winter, and settled down to card playing and love making in comfortable New York. Around the fires of the winter encampment at Morristown, New Jersey, clustered the ragged patriots, congratulating one another on the late victory. The danger was lifted. The crisis was over.

Secure in Philadelphia, Paine celebrated the new strength of America in *Crisis II,* on the 13th of January. A plain American citizen, he looks down upon Lord Howe with contempt and mockery. He congratulates the Americans on their noble resistance to the "unhallowed foot of the invader." "What are salt, sugar and finery to the inestimable blessings of 'Liberty and Safety'? Or what are the inconveniences of a few months to the tributary bondage of ages?" Striking back at personal vilification by the Tories, Paine proudly asserts that he is actuated by "a fixed, immovable hatred I have, and ever had, to cruel men and cruel measures," and "My pen and my soul have ever gone together."

Having thrown himself into the cause without reservation, Paine had no income, not even the pittance of a regular soldier. He had given *Common Sense* to America gratis and he was near the end of his resources. The defect was now remedied. On the 17th of April, 1777, Congress took up the question of reorganizing the Committee of Secret Correspondence as the Committee of Foreign Affairs, with an official secretary. For this important confidential post, John Adams nominated Paine, "supposing him a ready writer and an industrious man." President Witherspoon of Princeton objected that he knew Paine as originally a Tory and as a heavy drinker and bad character. General Roberdeau defended his former secretary and "No one confirmed Witherspoon's account," Adams recorded in his autobiography. Paine was elected to the office, with a salary of $70 a month.

In the stock-taking *Crisis III,* on the 19th, the new secretary mused, "Truly may we say that never did men grow old in so short a time." Two years previously, he was a humble Quaker hoping for a quiet corner in the American colonies—to-day, a distinguished officer in the revolutionary government of the United States. America, too, had been growing up fast. Excepting the Loyalist faction, she had broken forever with "the savage obstinacy of the king, and the jobbing, gambling spirit of the court." America now sees that the present war is the sole path to independence and enduring peace. Paine broadly appeals to all classes to unite in the common struggle for liberation from the imperial oppressor. "On the whole, if the future expulsion of arms from one quarter of the world would be a desirable object to a peaceable man; if the freedom of trade to every part of it can engage the attention of the man of business; if the support or fall of millions of currency can affect our interests; if the entire possession of estates, by cutting off the lordly claims of Britain over the soil, deserves the regard of landed property; and if the right of making our own laws, uncontrolled by royal or ministerial spies or mandates, be worthy our care as freemen;—then are all men interested in the support of independence; and may he that supports it not, be driven from the blessing, and live unpitied beneath the servile sufferings of scandalous subjection!" America must not indulge "a bastard kind of generosity" to the enemies at home. "In the present crisis, we ought to know, square by square and house by house, who are in real allegiance with the United Independent

41

States, and who are not." It was a hard inquisitorial program, but it led to independence.

At every critical juncture of the Revolution Paine was to come forth with a *Crisis* paper signed Common Sense, with imperturbable confidence inspiring the Americans to an ultimate success "as certain as fate." The Loyalists ineffectually poured out their spleen on "our hireling author," "true son of Grubstreet," "the famous Crisis-writer, who boasts himself to be the author of 'Common Sense,' a pedantic schoolmaster, not worth sixpence, nor possessing as much property in the country."

> Champions of virtue, we'll alike disdain
> The guards of Washington, the lies of Payne.

"The lies of Payne" were bread and meat to the American cause. No agitator has ever achieved a more thorough success. Printed on any available scraps of paper—gray, brown, yellow—the *Crisis* pamphlets were to be found everywhere, like newspapers. They were fastened together with army orders, as part of the military program; they were sent throughout the country packed in trunks with American flags, as rallying-points of battle; they accompanied American envoys into all the courts of Europe, frequently as official communications. "Have you read the latest *Crisis?*" "What does Common Sense think to-day?" So the conversation ran among the soldiers and their supporters at home. Thomas Paine is the authentic spokesman of the American Revolution and the thirteen *Crisis* papers are its articulate soul.

CHAPTER V

BATTLES AND ALARMS

THE winter and spring truce of 1776-77 came to an end. On the 13th of June the British army moved into New Jersey, maneuvered aimlessly back and forth for two weeks, and returned to New York. Then, to the amazement and perplexity of Washington, Howe piled his 18,000 troops on transports and, after dawdling a month between New York and Sandy Hook, disappeared into the Atlantic. The mighty fleet of 300 ships loomed up suddenly at the entrance of Delaware Bay, faded out again, and finally landed on the 21st of August at Elkton on the Chesapeake. Washington decided to defend the capital city by an offensive. He marched his troops through Philadelphia in an impressive parade, the jaunty green sprigs in the hats of the patriots contrasting grotesquely with their rags and protruding toes, but their bold weather-beaten faces inspiring the Congress and stirring uneasy tremors among the British sympathizers. The fighters hastened southwards to meet the enemy.

On the 11th of September, as Paine in Philadelphia was preparing a despatch from the Committee of Foreign Affairs to Franklin and the other American envoys in France, a messenger came with news of the American defeat at the Brandywine River. Immediately Paine dashed off the brief *Crisis IV*, putting the best front on the new catastrophe and reasserting the American idealism: "We fight not to enslave, but to set a country free, and to make room upon the earth for honest men to live in." Let not the brave Americans be dismayed by "a band of ten or twelve thousand robbers," for "the nearer any disease approaches to a crisis, the nearer it is to a cure. Danger and deliverance make their advances together, and it is only the last push, in which one or the other takes the lead."

The British descent upon the capital city was now imminent. Only a demoralized American army stood guard for disunited and helpless Philadelphia. On the 19th of September, at one o'clock in the morning, came the first alarm that the British had crossed the Schuylkill. "The confusion, as you may suppose," Paine wrote later to Franklin, "was very great. It was a beautiful still moonlight morning and the streets as full of men, women and children as on a market day." The alarm was false, but in a few days Howe out-maneuvered Washington at the Schuylkill and slipped across the river without losing a man. Philadelphia was doomed. Without bothering to take a vote, Congress and its retinue fled to York. On the 26th a forward detachment of the British army under Cornwallis marched into the rebel capital, the fiercely mustached Hessians glowering to right and left for plunder.

With the city taken, Congress in flight, and communication cut off by the British, revolutionary pamphlets could neither be printed nor circulated. Paine put away the pen of Common Sense and went to the scene of war. He set out on horseback along the uncertain countryside northwards in quest of Washington, riding high up in the country almost in circles rather than risking to ask questions of the local farmers. On the 2nd of October he came upon the American camp of General Nathanael Greene. The Battle of Germantown began on the 4th.

The next day, at 5 o'clock in the morning, Paine headed for the battlefield. "I met no person for several miles riding," Paine tells Franklin, "which I concluded to be a good sign; after this I met a man on horseback who told me he was going to hasten on a supply of ammunition, that the Enemy were broken and retreating fast, which was true. I saw several country people with arms in their hands running across a field towards German Town, within about five or six miles, at which I met several of the wounded on waggons, horseback, and on foot. I passed Genl. Nash on a litter made of poles, but did not know him. I felt unwilling to ask questions lest the information should not be agreeable, and kept on. About two miles after this I passed a promiscuous crowd of wounded and otherwise who were halted at a house to refresh. Col. Biddle D.Q.M.G. [Deputy Quarter-Master General] was among them, who called after me, that if I went farther on that road I should be taken, for that the firing which I heard ahead was the Enemy's." Almost in sight of success the Americans had lost. Again Howe failed to follow up his victory; instead of pursuing the Americans, he returned to comfortable Philadelphia. The next morning Paine had breakfast with the officers at Washington's headquarters, where the downcast council analyzed the defeat, blaming the fog and the inexperience of the troops.

American fortifications had been established on the Delaware just below the city—Fort Mifflin at Mud Island on the Pennsylvania side, Fort Mercer at Red Bank on the Jersey side—to prevent the British fleet from bringing supplies and reenforcements to Howe. But the *chevaux de frise* which had been laid across the Delaware between the two forts to check the British fleet, worked out a back channel, through which the enemy ships now sailed to join the land batteries in a successful bombardment of Fort Mifflin. What was left of the fort had to be abandoned to the British, and on the 18th of November 5,000 British under Cornwallis crossed to New Jersey and took Fort Mercer without meeting any resistance. Two thousand Americans under General Greene, with Paine at his side, looked on from a safe distance and marched back to the main army. Howe had cleared the Delaware.

On the 19th of December the American army dug in for the winter on a steep hill at Valley Forge. While the British frolicked with the loyalists in Philadelphia, the exhausted Americans after their disastrous campaigning pushed grimly through the bleak rigors of winter. One joyous ray flickered over the scene: the Northern army under Gates had taken Burgoyne and 3,000 prisoners at Saratoga on the 17th of October. But, even so, how long could the Americans last?

For the winter, at least, the test was deferred. Howe had no desire to disturb his Philadelphia entertainment by any marches over snow-covered country, even though a sortie to Valley Forge twenty miles away would almost certainly have destroyed or scattered the American army.

At the end of January, after a few weeks with his friend Colonel Joseph Kirkbride in Bordentown, New Jersey, Paine traveled on horseback in a wide circuitous route to the encampment at Valley Forge. From Valley Forge he went to Lancaster. On the 12th of February Paine's old friend, Christopher Marshall, noted in his Diary: "Just as I lockt front door to prepare for bed Thos. Payne came. So there was supper to get for him having been thus recruited had his bed warmed then to bed after he sat some time regaling himself." For the rest of the winter of 1777-78 Paine divided his time between the State Assembly at Lancaster and the Federal Congress at York.

In York Paine found the Congress in a cheerful and aggressive mood. The victory at Saratoga had accelerated the negotiations with France and news of the formal alliance was momentarily expected. It was hoped that if the British remained inactive for a few months longer, a French army and a French fleet would add enough energy to America to sweep the invader out of the country. But a powerful faction in Congress felt that in order for the next campaign to bring the final victory, a more aggressive commander than Washington was needed. Samuel Adams, Richard Henry Lee, Dr. Rush, and others were active behind the scenes in throwing on Washington the blame for recent defeats and urging that he be supplanted by Gates, the hero of Saratoga. Congressional confidence was mixed with factional unrest. It was time for another message from Common Sense, to abate the differences, support the arm of Washington, and direct the vigor of a united people against the common enemy.

Crisis V, in March, 1778, holds up British pretensions to the proud scorn of a democratic and freedom-loving nation. The British army has made one mistake after another and is busy getting nowhere. The seizure of Philadelphia, which Paine had regarded at the time as a calamity, he now dismisses as inconsequential. On the other hand, the apparent American defeats are really strategic victories and the American patriots have all done nobly under "the unabated fortitude of Washington."

47

There is in *Crisis V* an undercurrent of sadness, out of which Paine reasons into a more intensified determination. Two years of war, its desolation, its horror, had not been to his liking. But America "has taken up the sword of virtuous defence; she has bravely put herself between Tyranny and Freedom, between a curse and a blessing, determined to expel the one and protect the other." To turn back now is unthinkable. America must drive forward, without hesitation, without compromise, to a swift conclusion of this hellish business, for "The Will of God hath parted us, and the deed is registered for eternity. . . . Vigor and determination will do any thing and every thing. We began the war with this kind of spirit, why not end it with the same? Here, gentlemen, is the enemy. Here is the army. The interest, the happiness of all America, is centered in this half-ruined spot. Come and help us. Here are laurels, come and share them. Here are Tories, come and help us to expel them. Here are Whigs that will make you welcome, and enemies that dread your coming."

His appeal and the advent of spring brought new enrolments into the American camp at Valley Forge for the campaign of 1778. On the 6th of May, Washington made formal announcement of the alliance with France, and the men went wild with celebration, throwing their hats in the air and shouting huzzahs to the indomitable and majestic leader whom they would follow even into the mouth of hell.

In Philadelphia, too, a celebration was staged by the British army on the 18th. Howe was being fêted before going home to explain his ambiguous manner of waging war. Elaborately decorated barges floated down the Delaware, fake medieval knights jousted in fake tournament for the damsels, enough fireworks were shot off to have battered ten Valley Forges into débris. It was the last British carnival in the Quaker City. The British had to leave Philadelphia quickly since a great French fleet was on the way to block up the Delaware. On the 18th of June the British troops under Clinton departed on a devious land-and-water route towards the more advantageous base in New York, while the main American army followed along the line of march in wary pursuit.

As the British army trailed out of Philadelphia, an American detachment rushed in, capturing a few stragglers. Penn's trim city was a sorry sight after nine months of British occupancy—piles of rubbish in the streets, garden fences torn down for firewood, patriot homes gutted or in ashes. Before the avenging wrath of the revolutionists, many a loyalist wished he had gone with the 3,000 who had fled with Howe. Paine was in the vanguard taking the pledge of the Patriot Society to bring all Tories to justice. Since the chief culprits were gone, the reign of terror was brief and fairly moderate. Every one else being acquitted, the court made an example of two Philadelphians who had served the enemy—a watcher at the city gate and a canvasser for enlistments. Roberts and Carlisle were paraded through the city, tied by ropes around their necks to the back of wagons bearing their own coffins, and were publicly hanged. The memory of these two has been watered by the tears of gentle-hearted historians whose sympathies do not reach into the furious hearts of the American soldiers grieving for their comrades slain on the battlefield or frozen to death in camp.

The capital city with its divided loyalties settled down to superficial harmony. These were busy, thriving days for the secretary of the Committee for Foreign Affairs, what with elaborate French negotiations and general European interest in the American struggle. The American cause was not faring so triumphantly as had been hoped. After the indecisive Battle of Monmouth on the 28th of June, 1778, Washington rested at White Plains. The French fleet under D'Estaing lumbered ineffectively between New York and Newport and French soldiers got into sordid scraps with Americans. The new British commander, Clinton, a thoroughgoing practitioner of war, made sudden excursions out of New York to ravage prosperous towns and farmhouses, and incited the Six Nations to frightful massacres in upper Pennsylvania and western New York. Meanwhile, the British Commission in New York repeatedly reminded the Americans in seductive proclamations that Britannia was ready to forgive and forget if her erring children would come back to the fold.

In order to break the dangerous Franco-American alliance, British policy had taken a liberal turn. The British Commissioners were instructed to promise almost everything short of absolute independence. In Congress a pro-British faction, built on the ruins of the anti-Washington cabal, raised its head to urge that the Americans repudiate their connection with the ancient enemy, France, and return to the mother country, England.

On October 20, in *Crisis VI,* Paine denounced the scheme of reconciliation. He flung back the pious favors of the British Commissioners by a blunt assurance: "Your cargo of pardons will have no market. . . . What sort of men or Christians must you suppose the Americans to be, who, after seeing their most humble petitions insultingly rejected; the most grievous laws passed to distress them in every quarter; an undeclared war let loose upon them, and Indians and negroes invited to the slaughter; who, after seeing their kinsmen murdered, their fellow citizens starved to death in prisons, and their houses and property destroyed and burned; who, after the most serious appeals to heaven, the most solemn adjuration by oath of all government connected with you, and the most heart-felt pledges and protestations of faith to each other; and who after soliciting the friendship, and entering into alliance with other nations, should at last break through all these obligations, civil and divine, by complying with your horrid and infernal proposal." He champions the French alliance as "open, noble, and generous."

On November 21, Paine pursued the departing Commissioners across the Atlantic with *Crisis VII,* addressed to The People of England. Surely, he reasons, the reverses of the American war should open the eyes of Englishmen to the realization that Britannia is not always right and on the side of the Gods. England has senselessly ruined her own trade by attempting to strangle her best customer. "Samson only told the secret, but you have performed the operation; you have shaven your own head, and wantonly thrown away the locks." Why do the English people permit this shameful waste of their human and economic resources? Paine asks a few plain integrated questions rising to a revolutionary climax: "1st, What is the original fountain of power and honor in any country? 2d, Whether the prerogative does not belong to the people? 3d, Whether there is any such thing as the English constitution? 4th, Of what use is the Crown to the people? 5th, Whether he who invented a crown was not an enemy to mankind? 6th, Whether it is not a shame for a man to spend a million a year, and do no good for it, and whether the money might not be better applied? 7th, Whether such a man is not better dead than alive? 8th, Whether a congress, constituted like that of America, is not the most happy and consistent form of government in the world?" In this broadside Paine attempts to weaken the enemy by confusing the allegiance of her own citizens. He does more, he asserts an international program of liberation. This is a new note in Paine's writings. Out of the bitterness of the American struggle he was evolving a desire to help rid the whole world of the privileged order. His devastating questions were destined in the new phrasing of *The Rights of Man* in 1791 to be the slogans of world revolution.

CHAPTER VI

Une Tracasserie

ALTHOUGH in championing independence and democracy Paine had fired the hearts of the common soldiers in Washington's army, he had also made powerful enemies within the American lines. Secret British sympathizers hated him as the spokesman of treason, and New World aristocrats and big merchants feared the democratic implications in his writings. There was a tacit anti-Paine faction biding its time for a chance to destroy him.

When as Common Sense and Secretary to the Committee of Foreign Affairs, Paine raised his voice against a ramified international racket headed by Silas Deane, the first American envoy to France, he brought down upon his head a torrent of abuse and defamation without parallel in the Revolution. He lost his job and risked his life at the hands of his fellow citizens, while the fury of classes and factions raged around him as the center.

The Silas Deane affair is one of the unsolved mysteries in American history. The first French ambassador to the United States, Monsieur Gérard, who played an important rôle in the affair, properly termed it a mess (*une tracasserie*), and it has remained so to the present day. The tangled intrigues and motives of governments and agents are buried under a formidable chaos of letters and declarations—let alone a mass of vouchers and receipts stuffed in countless portfolios in Parisian archives, and whispered conversations

53

that have vanished into the air. In the present survey we are concerned only with the bearing of this imbroglio upon Thomas Paine. The record pertaining to him testifies to a truly heroic performance in which even the mistakes must be ascribed to selfless patriotism. The same cannot be demonstrated for his adversary, Silas Deane.

The Deane affair was already considerably advanced before Paine became involved in it. The Philadelphia fracas between Deane and Paine developed out of the early Franco-American negotiations, which must first be considered in brief perspective.

The French assistance to the insurgent British colonists was an incident in the protracted imperial struggle between England and France, and was directed toward preventing reconciliation. In the winter of '75-'76 the French Foreign Minister Vergennes appointed that amazing adventurer and playwright, Caron de Beaumarchais, as secret emissary to sound out Arthur Lee, the American agent in London. On his return Beaumarchais addressed Louis XVI, outlining a strategy of secret support for the Americans, "according as the situation of the Americans becomes more or less pressing, with the result that these aids, wisely administered, will serve not so much to terminate the war between America and England, as to sustain and keep it alive to the detriment of the English." As for payments by America, "that is of small consequence." For this program Beaumarchais got a million livres from the treasury in June, 1776. With these funds and another million from the King of Spain, he launched a quasi-independent commercial house under the name of Roderique Hortalez and Company, to send mysterious shipments of ammunition and clothing to an obscure consignee across the Atlantic. Thus, before the

Americans had made any formal request, France was committed to secret assistance. A messenger from Lee brought this good news to the Committee of Secret Correspondence in October.

Meanwhile the Committee, without the authorization or even cognizance of Congress, had appointed Silas Deane of Connecticut a secret commercial agent to France. Deane had no diplomatic experience, could not speak French, and had recently been defeated for reëlection to Congress. The Committee guaranteed Deane a five percent commission on purchases made for the American government, and ordered him to keep in touch with Lee. Deane also made private commercial contracts with enterprising American importers, particularly Robert Morris, who wrote him: "If we have but luck in getting the Goods safe to America the Profits will be sufficient to content us all."

Deane arrived in Paris in July, ignorant that the groundwork had been laid since his appointment. Vergennes would not deal officially with the rebel agent, but Beaumarchais sought him out and grandiosely announced his long-cherished desire "to aid the brave Americans to shake off the British yoke." The extensive, ready-made program was enough to make Deane reel, but he was not deceived about Beaumarchais' resources and reported to the Committee on the 15th of August that Beaumarchais was obviously acting on behalf of the French government. The British Ambassador Stormont, too, knew what was going on through a British spy employed in Deane's office, but his protests brought only bland denials from the Ministry. In spite of interference by British ships hovering in the Channel, most of the consignments from Roderique Hortalez arrived safely in America, and Silas Deane could congratulate himself on the overnight success of a mission which in fact could not possibly have failed.

So far, Beaumarchais had been a faithful servant of the King. But Beaumarchais had schemes for himself, and Silas Deane fell in with them. Why not charge the insurgents for the military supplies? The French government would not dare to acknowledge the secret aids, for fear of complications with Great Britain. Beaumarchais' clever notion to convert the French gift into an American debt to Roderique Hortalez was profitable to Deane, whose governmental contract did not stipulate for commissions on gifts. Everything would go well if the strait-laced Lee were kept out of the business. Hearing late in August that Lee was on the way to Paris, Deane did not make plans to welcome him, though the Secret Committee had ordered cooperation. Instead, he wrote a warning to Vergennes against Lee as being too much involved in the affairs of England. As Lee's enquiries about the progress of transactions which he had himself begun were turned off with evasions, his hot, suspicious disposition began to distrust the teamwork of Beaumarchais and Deane. The arguments were long and acrimonious, and as early as October 1, 1776, Deane was already building a defensive backfire in a complaint to the Secret Committee about "the black and villainous artifices of one or two of our own countrymen here."

In October, 1776, Lee and Franklin were appointed colleagues of Deane as an American Commission for open negotiations at the French court. Their instructions declared: "It will be proper for you to press for the immediate and explicit declaration of France in our favor, upon a suggestion, that a *reunion* with Great Britain may be the consequence of delay." Adopting this position with literal

fidelity, Lee was soon working at cross purposes with his
more complaisant colleagues, and confirmed the suspicions
of the French Ministry that he had some illicit understanding with the British. At the behest of the Ministry, Deane
and Franklin were obliged to keep much of their activity
secret from Lee; while Deane had his own secrets from
Lee and Franklin.

In October, 1777, the Commissioners wrote a joint report to the Secret Committee (now the Committee for Foreign Affairs, with Thomas Paine secretary) revealing a do-
nation from the French government. "But," they added,
"we are continually charged to keep the aids that are or
may be afforded to us a dead secret even from the Congress,
where they suppose England has some intelligence; and
they wish she may have no certain proofs to produce against
them with the other powers of Europe." They speak further
of "the assurances we have received that no repayment
will ever be required from us of what has already been
given us either in money, or military stores." In the same
package with this report, Lee inserted a letter detailing
his London conversations with Beaumarchais, *"an agent of
this court,"* who had promised free aids.

These two letters mysteriously disappeared from the ship,
and the duplicates did not arrive in Philadelphia until the
spring. Meanwhile the Foreign Committee had received dun-
ning letters from Beaumarchais and had dismissed them
as the mere pleasantries of the gallant French court whose
generosity Lee had reported in 1776. But early in December, 1777, there popped up in Philadelphia one M. de
Francey, agent of Beaumarchais, bearing an introduction
written by Deane without the knowledge of Lee or Franklin. Deane asked the Committee to make an immediate

financial settlement with this agent. M. de Francey left no doubt that Beaumarchais had really sent him across the Atlantic to collect the enormous debt of 4,500,000 livres. Some explanation was in order. Guided by the Committee, Congress recalled Deane on the 8th of December.

Before his letter of recall reached him, Deane tried to cover up the tracks of his double-dealing by signing a joint report of the Commissioners to the Foreign Committee concerning the claims of Beaumarchais. In February, 1778, they wrote: "We hear [it was certainly news to Franklin and Lee, but not to Deane] that he has sent over a person to demand a great sum of you, on account of arms, ammunition, &c. We think it will be best for you to leave that demand to be settled by us here, as there is a mixture in it of public and private concern, which you cannot so well develop." Silas Deane, however, would have to explain in America his mixture of public and private concern in France. Beaumarchais rushed to the assistance of his American partner. In a letter to the Foreign Minister Vergennes he lunged out at Lee and his "dissolute suppers" and wept copious tears for his "disheartened friend" Deane. Beaumarchais reminds Vergennes that Deane has always worked for the French alliance and can be useful to France in America; he should be supported by the French government.

If Vergennes balked at the colossal fraud attempted by his emissary, it was not for long, because the Minister had his own official duplicity to hide. No matter how transparent, the fiction must be publicly maintained that before the formal alliance in February, 1778, France had given no secret aids of any kind to the Americans—none through Beaumarchais and Deane, none through the Commissioners. The outward appearance of "national honor" must be preserved even at the cost of wholesale deception and legitimized theft of public funds. Vergennes gave Deane a formal testimonial and provided him with an impressive traveling companion in his own secretary, M. Gérard, who had handled the details of the American negotiations and was going out to America as the first French ambassador. Their departure on the French fleet at the end of March was kept secret from Lee, who proceeded to attack Deane in a barrage of denunciatory letters to the Foreign Committee.

Gérard and Deane sailed into Philadelphia in May, 1778. At the festivities over the alliance, the critics of Deane were vexed to see him sharing in the adulation under the wing of the French Ambassador. Gérard, minimizing the strength of the anti-Deane party, was relieved and wrote back to Vergennes that the fury let loose against Deane in Paris had produced no effect in Philadelphia, that Deane's enemies were confused, the majority in Congress were favorably disposed and would soon heap honors on their French agent. But, he continued uneasily: "I limit myself on my side, My Lord, to general compliments and I speak of Mr. Deane only to those who speak to me of him first; I hope much that I will never find myself mixed up in this mess or any other."

The Deane affair in Philadelphia stood in an ambiguous position through the summer and fall of 1778. Congress, proceeding on the well-founded suspicion that British agents were among its membership, had been reconciled to ignorance about the secret doings of its own committees. Congress was confused, while the Foreign Committee, unwilling to offend the French Ambassador, gave no hints to direct action. Deane, however, felt that he had the whip hand over Congress in that any censure of him would inevitably involve the reputation of the French court. Now was the moment to press for a vote of thanks, for payment of commissions, and for reappointment. Deane and his commercial partizans in Congress forced a hearing in August. But they had underestimated the vehemence of the Lee faction. Under fire, Deane admitted that he had left his vouchers and receipts in France and he positively refused to answer certain questions as tending to incriminate him. He left in discomfiture.

But finding his friends in Philadelphia many and powerful, he passed quickly from uneasiness to a cocky assurance that nothing could stop him. He continued to badger Congress for immediate approbation and a renewed European mission. He spoke darkly of drawing "the sacred Vail" and stripping the corrupt Congress "to the open View of their Countrymen," and he bluntly accused Lee of insanity. Wearying of Deane's continual charges of undeserved neglect, Congress decided on December 1st to grant him another hearing. Deane thanked Congress but disregarded its invitation, and without consulting the French ambassador —who would certainly have dissuaded him—published in the Philadelphia papers on the 5th of December *The Address of Silas Deane to the Free and Virtuous Citizens of America*. The *tracasserie* which Gérard had hoped to suppress was out in the open.

"What I write to you, I would have said to your Representatives," Deane lyingly began; "their ears have been shut against me, by an attention to matters, which my respect for them induces me to believe were of more importance." He asserted that Arthur Lee and his brother William Lee, another American agent in Europe, were secretly scheming in collusion with England, while their brother Richard

Henry Lee had held shady meetings with the British agent Berkenhout in Philadelphia. Deane was under suspicion, not the Lees. Instead of meeting their charges, Deane blustered. "To honor them with the emotions of anger would be degrading to that character which I hope always to maintain."

Riding the wave of the popular response to Deane's martyr pose, his friends in Congress more insistently demanded that he be given his due. Sick of their machinations, Henry Laurens of South Carolina resigned the presidency of Congress. Who would answer the Deane gang? Arthur Lee and William Lee were in Europe, Richard Henry Lee was at the moment in Virginia. Congress was ignorant of the details and could hardly descend to a public debate with its agent.

It was Thomas Paine who filled the breach against Deane. On December 14, 1778, in a succinct letter *To Silas Deane, Esq're,* in the *Pennsylvania Packet,* Paine reproached Deane for confusing the nervous public mind at this critical time. He observes that Deane cannot get out of his personal difficulties by attacking the absent Lees or playing fast and loose with the good name of Congress. He summarizes the case against Deane: "It was the intricacy of Mr. Deane's *own official* affairs, his multiplied contracts in France before the arrival of Dr. Franklin or any of the other Commissioners; his assuming authorities, and entering into engagements, in the time of his Commercial Agency, for which he had neither commission nor instruction; and the general unsettled state of his accounts, that were among the reasons that produced the motion for recalling and superseding him,—Why then does Mr. Deane endeavour to lead the attention of the public to a wrong object, and bury the real reasons, under a tumult of new and perhaps unnecessary suspicions?"

Paine's letter did not end the controversy. It merely gave Deane's partizans a conspicuous target in Philadelphia. On the 21st a writer signing as Plain Truth tried to salvage Deane and denounced Paine as "almost below the level of hireling writers." This broadside was reenforced by Deane's lengthy address at the Congressional hearing which his friend John Jay, the new President, now arranged for him. Deane drew an unrestrained picture of his great sacrifices and services, to be taken on faith in the absence of receipts and vouchers left somewhere in France. Strongly recommending the claims of "Monsieur Beaumarchais, a gentleman to whom I owe much, my country more," Deane hid from Congress the fact which he had imparted in one of his first reports to the Foreign Committee, that Beaumarchais was a direct agent of the French court.

It was imperative, to defend his own position and to expose Deane in all his treachery, that Paine should come forward with more damaging revelations. The situation called for "language as plain as the alphabet." On the 31st of December he began a series in the *Packet* entitled *To the Public on Mr. Deane's Affair*. "I desire the public to understand," he explained, "that this is not a personal dispute between Mr. Deane and me." Paine speaks "as one of the public, under the well-known signature of Common Sense," against a raid on the treasury and Congress by Deane and "his friend and associate, and perhaps partner too, Mr. Plain Truth." The central facts remain: Deane has not yet satisfactorily explained his dealings in France, he did not bring his receipts and vouchers with him, and he refuses to tell Congress specifically where they can be found. Yet

Deane has his prominent defenders. Why? Broadening the attack, Paine counsels "every State, to enquire what mercantile connections any of their *late* or present Delegates have had or now have with Mr. Deane, and, that a precedent might not be wanting, it is important that this State, *Pennsylvania should begin.*" It was time for Deane's partner, Robert Morris, former member of Congress and the richest man in Pennsylvania, to lift up his ears.

On January 2, 1779, Paine proceeded to blast Deane's pretensions—"The Saviour of his Country—the Patriot of America—the True Friend of the Public—the Great supporter of the cause in Europe." The real facts may be "a nice point to touch upon," but there is no further necessity for beating about the bush. France and England are now irrevocably at open war. There is no longer any point in hiding from the public the correspondence of the Foreign Committee. Paine, secretary to the Committee, reveals that Deane himself was one of the Commissioners who signed the letter on February 16, saying that the French aids involved a mixture of "public and private concern." Deane was then and is now attempting to confuse and deceive the public. "If Mr. Deane or any other gentleman will procure an order from Congress to inspect an account in my office, or any of Mr. Deane's friends in Congress will take the trouble of coming themselves, I will give him or them my attendance and show them in a handwriting which Mr. Deane is well acquainted with [Lee's], that the supplies, he so pompously plumes himself upon, were promised and engaged, and that as a present, before he ever *arrived* in France."

Here was the beginning of Paine's transgression. The solid welfare of America seemed to him more important than any fine-spun and immaterial imputations of "dishonor" to the French court. The French ambassador, however, feeling embarrassed at the prospect of a complete exposé, protested to his good friend Common Sense against the tendency of his writings. In a private reply, January 2, Paine assured Gérard that he was acting as an individual, not as an officer of the American government, and that he did not belong to the anti-French faction or express their views. Thanking Paine, Gérard declared to Congress on the 4th of January the official French view: "That all the supplies furnished by M. de Beaumarchais to the States, whether merchandise or cannons and military goods, were furnished in the way of commerce, and that the articles which came from the King's magazine and arsenals were sold to M. de Beaumarchais by the department of artillery, and that he has furnished his obligations for the price of these articles."

If Gérard concluded that after their polite correspondence Common Sense would retire from the public discussion, he was mistaken. Continuing his series on the 5th, Paine poured the rough scorn of an American soldier upon Deane's "sufferings" and "sacrifices" for the American cause. "It fell not to his lot to turn out to a Winter's campaign, and sleep without tent or blanket. He returned to America when the danger was over, and has since that time suffered no personal hardship. What then are Mr. Deane's *sufferings* and what the sacrifices he complains of? Has he lost money in the public service? I believe not. Has he got any? That I cannot tell." Paine also reasserted for America, "Those who are now her allies prefaced that alliance by an early and generous friendship." The statement could not be ignored by Gérard. On that same day he rushed a formal protest to Congress against these "indiscreet assertions" by an American public official. He asked Congress "to take measures suitable to the circumstances."

Had Congress known the true facts and been willing to act disinterestedly, there was one obvious policy to pursue—disavow the publications of Common Sense, wink at Paine and Gérard, and put off the claims of Deane and Beaumarchais indefinitely. But Congress was ignorant of its own secrets and was torn by the interests of conflicting factions—the pro-French, the pro-British, the friends of Paine, the partners of Deane. Paine sent in a memorial on the 6th, "understanding that exceptions have been taken to some parts of my conduct." He requested a hearing. Summoned before Congress, he was asked whether he was the author of *Common Sense to the Public on Mr. Deane's Affair*. He answered, "Yes, I am the author of all these pieces," and was immediately ordered to leave. Continuing the matter in secret session, Congressional debate waxed hot and furious in a swirl of motions and counter-motions, none of them put to a vote: that the publications were ill-judged and indiscreet, that Congress did not sanction them, that Congress never received military stores as a present from France or any other court or person in Europe, that a committee be appointed to investigate the whole matter.

Paine's friends informed him of the proceedings. The next day he submitted another memorial, demanding his right to a copy of the charges and an opportunity to answer them. "I have obtained fame, honor, and credit in this country," the $70-a-month Secretary said. "I am proud of these honors." They cannot be taken away by "any unjust censure founded on a concealed charge." But Congress was in the ludicrous position of being afraid to hear the

65

truth. The previous motions were brought up, and new, more damnatory ones introduced: that the publications were an abuse of office, that Paine be dismissed from his position, that the French ambassador be consulted to suggest a more suitable punishment. Paine's friends—Henry Laurens, General Roberdeau, and others—fought every inch of the way and urged the Deane party in the name of common decency to allow Paine to defend himself.

At this arose Gouverneur Morris, New York aristocrat and staunch friend of Deane and Robert Morris (to whom he was related only in political kinship). Why all this pother about rights and privileges, when all that is proposed is "to turn a man out of office who ought never to have been in it"? He swelled along in lofty contempt at Paine's social origins: "What would be the idea of a gentleman in Europe of this Mr. Paine? Would he not suppose him to be a man of the most affluent fortune, born in this country of a respectable family, with wide and great connexions, and endued with the nicest sense of honor? Certainly he would suppose, that all these pledges of fidelity were necessary to a people in our critical circumstances. But, alas, what would he think, should he accidentally be informed, that this, our Secretary of Foreign Affairs, was a mere adventurer *from England,* without fortune, without family or connexions, ignorant even of grammar? . . . And yet, Sir, this is the man whom we would remove from office, and this is the man, who has been just now puffed as of great importance." The speech of Gouverneur Morris is an eloquent testimony of what the Spirit of '76 meant to one of the haloed Founders of Our Country, whose hand was destined to write the American Constitution, and to a large section of the leading "gentlemen" in Congress. They were quite ready and eager to scuttle the author of *Common Sense* and *The Crisis*. By a vote of 8 to 4, Rhode Island divided, Congress decided that Paine should not be heard.

The next morning, the 8th of January, 1779, before a motion for dismissing Paine from his official post could be made, Congress had Paine's resignation. He made a ringing affirmation of his recent conduct.

"My wish and my intentions in all my late publications were to preserve the public from error and imposition, to support as far as laid in my power the just authority of the Representatives of the People, and to cordialize and cement the Union that has so happily taken place between this country and France.

"I have betrayed no Trust because I have constantly employed that Trust to the public good. I have revealed no secrets because I have told nothing that was, or I conceive ought to be a secret. I have convicted Mr. Deane of error, and in so doing I hope I have done my duty."

Paine having slipped through their fingers, the Deane party angrily demanded to know how he had come to get a look at the Journal. Charles Thomson, Secretary to Congress, declared that he had shown the Journal to nobody, had taken it home the night before and brought it into Congress in the morning. A motion was made and argued to poll the members for the secret, whereupon Henry Laurens revealed that he had told Paine of yesterday's proceedings. Laurens, the former President of Congress, was too big to be chastised. A motion was offered on the 9th that the motion not to hear Paine on the 7th "did not imply, nor can it be justly construed to imply, that Congress had

67

determined that Mr. Paine was not to be heard." This bare-faced lie was spread on the record as the sense of Congress by a vote of 11 to 1, Rhode Island again divided. Congress had, after a fashion, washed its hands of Silas Deane and Thomas Paine.

CHAPTER VII

CLASS WARFARE IN PENNSYLVANIA

THE Deane affair was not over. It simply shifted from the halls of Congress to the streets of Philadelphia. While the international war was comparatively at a standstill in 1779, Pennsylvania was in the throes of a class war between the common people and the economic royalists of the day.

In an unremitting stream of newspaper articles Thomas Paine, now an ordinary clerk in a brokerage house, struck out at the Deane clique. Men are making profits out of the prerogatives of office, out of the sufferings of their fellowmen. Not public spirit, but private greed, motivates the Deane-Morris crew. "To what a degree of corruption must we sink," he demanded, "if our Delegates and Ambassadors are to be admitted to carry on a private partnership in trade? . . . Is it right that Mr. Deane, a servant of Congress, should sit as a Member of that House, when his own conduct was before the House for judgment? Certainly not. But the *interest* of Mr. Deane has sat there in the person of his partner, Mr. Robert Morris, who, at the same time that he represented this State, represented likewise the partnership in trade. . . . One monopolizer confederates with another, and defaulter with defaulter, till the cause becomes a common one." Deane and his literary advocate, Philalethes, brazened out a strained defense, while Paine lashed forth time and again at the grafters and profiteers.

For his unequivocal stand on Deane and his associates,

Paine was in mortal danger. Something of the risk which he took whenever he went out on the streets in the winter of '78-'79 is shown by the incident which John Joseph Henry smugly relates. A number of men—among them Matthias Slough, a member of the state legislature—were returning from a banquet one night when they saw Paine coming towards them down Market Street. " 'There comes Common Sense,' says Slough, 'I shall common sense him.' As he approached the party, they took the wall. Mr. Slough tripped him, and threw him on his back into a gutter, which at that time was very offensive and filthy." Henry observes that these persons were all "men of eminence in the state."

The personal attention by these "men of eminence" was a recognition of Paine's power with the populace. The common people of Pennsylvania rallied to his support because his exposé of the Deane-Morris cabal pointed to the source of their own miseries—food scarcity, rising prices, and profiteering. "Personal disinterestedness and pecuniary integrity," Gérard reported to Vergennes, "have shed no lustre on the birth of the American republic." The deep-seated social conflict in Pennsylvania now revolved about Paine and Deane as symbols.

The political and economic issues were inseparable. Politically, the merchants and aristocrats had been checked by the democratic State Constitution and the democratic single-house legislature to which the Philadelphia artisans and western frontiersmen clung with fierce loyalty. Ever since the revolutionary enactment of the State Constitution in July, 1776, these two opposing groups—the Constitutionalist masses and the Anti-Constitutionalist reactionaries—had been engaged in a continuous conflict which often took on the lineaments of civil war. On the 24th of March, 1779, the aristocratic minority, led by Robert Morris, organized themselves into a Republican Society to get rid of the Constitution which had given power to workers and farmers. James Wilson, lawyer and real-estate speculator, published in the *Packet* of the 25th a blast against the democratic Constitution as the source of Pennsylvania's troubles. Timothy Matlack, spirited Fighting Quaker and secretary to the Supreme Executive Council, replied with a warning to the enemies of the Constitution lest they overstep the line into conspiracy. On the 30th the Constitutional Society was formed, with Captain Charles Willson Peale, the celebrated painter, as Chairman.

Now the people's fight against economic oppression— the "forestalling" and "engrossing" of commodities—was intensified. On the 27th of May a mass meeting was held in the State House yard. The meeting, led by General Roberdeau, declared that profiteering, hoarding of commodities, and high prices must end and that the people should take direct action, if necessary. A Committee of Inspection was chosen, consisting of Matlack, Rittenhouse, Peale, Colonel J. B. Smith, and Thomas Paine. Leading merchants were ordered to appear before this extra-legal tribunal to justify their business methods. A company of soldiers lately returned from Fort Mifflin swore to enforce the orders of the Committee.

Feeling ran high. And Paine was the special target of reactionary attacks. On the 9th of July, in the *Evening Post,* a writer signing as Cato launched into a ferocious personal denunciation. "Who was an Englishman? Tom P——. Who was a Tory? Tom P——. Who wrote the Crisis, and abused Howe? Tom P——. Who was made secretary to the committee of foreign affairs? Tom P——. Who recommended him

to that office? . . . Who betrayed state affairs? Tom P——.
For whom did he betray them? . . . Who has traduced
the tried friends of America? Tom P——. Who has endeavoured to raise suspicions against congress? Tom P——.
Who was a committee man? Tom P——. Who proposed a
resolution to the committee to prevent supplies from going
to the army? Tom P——. Who maintains Tom P——? Nobody knows. Who is paid by the enemy? Nobody knows.
Who best deserves it? Tom P——." On the 22nd A Friend
to Cato and to Truth peered maliciously into Paine's first
mental gropings in America in 1775, his "throwing off the
Tory, and commencing Whig." Two days later Cato sneered
at "the great, the glorious, magnificent, magnanimous,
most monstrous Tom."

On the evening of Cato's latest outburst, a few Constitutionalists, accompanied by a file of soldiers, called upon Benjamin Towne, publisher of the *Post,* and demanded Cato's
real name. Towne hesitated, until his visitors asked him
whether he would like to hang from a tree. Cato, they
discovered, was Whitehead Humphreys, a local merchant.
Marching over to Humphreys' house, the crowd broke in,
handled the furnishings unceremoniously, and, brandishing
clubs and muskets, hurled their warnings at Humphreys
and withdrew. Cato stopped writing.

The people of Philadelphia came together on the 26th
of July in a mass meeting in the State House yard to hear
a report by the Committee of Inspection, of which Paine
was a member. The Committee submitted its findings on
Robert Morris, who had been suspected, in collusion with
a Mr. Solikoff of Baltimore, of cornering the market in flour
while Philadelphia was suffering the hardships of war. In
spite of the mass pressure for a violent decision, the Com-

mittee reviewed the facts temperately and concluded: "As we are not authorized to condemn, so neither can we justify; and are persuaded that when Mr. Morris reflects on the uneasiness which such a mode of purchasing has occasioned, that he will take measures in future to prevent the same consequences, for tho', as a merchant, he may be strictly within rules, yet when he considers the many public and honorary stations he has filled, and the times he lives in, he must feel himself somewhat out of character." Attempting to speak in behalf of Morris, General John Cadwalader was silenced by the menacing crowd. A small section withdrew to the yard of the College of Philadelphia, and here, with Morris in the chair, dutifully passed a resolution endorsing him. Morris, however, having a good weather eye, soon afterwards got rid of the flour and could rest more securely behind the mahogany doors of the grandest mansion in America.

It had been an exhausting time, and Paine fell sick with a "fever." He took no active part while the Pennsylvania Assembly stiffened its regulations against the enemies of the State Constitution, the popular meetings continued and grew more bitter, and shirt-sleeved radicals pasted placards all over town denouncing Wilson, Morris, Deane, and their fellow aristocrats. In the long solitary hours of sickness, the poverty-stricken clerk might well brood on the amazing outcome of his dreams for personal well-being in America. The future seemed suddenly bleak and shabby. Writing to Henry Laurens on the 14th of September, Paine sighs, even while he jokes about it, for those material comforts which are denied him. He cannot even afford to hire a horse for the exercise which he needs. He beats his brains for ways of making money. He will bring together all his writings.

He will write a complete History of the Revolution, copiously illustrated, treating the English phase as well as the American, and "an abridgement afterwards in an easy agreeable language for a school book." But meanwhile? The words come haltingly. He would like "to borrow something of a friend or two in the interim."

Sick and worried, Paine wrote bitter letters to President Reed and the Supreme Executive Council about the indifference of the State to his welfare. He pointed out that his plight was a matter of concern for the future of the Revolution. "I cannot but observe," he wrote to the Council on the 28th of September, "that the Course of four years have produced no other signature universally known and read here and abroad except that under which I have constantly published, and should my situation be rendered such as shall oblige me to discontinue the part I have hitherto acted, it will not be easy to establish a new Signature that shall collect and keep the Sentiments of the Country together, should any future emergency arise, which to me appears very probable." The following day President Reed, a smooth politician, unwilling to make Paine an issue with the Anti-Constitutionalist minority in the government, wrote to the French ambassador inquiring whether it would be agreeable to him that Pennsylvania do something for Paine. Gérard being out of town, the matter was left temporarily in suspense.

Any hesitancy in the minds of Reed and Gérard about aiding Paine was removed as the Constitutionalists of Philadelphia, with whom Paine was so intimately involved, surged violently forward to a more complete domination of the city. The "Fort Wilson Riot" occurred on the 4th of October. After a fiery meeting at noon in Byrne's Tavern a furious crowd of militiamen and hot-headed townsfolk swept along Walnut Street, proclaiming with boisterous lungs and pounding drums that they were going to visit James Wilson, intellectual leader of the Anti-Constitutionalists and author of their chief pronouncements. Arriving at the mansion on the corner of Third Street, the mob found Wilson and some thirty supporters ready. Orders to move on and defiant yells were exchanged, and shooting broke out. The maddened people were about to break into the house with hammers and bars when President Reed, disheveled and panicky, galloped up with members of the City Horse and dispersed them. Several wounded and one killed on each side bore witness to the blood-soaked hatreds of classes and parties within the American fold.

The State elections took place on the 12th of October. Paine was not running for office; but he had been the central and symbolic issue of the campaign. The Constitutionalists, carried along by the democratic suffrage, won a smashing victory at the polls. Philadelphia went completely Constitutionalist, and the Anti-Constitutionalist minority from the counties was reduced almost to nothing. Robert Morris was supplanted in the Assembly by the radical Judge George Bryan, sharing primacy in the new government with Peale, chairman of the Constitutional Society. To the aristocrats and big merchants and their adherents it seemed that the twilight of the gods was plunging into utter darkness. Dr. Benjamin Rush, whose concept of independence did not include democracy, groaned on the 24th of October in a letter to General Charles Lee that "Poor Pennsylvania" was now governed by a "mobocracy" and that "all our laws breathe the spirit of town meetings and porter shops." "My family & my business now engross all

75

my time," Rush concludes. "My Country I have long ago left to the care of Timy Matlack—Tom Paine—Charles Willson Peale & Co."

At the first session of the new government, the grateful Assembly elected Paine its Clerk. The wheel had turned full circle and he was again officially in public life. On the 17th of November, Congress gave a last audience to Monsieur Gérard, now diplomatically sick and glad to retire after a strenuous year with the Americans. One feature of the ceremony was the entrance of the entire Pennsylvania Assembly with their Clerk Paine, quietly triumphing over the House and the ambassador who had both consigned him to disgrace and oblivion. "As to myself," Paine writes Henry Laurens on the 21st, "thank God, I am well and feel much pleasanter than I did—The Clerkship is not much but it is something like business and has released me from that burden of idleness, uneasiness and hopeless thinking that got so much the upper hand of me for these three or four months past."

The crucial year 1779 was now drawing to an end, sweeping into memory the conflict of Deane and Paine. Deane, rejected by Congress for making a private racket out of official opportunities, left America in high dudgeon and became an open enemy of the American cause. Safe in Europe, he attempted the seizure by litigation of American governmental property, held secret meetings with British emissaries, formally renounced his American citizenship, and received and returned the visits of the traitor Benedict Arnold. Paine, supported by the masses whom he had championed, rededicated himself to the work of the American Revolution—"to make room upon the earth for honest men to live in."

CHAPTER VIII

FOR. NATIONAL UNITY

TO A Philadelphia patriot in the winter of '79-'80 the prospect for the Revolution was dark. The main British and American armies were stalemated in New York and White Plains, the Americans increasingly demoralized by hunger and cold. The French were mainly occupied with defending their own in West Indian waters. The British campaign in the South had brought Georgia under complete control and was moving into South Carolina. British raiding parties tore through the countryside up and down the coast, plundering the crops, slaughtering the cattle, burning the houses, raping and killing. Anarchy reigned in wide sections of the country, and British sympathizers pleaded openly for a return to the peace of the King.

The facts themselves gave little justification for Paine's boast in *Crisis VIII* (March, 1780) that "America is beyond the reach of conquest." Anxiously and impotently the patriots looked to the South, where Clinton's siege and Tarleton's cavalry charges were breaking down the American defenses at Charleston, South Carolina. Charleston fell on the 11th of May, and South Carolina passed under a military dictatorship. At White Plains, the starving remnants of Washington's army were coming to the end of human endurance. Contractors refused to deliver more supplies, and what was available could not be hauled for lack of wagons. The mutiny of two regiments, though suppressed,

77

was an ominous token that American resistance might soon fall to pieces at every strategic point of conflict.

On the 28th of May Washington appealed in his last desperate straits directly to the Executive Council of Pennsylvania, which transmitted his letter to the Assembly. Sitting behind locked doors, the Assembly listened to the straightforward forecast of immediate disaster being read by the Clerk. The army, said Washington, were devoted to the cause of America, but it was humanly impossible for them to carry on much longer against their privations. "I assure you," he reported, "every idea you can form of our distresses will fall short of the reality. There is such a combination of circumstances to exhaust the patience of the soldiery that it begins at length to be worn out, and we see in every line of the army the most serious features of mutiny and sedition." As Paine finished reading, a dead silence fell upon the House. What could they do? The Quakers and Tories were cheating on their tax returns, and many delegates had already pledged themselves to reduce the terrific financial burden of the war. "It appears to me in vain to contend the matter any longer," said one delegate, while another feebly protested, "Don't let the house despair."

Money, food, clothing were needed. Leaving the assembly hall, Paine drew out one thousand dollars (paper money) due him on salary. He sent half that sum to a leading merchant, Blair McClenaghan, with a plea for a revival of interest among the rich and powerful to rescue "the fairest cause that Men ever engaged in." "It is now hard times with many poor people," he observes, and only the "Merchants and Traders," who have the largest stake in the Revolution, can save the day. "I enclose 500 dollars as my

78

mite thereto, and if that is not sufficient I will add 500
more, tho' the little gratitude I have received does not lay
it upon me as a duty, neither do my circumstances well
admit of it; but I have an affection for her cause that will
carry me as far as the last ability will enable me to go."
Putting aside the political differences of the past year, Paine
declares his readiness to cooperate with any patriotic society "no matter who may complete it."

That evening, at the coffee-house, McClenaghan elaborated on Paine's suggestion before a wealthy group, and
they proceeded to action. On the strength of their bonds the
Bank of Pennsylvania was started to supply the army with
provisions. McClenaghan and Robert Morris subscribed for
£10,000 each, and other prominent subscribers were James
Wilson, President Reed, and Dr. Rush. The wives of more
modestly circumstanced patriots like J. B. Smith and Dr.
Hutchinson organized "The American Daughters of Liberty" and went from house to house, collecting funds and
provisions for Washington's army.

The danger was temporarily averted. In *Crisis IX* (June
9) Paine hails the fact that "The reported fate of Charleston, like the misfortunes of 1776, has at last called forth a
spirit, and kindled up a flame, which perhaps no other event
could have produced." It may serve "to rouse us from the
slumber of twelve months past, and renew in us the spirit
of former days." A final push and we have won. The enemy
are exhausting themselves by "piecemeal work," a united
Europe is with us, and America must surely triumph since
these developments in Pennsylvania prove that her cause
is based "on the broad foundation of property and popularity."

Yet the American cause kept wavering between hope and

79

increasing despair. In mid-July, a French fleet arrived at Newport with 6,000 troops under Rochambeau, but Clinton was in turn reenforced by British warships. The second French fleet was blocked up in Brest, and Rochambeau would not venture alone to cooperate with Washington in an attack on New York. The attempt by Gates to salvage the South received a severe setback in August when he met the British at Camden, South Carolina. In September the treason of Benedict Arnold came fearfully close to throwing the strategic fort at West Point into the hands of the enemy.

Paine appreciated the desperate situation. The Revolution could not succeed without the full, united effort of all—rich and poor, state and state, America and France. He continued to urge the fundamental doctrine of unity.

The *Crisis Extraordinary* (October 6, 1780) appeals to the merchants "on the simple ground of interest" to support the Revolution. Paine proves by an elaborate display of facts and figures that it is cheaper to uphold the Revolution than, after the defeat, to pay the British debt and submit to the British restrictions which will fall upon Whigs and Tories without distinction. He sketches the octopus-like ramifications of the British tax system, which squeezes revenue even out of the light from heaven by exacting eighteen pence sterling per window annually. "In short, the condition of that country, in point of taxation, is so oppressive, the number of her poor so great, and the extravagance and rapaciousness of the court so enormous, that, were they to effect a conquest of America, it is then only that the distresses of America would begin. Neither would it signify anything to a man whether he be Whig or Tory. The people of England, and the ministry of that country, know us by no such distinctions. What they want is clear, solid revenue, and the modes which they would take to procure it, would operate alike on all." It is good business to endorse a funding of the currency. "Support that measure, and it will support you," he says, in the prudential spirit of Franklin's Poor Richard. Further, the appeal is interlarded with phrases about "the purity of the cause" and "honor, fame, character." When profit and patriotism coincide, the combination is irresistible.

Public Good (December, 1780) appeals to the states for unity. The individual states must get rid of their ancient antagonisms and jealousies and work together for their common needs as a nation. They had come to the Revolution with the concept of provincial rather than national sovereignty. Seven states—Virginia, the Carolinas, Georgia, New York, Massachusetts, and Connecticut—had overlapping sea-to-sea charters and would not yield to ownership and control by the Federal Government over the western lands as proposed by the Committee on the Articles of Confederation in July, 1776. On this rock all attempts at a legitimized federal union foundered. Without definite powers of any kind, the makeshift Revolutionary Congress stumbled through the gigantic task of waging the war for freedom. The sovereign states contributed according to their individual fears and whims, and the Articles of Confederation, in spite of its pathetic slightness and inadequacy, remained for five years a mere adventurous dream of the Committee.

The chief contention was between the claims of Virginia and the interests of Maryland. In her State Constitution of 1776, Virginia moderated her sea-to-sea pretensions into a claim upon all the lands east of the Mississippi within the old charter limits—a vast fertile territory embracing what has since become the states of Michigan, Wisconsin, Ohio, Indiana, and Illinois. Pennsylvania had extensive unoccupied stretches within her own borders. By selling their wild lands, Virginia and Pennsylvania could pay off their debts and finance elaborate governmental administrations without the imposition of taxes. Hemmed in between the two, Maryland feared that her own citizens would be lured away by her more attractive neighbors. Other small states—Delaware, New Hampshire, New Jersey—readily signed the Articles of Confederation, which promised them equal representation with the large states. Maryland alone held out until the states should cede their western lands to the Federal Government. Unperturbed, Virginia insisted on her "rights" and proceeded to open up land offices and give away land bounties. The resultant ill-will was a paralyzing handicap to the Revolution, and an ominous portent no matter which way the war might end.

It hardly needs to be argued that the health and internal peace of America depended on the Federal absorption and exploitation of the western lands and on the establishment of new states having a parity with the seaboard. Until Virginia relented, however, no other state dared to renounce its own claims. The continual petitions by Congress had no effect in themselves. More convincing arguments were furnished by the hazardous course of the Revolution, frequently making the whole squabble appear like an academic irrelevance, and by the ruthless southern campaign of Clinton and Cornwallis creeping up on Virginia. In September, 1780, Congress appealed again, and in December Thomas Paine laid bare all the fallacies of Virginia's case in his pamphlet *Public Good*.

Paine proceeds in a closely integrated pattern of arguments, the details of which have now only an antiquarian interest. First, the claims of Virginia are not founded on rights. Second, the claims are unreasonable. And, third, if the claims were admitted, detrimental consequences would result even for Virginia. "The United States now standing on the line of sovereignty," he concludes by urging "a continental convention, for the purpose of forming a continental constitution, defining and describing the powers and authority of Congress."

While his call for a national constitutional convention was still seven years ahead of its time, Paine's assertion of national governance over western lands was a push towards the further development of national unity. In January, 1781, Virginia renounced her western claims and Maryland ratified the Articles of Confederation, making it the law of the land.

CHAPTER IX

THE FRENCH GIFT

BY THE end of 1780 Paine as pamphleteer had probed to all the fundamental needs and mainsprings of action in America. *Common Sense* had made the young nation conscious of herself, her strength, and her revolutionary will. The first *Crisis* papers had inspired Americans with renewed hope in the ultimate triumph of America despite the terrific defeats of Long Island, Brandywine, and Germantown. His newspaper series during the conflict with Deane in 1779 had stayed the hands of colonial profiteers and had revived popular enthusiasm for the original idealism of the American cause. His pamphlets in 1780 had made a frank appeal in behalf of national unity to the enlightened self-interest of the wealthy classes and of the individual states. The circuit of American canvassing was complete.

But all this was not enough. It was painfully evident that America, divided and weak, would be unable by her own bayonets to win victory on her own soil. England must be made sick of the conflict by more subtle means, or France must give more energetic support.

In the fall of 1780, musing on the English newspapers which he had seen, with their garbled and unfavorable picture of the American position supplied by refugee loyalists and English politicians, Paine hit upon the bold scheme of returning incognito to England. There he would bring out a popularly toned publication purporting to be

84

the diary of an English traveler in America. "The simple point I mean to aim at," he explained to General Greene, "is, to make the acknowledgment of Independence a popular subject, and that not by exposing and attacking their errors, but by stating its advantages and apologizing for their errors, by way of accommodating the measure to their pride." Paine resigned the Clerkship to carry out this plan. But the treason of Arnold and the execution of his British accomplice André now occurred, and the atmosphere was heavy with danger of reprisals. If Paine were caught in England, he might grace the hangman's rope in the old Tyburn of London. General Greene and President Reed urged him to give up his scheme, and reluctantly he did so.

Here he was again, through his public zeal, out of employment and with no job in sight. However, his pockets were not yet empty, and the times were too exciting and critical to think much about self. He followed with keen interest the acrimonious debates which raged in Congress during the winter of 1780-81 over the reputed generosity of Louis XVI. French credits, Rochambeau's men loitering in Newport, the French fleet far away in the West Indies, had wrought no miracle of deliverance. The irrepressible anti-French faction, inflamed by Arthur Lee and Ralph Izard (another former envoy in Europe), argued that France was trying to get off too cheap while the Americans were grappling with her ancient enemy England, and that Franklin was not pressing American demands with enough diligence. As a compromise in the debate on foreign affairs, Congress decided to send a special envoy to ask the French court for an enlarged fleet and a gift of 25,000,000 livres in specie.

The man chosen was Colonel John Laurens, a chivalrous

young South Carolinian only twenty-six years old. His father, Henry Laurens, had been intercepted by the British on his way to Holland, and was imprisoned in the Tower of London. Young Laurens was a fanatical patriot, unskilled in diplomatic subtleties. He appealed to his friend and counselor, the forty-three-year-old Paine, to accompany him to France. Laurens wanted Paine to travel as his official Secretary, but it soon became apparent that such a proposition must not be pushed in Congress. Not to embroil the situation, Paine decided to go along as an unofficial companion.

On the way to Boston, Laurens received the hearty endorsement of Lafayette and Rochambeau and a letter from Washington to Franklin, intended to be shown to the French ministry. Reviewing the American situation, Washington emphatically declares: "What I have said to him [Colonel Laurens] I beg leave to repeat to you that, to me, nothing appears more evident than that the period of our opposition will very shortly arrive if our allies can not afford us that effectual aid, particularly in money and a naval superiority, which are now solicited." Embarked on the most crucial mission of the war, Paine and Laurens set out from Boston on the frigate *Alliance,* February 11, 1781.

The *Alliance* had a hazardous voyage across the wintry seas. It sailed along smoothly for four days until, at about nine o'clock of a black night, "from a sudden tremulous motion of the ship attended with a rushing noise, the general cry was that she had struck, and was either aground or on a rock." The ship, the voyagers discovered, was being tossed by ice-clogged waters, "a tumultuous assemblage of floating rolling rocks." A severe gale came up, and before the sails could be taken in, one was torn in half. At eleven o'clock, the larboard quarter gallery was swept away, a minute after Laurens had left it. At dawn they could see "an island of ice which appeared out of the water like a mountain," and they wondered how close they had been to disaster in the darkness. Storms were not their only danger. A few weeks later, sighting two British vessels, the passengers turned out under the command of Laurens for the prospective encounter, but the British fled. The next day the *Alliance* sighted two other vessels, gave chase, and captured without a fight a Scotch cutter and her unjustifiable prize, a Venetian freighter. On March 9, they arrived safely at L'Orient.

Two days later Paine wrote to his Philadelphia friend, Dr. James Hutchinson, describing the voyage. He reported with characteristic optimism that European conditions are improving for America, a French fleet will soon leave Brest, and all that is necessary is to "be forward in filling up your Army and fear nothing." "I find myself no Stranger in France," he writes, "people know me almost as generally here as in America, the Commandant of L'Orient paid me very high Compliments on what he called the great Success and Spirit of my Publications."

Laurens went immediately to Paris, while Paine proceeded to Nantes with Franklin's nephew Jonathan Williams, an American commercial agent and one of the objects of Lee's tirades. "I traveled with Mr. Payne from L'Orient hither," Williams writes to Franklin from Nantes, April 18, 1781. "I find he is a strong enemy to Mr. D[eane]; he professes not to be so to you, but, on the contrary, expresses himself respectfully of you. He says, however, he laments that you should be the friend and supporter of Mr. D[eane]. I suspect he is a little of a Leeite, tho' he professes no attachment to him; but I am sure he is attached to Iz[ard], and they, you know, run in the same line. We agree exceedingly well together, and are growing intimate. I confess I like him as a companion, because he is a pleasant, as well as sensible, man, and I trust, however, that when he has been a little longer in Europe, and is made acquainted with Lee's rascality, he will, like other good men, despise the wretch."

In Nantes it was Paine's misfortune to meet an American merchant by the name of Elkanah Watson. Many years later, after Paine the deist and world-democrat had become the universal butt of respectable vilification, Watson recalled this meeting in a book of reminiscences entitled *Men and Times of the Revolution.* He described Paine as "coarse and uncouth in his manners, loathsome in his appearance, and a disgusting egotist." And he said that the Mayor of Nantes, calling to pay homage, left in unseemly haste because Paine's offensive odor "perfumed the whole apartment." With the bait of a clean shirt and some English newspapers, Watson, according to his own account, cajoled Paine into a bath and directed the attendant in French (which Paine did not understand) to increase the heat until *"le Monsieur était bien bouilli."* This is Watson's backward glance at the man whom Williams found so "pleasant, as well as sensible." One may take it or leave it.

From Nantes Paine rejoined Laurens in Paris. Visiting Franklin at Passy, he tried to wipe away his old patron's lingering faith in Deane. He spent pleasant hours with the American group in Jonathan Williams' circle at St. Germain. He took no public part in the American mission.

Laurens himself was a most unwelcome visitor at Versailles. He cut through the red tape of diplomacy in which the adroit and devious Franklin did not object to being wound. Every day he stormed the Ministry as if it were an enemy fortress. The patriot cause was desperate, he warned, and touching his sword significantly, he assured Vergennes that the resentful Americans might unite with the British against His Christian Majesty. Lee, Izard, and John Adams were the most obsequious courtiers compared with this hot-headed youngster. Vergennes broke down and promised Laurens 6,000,000 livres and the French guarantee of a Dutch loan of 10,000,000 livres, but no more. And he refused to give specific information about the size of the French fleet for the coming summer.

Paine and Laurens sailed from France on the 1st of June in the frigate *La Résolue,* carrying in its hold 2,500,000 livres of silver in double casks, and accompanied by two ships freighted with military provisions. Heavy storms and fear of British cruisers made the voyage rough and devious, and they finally landed in Boston, instead of Philadelphia, on the 25th of August. The casks of silver were packed in sturdy oaken boxes, which were strapped and welded to the axles of sixteen powerful ox-carts; and the precious caravan, under a strong mounted convoy, plodded westward through the wild country and down to Philadelphia. Riding the post-road to New York, Paine's sulky broke down just after leaving Providence. Laurens, eager to bring the good news to Washington and to get back into the fight, gave Paine six guineas and went ahead alone. With the six guineas Paine had to pay the personal expenses of himself and a servant of Laurens and the upkeep of two horses for some three hundred miles of slow travel. At Bordentown he was obliged to borrow a dollar to get on the ferry to Philadelphia.

The French gift was the conclusive economic weapon of the Revolution. Robert Morris, newly appointed Superintendent of Finance, had been striving mightily to put American finances on a hard-money basis. He had called upon wealthy patriots to deposit their specie in the Bank, and had sold state contributions of flour and other goods in foreign ports for cash. All this, however, was slow and insufficient. The French money was a spectacular providential grant, which could be spectacularly exploited for popular support. Morris had the silver piled high on the counters of the Bank, and he put his men to trundling it busily back and forth from the vaults. America appeared fabulously rich, powerful. The soldiers could march to the siege of Yorktown with the novel, inspiriting sensation that all their needs would be quickly and generously supplied.

While Washington and Rochambeau by land and De Grasse by water were closing in on the amazingly incompetent Cornwallis at Yorktown, a minor inharmonious ripple of defeatism was being stirred up in America by the latest anti-patriotic endeavors of Silas Deane. From Paris that gentleman was scribbling letters wholesale to his old associates in America counseling surrender. To his brother Barnabas, Deane declared, "Peace only can save us from absolute ruin," and to James Wilson, "Independency must prove a curse rather than a blessing to us." These letters were gleefully published in the loyalist press of New York in order to dishearten the patriot forces. Deane stood before the eyes of the world as a renegade. Giving him up at last, Franklin correctly predicted to Jay that Deane's conduct "must ruin him forever in America and here. I think we shall soon hear of his retiring to England and joining his friend Arnold."

It was naturally a sweet personal satisfaction to Paine to
see the old adversary self-condemned and his former associates doing penance. Writing triumphantly from Philadelphia on the 26th of November to Jonathan Williams in
Nantes, Paine reports: "Mr. Robert Morris assured me that
he had been totally deceived in Deane, but that he now
looked upon him to be a bad man, and his reputation totally
ruined. Gouverneur Morris hopped round upon one leg,
swore they had all been duped, himself among the rest,
complimented me on my quick sight,—and 'by God,' says
he, 'nothing carries a man through the world like honesty.'"
But there is greater news to tell. "Lord Cornwallis with
7,247 officers and men are nabbed nicely in the Chesapeake, which I presume you have heard already, otherwise
I should send you the particulars. I think the enemy can
hardly hold out another campaign." It is a happy and
friendly man who concludes his letter to Williams, recalling pleasantly those he had met six months before in
France: "Remember me to Mr. & Mrs. Johnstone, Dr.
Pierce, Mr. Watson & Ceasey and Mr. Wilt. Make my best
wishes to Mrs. Williams, Mrs. Alexander, and all the good
girls at St. Germain."

CHAPTER X

The Last Push

THE victory at Yorktown on the 19th of October, 1781, put out of the war a great British army second only to Clinton's troops in New York. America and France had cooperated perfectly. The air sweet with the aroma of victory, Philadelphia was given over to a round of celebrations for the conquering army and General Washington.

But, for Paine personally, the bright picture had its dark aspect. He was penniless. It is impossible to keep on celebrating Yorktown on an empty stomach. This is bitter material fact which idealists like Paine must reckon with sooner or later. The author of *Common Sense* and the *Crisis* papers turned squarely to General Washington.

Strange musings must have run through Paine's mind as he wrote at the head of his appeal "Second Street, Opposite The Quaker Meeting-House, Nov. 30, 1781." How far and to what an amazing destiny had he traveled from the quiet faith of his childhood in old Thetford! "It is seven years, *this day,*" he reflects, "since I arrived in America, and tho' I consider them as the most honorary time of my life, they have nevertheless been the most inconvenient and even distressing." During the common hardships of the Revolution, he relates, he had declined the customary profits of authorship for his fighting pamphlets and had not complained at the willingness of the country to let him starve and be abused by special interests. With the rising prosperity of the cause, his personal straits were painfully ironic and intolerable. "I am totally at a loss what to attribute it to," he says, "for wherever I go I find respect, and everybody I meet treats me with friendship; all join in censuring the neglect and throwing blame on each other, so that their civility disarms me as much as their conduct distresses me."

Appreciating the clear and just debt of America, Washington set the wheels in motion to relieve his petitioner, but for a time nothing positive was accomplished. Meanwhile, the trend of events indicated that the vitalizing tonic of *Common Sense* was still needed. The British still held New York, Charleston, and other points, and in accordance with the usages of war could claim these territories at any peace negotiations. De Grasse, instead of cooperating with Washington in an attack on Charleston that would repeat the Yorktown success, sailed off to protect French interests in the West Indies. The states were jealous of one another and restless under the financial burdens of the war, and the disgruntled soldiers were clamorous for their back pay.

A committee of the army appealed to Paine to formulate their demand upon the Revolutionary Government. It was impossible not to sympathize with them, but their attitude at this juncture had a seditious tendency. Paine called at the office of Robert Morris, the Superintendent of Finance, on the 24th of January, and left a note warning of this development. On the 26th, according to Morris's Diary, they "had a long conversation on various matters of a public nature." Paine mentioned incidentally his own difficulties, and Morris, recalling that Washington had spoken to him twice about doing something for Paine, expressed a hope that some arrangement might be worked out suitable to

93

the dignity and influence of the author of *Common Sense* and the *Crisis*.

Robert Morris and his assistant, Gouverneur Morris, held frequent meetings with Paine in the next few days regarding a subsidy for his literary work. Having tasted his mettle on previous occasions, they knew that the mere prospect of hunger would not compel him to prostitute his pen for factional purposes. "In all our conversations with him," Robert Morris confides to his Diary, "we have pointedly declared that we sought the aid of his pen only in support of upright measures and a faithful administration in the service of our country. We disclaim private or partial views, selfish schemes of any and every kind." Robert Morris conferred with Washington and Robert R. Livingston, Secretary for Foreign Affairs, and the three agreed that Paine should confidentially receive 800 dollars a year out of the secret-service money, payable quarterly. His writing assignment was stated generally "to prepare the minds of the people to such restraints and such taxes and imposts as are absolutely necessary for their own welfare" and "to comment from time to time on military transactions, so as to place in the proper point of view the bravery, good conduct, and soldiership of our officers and troops when they deserve applause, and do the same on such conduct of such civil officers or citizens as act conspicuously for the service of their country."

Their common interest in the Revolution had finally made fast friends and partners of Robert Morris and Paine. On the 28th of February Paine wrote Morris a cordial letter of acceptance. As to the Deane affair, in which Paine and Morris had been so violently at loggerheads, Paine says gracefully, "We have now got rid of two traitors

Arnold and Deane, and tho' the event so far as respects the latter, has proved me right, it has at the same time proved nobody wrong. That they were alone in their crimes every one must see, and thus the mischiefs of their secret defection being remedied in their detection, the minds kept asunder by their contrivance unite with ease, confidence and satisfaction." Paine asks that an advance be granted in order that he may straighten out his accounts.

The advance was promptly made and Paine was freed for a year from financial worries. During this year he wrote many newspaper articles anonymously or under various pseudonyms in order not to exaggerate minor issues, keeping his famous signature Common Sense for the great public messages.

On the 27th of November, 1781, George III, still obdurate for war despite the debacle at Yorktown, made a bellicose address to Parliament. After a comprehensive debate extending over several weeks, Parliament voted to continue the war. When the King's Speech came to America, Paine answered it in *Crisis X* (March 5, 1782). Of course, he says, the Speech is a mere nothing, "inquired after with a smile, read with a laugh, and dismissed with disdain." Yet, Paine warns, "perhaps one of the greatest dangers which any country can be exposed to, arises from a kind of trifling which sometimes steals upon the mind, when it supposes the danger past; and this unsafe situation marks at this time the peculiar crisis of America."

It is difficult to keep fighting spirits high when there is no fighting to be done. The war in America had fallen away to scattered skirmishing. Great Britain was engaged in a desperate, losing effort to preserve her empire in the West Indies, the Mediterranean, and India from the Spanish and French fleets. The comforting news of successive allied victories trickled slowly into Philadelphia. Anxiously the Americans scanned the international arena to which the conflict had spread. On the 17th of March Paine invited Washington and Morris to discuss the shifting tendencies at his apartment over "a few oysters or a crust of bread and cheese." Talking and writing filled his days.

The packets landing in May brought a load of great, indistinct news to which American policy must be vigorously adapted. It seemed that the British merchants, at last tiring of the expensive war, the rising national debt, the restricted markets, had forced the resignation of the North Tory Ministry and had installed the Rockingham Whig Ministry pledged to a truce with America. Realistic, hard-headed Americans like Washington took this information for what it was worth. They knew that the Rockingham Whigs, counting on the decline of American militancy in the comparative peace after Yorktown, might offer terms no more satisfactory than those of 1778 and would try to play off America and France by separate settlements resulting in a disastrous realignment of forces.

"I do not address this publication so much to the people of America as to the British Ministry, whoever they may be," says Common Sense in *Crisis XI* (May 22, 1782), "for if it is their intention to promote any kind of negotiation, it is proper they should know beforehand, that the United States have as much honour as bravery; and that they are no more to be seduced from their alliance than their allegiance; that their line of politics is formed and not dependent, like that of their enemy, on chance and accident." The torn and bleeding heart of America must not be trifled with by half-way and treacherous offers. "Can ye restore to us the beloved dead? Can ye say to the grave, give up the murdered? Can ye obliterate from our memories those who are no more?" France has rejected all previous attempts to separate her from America, and America will not desert her great benefactor. "Let the world and Britain know," America's spokesman declares, "that we are neither to be bought nor sold; that our mind is great and fixed; our prospect clear; and that we will support our character as firmly as our independence."

In September appeared Paine's *Letter to the Abbé Raynal,* on which he had been working at intervals ever since the fall of the previous year, when he had borrowed from Robert Morris a copy of the Abbé's *Observations on the Revolution in America.* Raynal, a distinguished luminary among the Encyclopedists in France, an abbé by convenience, was one of those rare individuals whose idealism is so refined as to eventuate in a comprehensive skepticism and an active encouragement of the most reactionary forces. Under the guise of an Olympian impartiality, the mercurial passages of his pamphlet subtly ridiculed the pretensions of America and the motives of France while exalting Great Britain, "like the stout oak to which Horace compares the Romans, which, smitten by the axe and hacked by the steel, grows under the strokes, and draws fresh vigor even from its wounds." The Abbé's declamatory style and philosophic reputation, added to the persecution inflicted upon him by the French government, made the *Observations* an international literary event. It was quoted at length in one of Deane's intercepted letters and was reprinted extensively in America, even in the patriot newspapers.

To Paine's quick mind the *Observations* provided an opportune occasion for the practical fusing of two publications which he had long contemplated—a rationale of the Revolution addressed to European readers, and a narrative of the heroic American campaigns. After a courtly salutation to the renowned philosopher, Paine examines his leading tenets. At one point the Abbé says, "The whole question was reduced to the knowing whether the mother country had, or had not, a right to lay, directly or indirectly, a slight tax upon the colonies," yet elsewhere he considers the Stamp Act "an *usurpation* of the Americans' *most precious and sacred rights.*" It was a whole series of such usurpations, says Paine, which brought the Americans face to face with the real question, "Shall we be bound in all cases whatsoever by the British parliament, or shall we not?" and provoked an epochal Revolution the like of which the world had never seen. Because the Abbé skips lightly over the American victories at Trenton and Princeton in December, 1776, as "accidental," Paine gives a detailed account of that phenomenal campaign in which he had himself participated, and glorifies the peerless patriots who, after their heroic labors, lay down to rest on "the bare and frozen ground, with no covering than the sky." The continental paper money, which the Abbé deplores as an act of "despotism," was really a kind of war tax imposed by the people upon themselves for the preservation of "*their* independence," "*their* property," and "*their* country." Furthermore, the Americans were not weakening in 1778 and would have continued the war even without the French alliance.

These are all facts, demonstrable and obvious. Paine now pursues the Abbé into the airy region of "philosophical reflection." Raynal has roundly declared, "Philosophy, whose first sentiment is the desire to see all governments just and all people happy, in casting her eyes upon this alliance of a monarchy, with a people who are defending their liberty, *is curious to know its motive. She sees at once, too clearly, that the happiness of mankind has no part in it.*" Paine has to strain considerably in order to nullify this contention. Personally, having been victimized by official French double-dealing in the Deane affair and having been a prominent agent in the brow-beating Laurens mission, he could have no illusions about the motive of Louis and his Ministers. But he had consistently presented France in the *Crisis* papers as a noble and generous ally, and he must now maintain that position for the sake of harmony and the enhanced good-will of European governments. Paine makes a strong point, that purposes are hidden in "the barren cave of secrecy" but consequences are clear and unmistakable, and the consequences of the alliance are "a continued good to all posterity." "That demon of society, prejudice," keeping nations apart, has caused misunderstanding and war, and the American Revolution and the alliance with France are the most powerful solvents of prejudice. The future peace and happiness of mankind depends on "a total reformation" and "an expanded mind" in England to "reform her manners, retrench her expenses, live peaceably with her neighbors, and think of war no more."

The *Letter to the Abbé Raynal* had a wide, harmonizing influence in Europe at the time of the peace negotiations. In England, as "a gentleman in a high character in France" writes on the 14th of December, the pamphlet was presented to Burke, the Duke of Richmond, and Secretary Townshend, and "has since been largely reprinted, and rapidly vended in London." Across the Channel, under the paternal eye of His Majesty's Government, laudatory reviews were printed in the *Courier de L'Europe* and the *Journal of Annual Literature*. "An American gentleman in France" writes back home on the 3rd of February, 1783: "I could not help thinking of our old friend COMMON SENSE. And I tell you plainly, that even those who are jealous of, and envy him, acknowledge that the point of his pen has been as formidable in politics as the point of the sword in the field. I have lately traveled much, and find him everywhere. His letter to the Abbé Raynal has sealed his fame; and I am firmly persuaded that all the prolix writings of the present age, put together, will not contribute so effectually to eradicate ancient prejudices and expand a liberality of mind as his laconic epistle."

After seeing his *Letter* through the press in Philadelphia, Paine withdrew for two or three weeks to visit with his friends Kirkbride and Borden in quiet Bordentown across the Delaware in New Jersey. From this retreat he sent fifty copies of the *Letter* to Livingston, fifty to Morris, and fifty to Washington. To the latter he writes on the 7th of September, "I fully believe we have seen our worst days over." Since the British "have now had seven years' war, and are not an inch farther on the Continent than when they began," they must be ready to conclude that the fates are unalterably set against a British victory.

Paine was correct in his view of general British sentiment, but the old irreconcilables in London had not yet given up hope. In September disquieting news came to Philadelphia. Rockingham was dead and a new Ministry was being formed by the Earl of Shelburne, excluding Burke, Fox, and other staunch friends of America. Averse to granting independence, Shelburne declared on the 10th of July: "Whenever the parliament of England acknowl-

edges that point, the sun of England's glory is set forever."
Crisis XII (October 29, 1782) is addressed to the Earl of
Shelburne and, by inference, to all other mealy-mouthed
politicians in England and America who think that at this
late date mere expressions of love and forbearance can melt
the two peoples into their former unity. There is profound
emotion, the long-rankling sorrow that embitters the heart,
in Paine's words: "The situations of the two countries are
exceedingly different. Ours has been the seat of war; yours
has seen nothing of it. The most wanton destruction has
been committed in our sight; the most insolent barbarity
has been acted on our feelings. We can look round and
see the remains of burnt and destroyed houses, once the fair
fruit of hard industry, and now the striking monument of
British brutality. We walk over the dead whom we loved,
in every part of America, and remember by whom they
fell." The British cause is hopeless. How long will the
British government force "this silly, foolish, and headstrong
war" upon "the laboring farmer, the working tradesman,
and the necessitous poor in England, the sweat of whose
brow goes day after day to feed, in prodigality and sloth,
the army that is robbing both them and us?" In short, "As
America is gone, the only act of manhood is *to let her go.*"

In spite of the unqualified optimism of this pronouncement, independence was far from being an accomplished
fact. Backsliding and sectionalism in America were menacing the success of the Revolution at the same time that a
less favorable Ministry took over the reins of office in London. The five-percent duty on imports, which Congress had
proposed that the states should levy in order to meet the
Federal foreign debt, was generally unpopular and was flatly
rejected by Rhode Island.

On the 23rd of November Paine began a series in the Philadelphia papers on the five-percent duty. In order that the domestic dispute might not be given undue international notoriety, he signed himself not Common Sense but A Friend to Rhode Island and the Union. He stressed the imperative need of allegiance to "the principle of union," which is "our magna charta—our anchor in the world of empires." The fear of a congressional despotism, he argued, is a carry-over from colonial troubles with British tyranny, and has no place in "this country where every man is an elector, and may likewise be elected."

Paine did not rest with this. He appointed himself a committee of one to go to Rhode Island and argue with the people directly. Borrowing a horse from a New Jersey friend, and with no additional financing from the Federal Government, he set forth in the dead of winter on the snow-covered trails. At Providence he met difficulty in getting his pieces published, and he was subjected to the jeers and sarcasms befitting an impertinent outsider. He could accomplish nothing.

The times were precarious in the extreme before the final deliverance. The French army under Rochambeau had gone off to the West Indies, leaving Washington depleted at Newburgh on the Hudson. By his own plea to a committee of officers, Washington staved off a conspiracy to declare a military dictatorship and force payment to the soldiers out of the populace at the musket-point. And then, crashing through the utter blackness like the wide radiance of a sudden dawn, came the epoch-making, awe-inspiring news: Peace and Independence. On the 16th of April, the tidings were proclaimed from the court house in Philadelphia to an immense, rejoicing crowd. On the 19th of April, exactly eight years after the Battle of Lexington, Washington announced to the army that their work was done. And on that same wonderful day, if any soldiers or civilians were in the mood for reading at all, they might ponder on the final message of Common Sense—*Crisis XIII*.

As *Crisis I* incarnates the fighting Spirit of '76, so *Crisis XIII* captures forever the grand hopefulness of the Spirit of '83, when a new nation emerged from the shambles of war into the unchallenged control of her own destiny. " 'The times that tried men's souls' are over—and the greatest and completest revolution the world ever knew, gloriously and happily accomplished." In the Biblical phraseology which men use to convey their deepest feelings, Paine rejoices that America "is now descending to the scenes of quiet and domestic life. Not beneath the cypress shade of disappointment, but to enjoy in her own land, and under her own vine, the sweet of her labours, and the reward of her toil." No nation has ever had a fairer start. "She has it in her choice to do, and to live as happily as she please. The world is in her hands." A vista of unending peace and prosperity beckons if America will never abandon her true safeguard, "the union, that great palladium of our liberty and safety." Paine writes his ideals of national progress in capital letters—"UNION OF THE STATES," "UNITED STATES," "AMERICANS."

Before the writing bond is broken, a last personal word to these people whom he has served with all his energies for seven arduous years, and whom he has loved as a great collective being with its face turned to the vision of human liberty. "As the scenes of war are now closed, and every man preparing for home and happier times, I therefore take my leave of the subject. I have most sincerely followed it from beginning to end, and through all its turns and windings: and whatever country I may hereafter be in, I shall always feel an honest pride at the part I have taken and acted, and a gratitude to nature and providence for putting it in my power to be of some use to mankind."

CHAPTER XI

Thomas Paine, Esquire

THE high tension of the revolutionary epoch was followed by no utopia but by the drab spaces of the so-called critical period. The biographies of the great American revolutionists become largely the chronicles of private individuals in a confused and prosaic society.

As Paine rested at the home of his friend Kirkbride in Bordentown, he could look back with high satisfaction upon a great revolutionary career. He had known the dangers and miseries of a soldier's life. He had refused to make money out of his revolutionary pamphlets, which circulated in thousands of copies; in fact, he had incurred expenditures for *Common Sense* amounting to 39 pounds, 11 shillings. He had worked in governmental posts at low salaries, paid in paper money and at irregular intervals, and he had gone on important public missions to France and Rhode Island at his own volition and without governmental outlays. No money-grubbing writer could have created that incomparable series of pamphlets which, at every juncture of the Revolution, nerved the trigger-fingers of the soldiers and inspired the people at home with hope and confidence and the religious joy of sacrifice.

Now that the Revolution was a success, where did Paine stand? He was famous and he was poor. His total property was an unfurnished house and a small strip of land in Bordentown. During the war money had meant virtually nothing to him; with peace it loomed up frighteningly as the most pressing concern of life. There was no job available for his literary and scientific talents in the war-torn country, or he lacked the temperament to seek it out. He turned for help to the national and state governments.

In June Paine appealed to Congress for some financial recognition of his services to the Revolution. But his plea was ill-timed. The poor distracted Congress would soon be running away from Philadelphia before the hungry wrath of a few insubordinate soldiers. Paine's letter was referred to a committee, and he was left to shift for himself as the long months rolled by. But he had staunch friends, and among them General Washington. In September, from the camp at Rocky Hill, near Princeton, to which Congress had fled, Washington invited Paine "to partake with me." "Your presence here," he wrote, "may remind Congress of your past services to this country; and if it is in my power to impress them, command my best services with freedom, as they will be rendered cheerfully by one who entertains a lively sense of the importance of your works."

When Paine visited the camp at Rocky Hill in November, Washington endorsed a memorial which Paine had prepared for submission to Congress. In December Paine followed Congress to New York and laid his memorial before the committee. In this petition he candidly lays bare the desperate situation that confronts him if the country will not come to his aid. "Trade I do not understand; land I have none, or what is equivalent to none. I have exiled myself from one country without making a home of another." He runs over the familiar highlights of his public services: *Common Sense,* the *Crisis,* the Deane affair, the Bank of Pennsylvania, the Laurens mission, the *Letter to*

106

Raynal, the Rhode Island tax dispute. "If, then," he proudly summarizes the matter, "the part I have chosen and acted has been of any benefit to America, it remains unacknowledged;—if it has not it requires none; or if it is consistent with the honor and character of a country to receive favors from individuals she is fully welcome to what she has had from me. But as to oblige and be obliged is fair and friendly, she has it in her choice, whether she will in return make my situation such, as I can with happiness to myself, and unconfined by dependence, remain in the rank of a citizen of America, or whether I must wish her well and say to her, Adieu."

While his petition was before Congress, and he needed all the good-will that he could muster, Paine boldly resumed the criticism of Rhode Island. In *The Supernumerary Crisis* of December 9, he denounced the "injudicious, uncandid, and indecent opposition made by sundry persons in a certain state to the recommendations of Congress last winter, for an import duty of five percent." His public spirit got in the way of his private plea, which was side-tracked by his enemies in Congress.

Back in Bordentown Paine whiled away the winter visiting with his friends, riding occasionally on his horse Button, and tinkering with mechanical experiments. In the spring he returned to his New York circle. On the 19th of April, a committee of the New York Senate recommended that he be given a farm in Westchester County because "his literary works, and those especially under the signature of Common Sense, and the Crisis, inspired the citizens of this state with unanimity, confirmed their confidence in the rectitude of their cause, and have ultimately contributed to the freedom, sovereignty, and independence of the United

States." The Senate and the Assembly assenting, Paine was presented with an estate in New Rochelle, formerly the home of a loyalist, Frederick Devoe.

The New Rochelle gift was a fine tribute from the State of New York, but it was after all not a livelihood. Unknown to Paine, Washington appealed to James Madison, Richard Henry Lee, and others to propose in the Virginia assembly a grant to Common Sense. The memory of *Public Good,* however, was too keen for Virginia to help such an unkind advocate of National as opposed to States' rights. Washington must then have spoken very earnestly to President John Dickinson of the Supreme Executive Council of Pennsylvania, for on the 6th of December the Council reported the conversation to the Assembly and expressed a hope "that you will, then, feel the attention of Pennsylvania is drawn towards Mr. Paine by motives equally grateful to the human heart, and reputable to the Republic." After some political backing and filling, Pennsylvania awarded Paine £500.

In the quiet village of Bordentown, with his sympathetic and understanding host Kirkbride, Paine's long-frustrated passion for practical science expressed itself. He hit upon an ambitious project, the designing of a great bridge.

Bridge-building was almost an unknown art in America. No attempt had been made at a permanent span over the large rivers of the seaboard, which could be crossed only by the ferry-boat and the scow. Such long bridges would have to be supported by piers, which would involve an incalculable amount of dangerous digging in mid-stream for rock bottom. Thick and close-set piers would interfere with navigation and might undo the purpose of the bridge by deflecting the river into new channels, or the spring thaws might shift the river bottom and bring the whole structure

108

down. Men came quickly to an impasse in thinking about permanent bridges.

Paine proposed a revolutionary departure from the traditional designs and materials. He would build a bridge across the Schuylkill River without piers, a single arch 400 feet long, and he would not use wood or even stone but cast iron. So large a single arch was a distinct innovation, and iron was practically unknown for bridge-building. Kirkbride set up his boarder in a workshop and Paine began putting together a model in wood and testing the stresses and strains on the abutments.

In the summer of 1785 Paine put away his tools and visited in New York. He hoped to win from the national government a definite statement in his favor and a reimbursement of his personal expenses in the Revolution, which he estimated at $6,000. By this time party malice had waned sufficiently for Paine's patriotic services to stand in a comparatively undisputed light, though Congress felt it necessary to pinch on the financial returns after admitting the national indebtedness. On the 26th of August a resolution was adopted "that the early, unsolicited, and continued labors of Mr. Thomas Paine, in explaining and enforcing the principles of the late revolution by ingenious and timely publications upon the nature of liberty, and civil government, have been well received by the citizens of these States, and merit the approbation of Congress; and that in consideration of these services, and the benefits produced thereby, Mr. Paine is entitled to a liberal gratification from the United States." On the 3rd of October Congress finally voted Paine $3,000.

While Paine was dickering with Congress, Benjamin Franklin returned to his fellow countrymen and "dear

Philadelphia" on the 13th of September, 1785. Paine hastened to add his voice to the congratulatory chorus on Franklin's homecoming. In a cordial letter from New York, September 23, he writes, "In making you this address I have an additional pleasure in reflecting, that, so far as I have hitherto gone, I am not conscious of any circumstance in my conduct that should give you one repentant thought for being my patron and introducer to America." Replying on the 27th, Franklin said, "Be assured, my dear friend, that instead of repenting that I was your introducer into America, I value myself on the share I had in procuring for it the acquisition of so useful and valuable a citizen."

In the course of the next few weeks Paine frequently visited with Franklin. The eighty-year-old Franklin found the scientist Paine good company, what with his bridge model, smokeless candles, and other ingenious contrivances. One day Paine dropped in and found Franklin poking around in his great library with his wonderful contraption, the mechanical arm-and-hand, for taking down and putting up books on high shelves. There may have been quizzical amusement in Paine's candid face; at any rate, Franklin saw the occasion for another of his lay sermons. "Mr. Paine," he said, "you may be surprised at finding me thus busily occupied at my advanced state of life. Many might think me an old fool to be thus busied in the affairs of this life, while making such near approach, in the course of nature, to the grave. But it has always been my maxim to live on as if I was to live always. It is with such feelings only that we can be stimulated to the exertions necessary to effect any useful purpose. Death will one day lay hold of me, and put an end to all my labours; but, till then, it is my maxim to go on in the old way. I will not anticipate his coming." It was a good lesson in vigorous living, and Paine took it to heart. In *The Age of Reason* he was to exalt Franklin as the paragon of rational existence because "Science, that never grows grey, was always his mistress. He was never without an object; for when we cease to have an object we become like an invalid in a hospital waiting for death."

This was what Paine desired for himself and what the volcanic age denied him—scientific pursuits and congenial friends. As far as fighting was concerned, he was content to rest upon his laurels as the universally admired Common Sense of the Revolution. And he had his laurels. The poet-physician Joseph Brown Ladd, for one, expressed the general opinion of Paine in his grandiloquent verses *The Prospects of America*:

> Immortal Payne! whose pen, surprised we saw,
> Could fashion empires while it kindled awe.
> When first with awful power to crush the foes,
> All bright in glittering arms Columbia rose,
> From thee our sons the generous mandate took,
> As if from heaven some oracle had spoke:
> And when thy pen revealed the grand design,
> 'Twas DONE, Columbia's liberty was thine.

It was pleasant to walk along the streets with Franklin and Dr. Rush, to be sighted as "Reason," "Common Sense," and "The Doctor." Pleasant, too, to attend a banquet at the Bunch of Grapes Tavern, given by the printers January 17, 1786, for Franklin's eightieth birthday, and to be toasted "Thomas Paine, Esq."

From this homage and bridge-building Paine was pulled away by the political dissensions of the period. America was torn by bitter internal conflicts and class warfare. The bond of a common enemy having been removed, the states reverted to their individual sovereignty. They established preferential trade restrictions against one another and could not make a united front for favorable commercial relations with European countries. The European continent had been accustomed by the restrictions of British mercantile policy not to trade with America, and now England closed her ports to the Americans as an alien people yet continued to sell her wares in the American market for solid cash. American importers were gradually draining the country of specie to make payments, the rate of interest rose, debtors were hard pressed and frequently thrown into prison. The great mass of people, the farmers, on whose shoulders the brunt of the burden fell, organized themselves and in some instances actually took up arms for paper money and stay laws. By sheer force of numbers they came to dominate the policies of a majority of the states, and in 1786 the Shays Rebellion in Massachusetts against courts and fore-closures almost overthrew the legally established govern-ment.

In Pennsylvania the chief object of popular wrath was the Bank of North America, a development out of the Bank of Pennsylvania, which Paine had helped to found in 1780. The stockholders of the Bank, taking alarm at the grow-ing stringency of conditions, had begun to retrench. The demand of the Bank for immediate and complete payment worked great hardships, and the debt-plagued farmers who constituted the bulk of the Constitutionalist party clamored that the monster be destroyed. The Assembly passed an act on the 10th of September, 1785, revoking the State charter of the Bank. The institution, however, refused to go out of business and limped along on the charter which had been granted by Congress.

To Paine the attempted destruction of the Bank by his Constitutionalist friends seemed a shameful spectacle. Far from regarding the embattled farmers as the latter-day fulfillers of the ideals of the Revolution, he saw them as the subverters of those ideals. The extreme economic radicalism of the eighteenth century is not the radicalism of Paine, but of conscious proletarian leaders like Shays in America and Marat in France. Paine's American record was consistent in its opposition to the special interest of classes. In 1776 he had been a principal advocate of the democratic Pennsylvania Constitution because it put the agricultural back-country on a plane of political equality with the commercial east. But in 1785 the assault on the Bank, coupled with a popular agitation for paper money, seemed to be upsetting the social balance so as to favor the farmers against the businessmen. In voicing his opposition to the agrarian movement in *Dissertations on Government, The Affairs of the Bank,* and *Paper Money* (February, 1786) Paine found himself in strange company and at outs with his most intimate political associates of the Revolution, but whatever else could be said against him, he had not betrayed his principles.

Although written and printed in the brief recess of the Assembly between December, 1785, and February, 1786, the pamphlet masses an elaborate structure of argument in behalf of temperate democratic government, the bank, and hard money. Seeking the true principle of distinction between despotic monarchies and free republics, Paine finds it in the difference between the arbitrary will of an individual and the democratic social compact of equal justice.

The legislature of a free people has a right to repeal any general statutes, but a contract between the state and the individual, honestly and openly arrived at, may not be abolished without mutual consent. With these premises, Paine proceeds to defend the Bank. He brightens up the halo of its origin in 1780 in "the distresses of the times and the enterprising spirit of patriotic individuals." The recent abolition of the Bank charter without a hearing was an undemocratic and underhand blow at the common welfare, for "The whole community derives benefit from the operation of the bank," which, by giving "a kind of life to what would otherwise be dead money . . . quickens the means of purchasing and paying for country produce" and invigorates the commercial system. And the attempt to make unredeemable paper into legal currency belongs in the realm of hocus-pocus with alchemy and the philosopher's stone. It is the artifice of the sharper and the dishonest debtor, bent on stealing by depreciation "the widow's dowry and children's portion."

Thus Paine plunged into the bank controversy on the side of the banking interest. In Bordentown, with his clangorous workshop, his assistant John Hall, his boy Joe, his horse Button and his carriage, Paine was a respectable and honored citizen. But in Philadelphia he was involved in an extremely bitter political fight and his revolutionary reputation was stripped off his shoulders. The opening of the Assembly on the 18th of February found Paine in Philadelphia. He attended the four days of hot debate on Robert Morris's motion to restore the charter of the Bank. On the fourth day John Smilie, a radical agrarian from Fayette County, introduced Paine's *Dissertations* with a sneering reference to the writer as "an unprincipled author whose pen is let out for hire." Paine almost leaped out of his seat among the spectators to shout "Liar!" at Smilie.

The charter was not yet restored, though the vote was close—36 to 28. Paine embarked on a series in the Philadelphia papers in favor of the Bank. Continuing in the vein of the *Dissertations,* he questioned the motives of the anti-bank leaders, warned that they were endangering the democratic form of government, and enlarged on the usefulness of a bank to all classes of society. In reply, a flaming democrat under the name of Atticus ridiculed Paine's "platitudes" about government and his fine-spun distinction between statutes and contracts, luridly depicted the menace of a moneyed power, and asserted the right of a legislature to revoke any charter which it has created. Atticus lashed out, "I cannot conceive, in the wide extent of creation, a being more deserving of our abhorrence and contempt, than a writer, who, having formerly vindicated the principles of freedom, abandons them to abet the cause of a faction; who exerts the little talent which Heaven has allotted him for the acquisition of his daily bread, to vilify measures which it is his duty to respect, and, who having reaped a recompence more than adequate to his deserts, prostitutes his pen to the ruin of his country."

Smarting under this bitter treatment from the camp of his former friends, Paine stuck to his newspaper siege through the summer. In August he took a parting shot at the paper-money craze: "If the honest and thinking men in the several parts of the Continent do not exert themselves to suppress this growing and delusive use of paper money, they will have no security for their liberty and property, and the consequences will be poverty and legislative tyranny." He retired to Bordentown and spent the next few months working on his bridge, with occasional visits to Philadelphia to help in the electioneering for advocates of the Bank. With the assistance of prominent names and the gradual easing of economic conditions, the energetic minority in behalf of the Bank won a narrow victory at the polls in October, 1786. The charter was restored in the following March.

On the whole, Paine was a congenial master in his Bordentown workshop, and Hall speaks of him habitually with affection and respect. On November 21, 1786, Hall writes: "I put on Mr. Paine's hose yesterday. Last night he brought in my room a pair of warm cloth overshoes as feel very comfortable this morning. Had a wooden pot-stove stand betwixt my feet by Mr. Paine's desire and found it kept my feet warm." But Paine was also passionately devoted to his brain-child, the bridge. Hall records a distressing experience on the 14th of December: "This day employed in raising and putting on the abutments again and fitting them. The smith made the nuts of screws go easier. Then set the ribs at proper distance, and after dinner I and Jackaway put on some temporary pieces on the frame of wood to hold it straight, and when Mr. Paine came they then tied it on its wooden frame with strong cords. I then saw that it had bulged full on one side and hollow on the other. I told him of it, and he said it was done by me—I denied that and words rose high. I at length swore by God that it was straight when I left it, he replied as positively the contrary, and I think myself ill used in this affair."

On the 22nd of December Hall put the completed bridge model on a sled and brought it into Philadelphia, where it was set up in the garden of Franklin's home in Market Street. A few days later, passers-by would have seen the interesting spectacle of Paine, Rittenhouse, and a friend named Glenworth standing and stamping on the model to test its strength. It held them easily. On New Year's Day Hall moved the model to the committee room of the Assembly, where it was viewed admiringly by the assemblymen and other amateur experts in engineering. "And then," wrote Hall with ecstatic vision, "to be canonized by an Act of State which is solicited to incorporate a body of men to adopt and realize or Brobdinag this our Lilliputian handy-work, that is now 13 feet long on a Scale of one to 24. And then will be added another to the world's present Wonders."

At Paine's request, the Assembly appointed a committee on the 20th of March to inspect the model. Within four days the committee submitted its report, stressing the importance of bridges and generally endorsing Paine. The Assembly thereupon voted to consider any propositions from him at the next session.

Paine feared that his bridge plan might be shunted off into honorable oblivion. Not only because he had political enemies in the Assembly, but because it would be more profitable for the backers of a Schuylkill bridge to get their designs out of old English engineering manuals rather than to deal with him. Wood was cheaper and more available than iron, and piers looked safer than a single arch with abutments. In order to have his plan accepted, Paine required more prestige than the authority of his own name and the sturdiness of his model. And prestige could come from none better than the French engineers, the greatest bridge-builders of the century.

Paine decided to take his model to France. Pennsylvania would do nothing about a bridge for at least a year, and he could be back by that time with credentials from the Academy of Sciences at Paris. Confiding his plans to Franklin in a letter on the 31st of March, 1787, Paine asked for some letters of introduction to leading Frenchmen. "As I had the honor of your introduction to America," he says with graceful recognition, "it will add to my happiness to have the same friendship continued to me on the present occasion." Franklin promptly sent over to Bordentown a package of about a dozen letters.

The young mechanic, Hall, had moved to a boarding house in Trenton. On the 20th of April, as he was looking out of the window, he recognized Paine's red coat in a carriage going by. He followed and greeted Paine, who had come to seek him out and settle his accounts. Paine invited Hall to ride back a short distance with him towards Bordentown, and as they rode along Paine discoursed jovially about the prospects of his bridge, Dr. Franklin, and the principles of fair dealing among nations. "Such and many more hints passed in riding 2 or 3 miles, until we met the stage," Hall noted. "I then shook hands and wished him a good voyage and parted."

So, with high spirits, Paine looked forward to his European voyage. At the age of fifty he stepped blithely forth upon what was destined to be the grand adventure of his career—to be for fifteen years at the very heart and center of the most tremendous ferment that the world had ever known.

CHAPTER XII

THE AMERICAN BRIDGE-BUILDER IN EUROPE

PAINE went on board the packet which pulled out of New York on the 26th of April, 1787, and reached Havre de Grâce on the 26th of May. Leaving his bridge model temporarily at the customs house as required by French law, he proceeded on a leisurely course to Paris.

When he arrived at Paris on the 30th of May, he paid his respects to the American ambassador, Thomas Jefferson, and began a round of visits in the old circle of Franklin's admirers. Though handicapped by his inability to speak French, he was soon on familiar terms with scientists, philosophers, and statesmen—Perronet, Veillard, Le Roy, Auberteuil, Morellet, Malesherbes, and others. The mathematician Le Roy, who spoke English fluently, appointed himself Paine's daily guide to the Parisian world. He escorted the great American to the naturalist Buffon and to various exhibitions of physical science which were popular at the moment.

The old order in France was not distinguished for efficiency. It took more than a month for the bridge model to get from Havre to Paris. The Academy of Sciences then appointed a committee consisting of Le Roy, Bossou, and Borda, to analyze the principles underlying the new structure.

While waiting for action on his bridge, Paine took a glance at the contemporary political situation. In the summer of 1787, the picture of French society had a delusive appearance of almost untroubled calm and of mild, reforming prospects. Not even Frenchmen could yet discern the first fissures of that tremendous earthquake by which the third estate, a self-conscious bourgeoisie and a hungry proletariat, would shatter the decadent feudal edifice and the privilege of birth. The financial crisis of Louis XVI's extravagant régime was not unprecedented or beyond amicable adjustment by the King and the privileged orders. Paine, like others, was disarmed into thinking that France could work out her problems easily.

On the 29th of August the committee presented a favorable report on Paine's bridge. They observed that the erecting of a single iron arch four hundred feet long was a project of such vast magnitude as to warrant serious doubts, but after considering the disposition of the various parts of the model they concluded "that Mr. Paine's Plan of an Iron Bridge is ingeniously imagined, that the construction of it is simple, solid, and proper to give it the necessary strength for resisting the effects resulting from its burden, and that it is deserving of a trial. In short, it may furnish a new example of the application of a metal, which has not hitherto been used in any works on an extensive scale, although on many occasions it is employed with the greatest success." The next day Paine set out for England. He left his bridge model in London with Sir Joseph Banks, President of the Royal Society, and went on to Thetford.

Except for the inexorable working of time, ancient Thetford had not changed. Here were the same old landmarks— the meeting-house and the pillory on Cage Lane, the Guildhall, Castle Hill, the Grammar School, the Catholic ruins. Here were the same old people—the peasants docile under their burdens, the pariah Quakers, the selectmen trafficking in government. With his mother, now in her ninetieth year, he mourned at the grave of his father, who had died the year before. In that autumn of 1787, Paine wandered among the musty vestiges of his childhood in a sentimental spirit, but he had gone too far afield ever to be reconciled to the gentle Quaker theory of human nature. It could be only too evident to Common Sense that loving-kindness would never persuade King George and his ministry to put the undemocratic system of England in order.

There was a prospect of erecting a new bridge across the Seine on Paine's plan. He settled an allowance of nine shillings a week on his mother, and after a brief visit to London, where he met the American ambassador, John Adams, he returned to Paris in mid-December. He did not spend all his time and energy trying to sell his bridge to the French Government. He began to familiarize himself with the turbid currents of pre-revolutionary France, and he formed a deep friendship with the American ambassador Jefferson that was to strengthen with the years. Like Franklin and Paine, Jefferson was a true child of the age—interested in the arts and sciences, liberal in politics and religion, inspired by great social dreams—and for his aristocratic origin he atoned by the zealous open advocacy of an extreme democratic position, even condoning the Shays Rebellion. Paine took frequent walks from his Paris lodging to Jefferson's home at Challiot. The two had many things to talk about—the bridge, the American constitution, French politics, Newtonian philosophy; and the Virginian listened attentively if dubiously to Paine's insistence on the priority of Federal power over States' rights.

Putting off his return to America for another year, Paine

crossed the Channel again in the summer of 1788 on the business of his bridge. One specific obstacle to the acceptance of his bridge for the Seine was that he had nothing to offer beyond a small model and the endorsement of leading scientists. Since practical iron construction was most highly developed in England, he might construct there a large-scale experimental rib or a real bridge which would carry more conviction to the officials in Paris and would also further his interest in Philadelphia for a bridge over the Schuylkill. In August he obtained a patent from the English Government. He made financial arrangements with the firm of Whiteside's in London and began to look about for a likely iron manufacturer.

Paine had a letter of introduction from Henry Laurens to Edmund Burke, who had befriended Laurens during his imprisonment in the Tower of London in 1781. There was a forthright ardent quality in the natures of Paine and Burke which drew them instinctively to each other and obscured any differences in social philosophy. To Paine Burke was the magnificent champion of American liberty, the author of grand phrases like "As for the people, it is never from a passion for attack that it rebels, but from impatience of suffering," and "I do not know the method of drawing up an indictment against a whole people." To Burke Paine was the author of a celebrated pamphlet which had helped to safeguard traditional British ideals in America; this keen-eyed pamphleteer was probably a good sensible American, like other Americans he had known— the Southern aristocrat Laurens, the Northern lawyers Jay and Adams. Burke escorted Paine on a summer tour to various iron works, entertained him as a guest at Beaconsfield for a week, and introduced him to the prominent

Whigs at London. "I am just going to dine with the Duke of Portland [titular head of the Whigs]," Burke writes to Wilkes on the 18th of August, 1788, "in company with the great American Paine, whom I take with me." John Adams having retired in disgust from the hostile Court of St. James, Paine became the unofficial American ambassador, on close terms with Burke, Portland, Fox, Sir George Staunton, and other Whigs who sympathized with his attempt to lift British prohibitions on American imports. He was friendly even with the Marquis of Lansdowne (to whom as the Earl of Shelburne he had addressed *Crisis XII*), and Lansdowne agreed with him in conversation against Pitt's adventuring in continental affairs.

Royall Tyler has left in *The Algerine Captive* a pictorial glimpse of Paine at this time—the spare figure in snuff-colored coat, olive velvet vest, drab breeches, coarse hose, large shoe buckles; the keen face under the tattered bob-tailed wig—a plain American, given to alternations of high and low spirits, gracious and richly entertaining in the play of ideas with congenial company.

In October, having come to suitable terms with the Walkers, the largest iron manufacturers in England, Paine left London for their foundry in Rotherham, Yorkshire. He began working with the Walkers' mechanics on a ninety-foot rib. In December, half the rib being finished, he gave instructions for erecting the complementary half and went down to London to be a spectator at the opening of Parliament.

Paine found the wrangle of parties at high pitch. King George had unequivocally gone out of his senses and was confined in a strait-jacket. Would the Prince of Wales automatically succeed him in a Regency? The Whigs hoped so, for the Prince was a fellow-rake and tippler with their Charles James Fox and would probably turn out the Tories and bring in a Whig ministry. The Tory Prime Minister Pitt defended his control of government by claiming that the Regent should be chosen by the vote of Parliament. As an American, Paine sided with the Whigs, who were favorably disposed towards America. As a democrat, however, he saw through the specious arguments of both the Whigs and the Tories, for he realized that it was immaterial to the great masses of Englishmen whether a monarch was forced upon them by hereditary succession or by an aristocratic parliament. While the debate raged, the King returned to his original senses and the kingly power, and the prospects of a Whig government and concessions to America disappeared.

In April Paine was back at the Walkers' iron foundry in Rotherham to test the completed ninety-foot rib. With the help of the Walkers' mechanics, using the wall of a furnace and the gable end of an adjacent brick building for abutments, he moved a load of six tons without any noticeable effect on the slender three-ton bridge. He arranged with the Walkers to fashion the parts of a five-ribbed bridge of 110-foot span and send them on to London. His personal hopes rose. He could already see in imagination a bridge across the Thames, a bridge across the Seine, the profitable sale of his patents in Europe, and a gala return to America.

In the letters from Jefferson during this year, from the summer of 1788 to the summer of 1789, lurked intimations of that epochal storm-cloud which would toss Paine's engineering schemes far into the background, keep him in Europe thirteen more years, and bring unparalleled glory and sorrow to the evening of his life. Jefferson's letters gave an optimistic and authoritative account of the progress of the French Revolution. On the 23rd of December, 1788, after the summoning of the Estates General, the dismissal of Brienne, the recall of Necker, Jefferson forecasts the party clashes in the Assembly and declares, "Upon the whole, if the dispute between the privileged and unprivileged orders does not prevent it, there is no doubt in my mind that they will obtain a fixed, free, and wholesome constitution." On the 17th of March, 1789, he describes the public mind as "ripened by time and discussion." On the 19th of May he anticipates the insistence of the third estate to vote by persons and not by orders and assures the success of this democratic endeavor in spite of "small troubles and ebullitions excited by the seceding noblesse and higher clergy." On the 11th of July he describes the tortuous and bullying tactics of the King's advisers, the "coolness, wisdom, and resolution" of the victorious third estate and the adherent nobles and clergy constituted as one body in the National Assembly. "The progress of things here will be subject to checks from time to time of course," he writes philosophically, two days later, about the street fighting in Paris, "whether they will be great or small will depend on the army, but they will be only checks." On the 17th of July, three days after the fall of the Bastille, he remarks, "This places the power of the States General absolutely out of the reach of attack, and they may be considered as having a carte blanche." On the 13th of September, in comparative calm, describing the course of reform legislation in the Assembly, he sums up, "I think there is no possibility now of anything's hindering their final establishment of a good constitution, which will in its principles and merit be about a middle term between that of England and the United States."

To the unrolling panorama of a liberal readjustment in the French system, Paine responded with a rising enthusiasm. "This will be to France like an Anno Mundi, or an Anno Domini," he writes on February 26, 1789. He began to look about him for signs of a similar awakening in English life, which would inaugurate an era of good-will between two great peoples living in a free social atmosphere under constitutional monarchies. "The people of this country speak very differently on the affairs of France," he reports September 18, 1789. "The mass of them, so far as I can collect, say that France is a much freer country than England. The Peers, the Bishops, &c., say the National Assembly has gone too far. There are yet in this country very considerable remains of the feudal system which people did not see till the revolution in France placed it before their eyes."

In the fall of 1789 Jefferson returned to America. His last European letter to Paine is dated October 14, shortly after the sensational march of the Parisian women to Versailles. He writes jubilantly, "The King, Queen, and National Assembly are removed to Paris. The mobs and murders under which they dress this fact are like the rags in which religion robes the true god."

Shortly after Jefferson's departure Paine was again in Paris. Things had moved forward amazingly in little more than a year—the adoption of the liberalizing principles in the Declaration of the Rights of Man, the confiscation of church property to meet the financial crisis, the overwhelming vote for a democratic single-chamber assembly, the drastic limitation of royal power. Paris had succeeded Versailles as the seat of government, and the Assembly met in the long hall of the Riding School under the critical eyes

f the Parisian populace in the galleries. Political schemes
nd speculations were the common, absorbing topics—in
he fashionable salons, the political clubs, the party news-
apers, the impromptu forums among the cluster of amusement places and cafés known as the Palais Royal. It was
he revolutionary ferment of Philadelphia and the Conti-
ental Congress in 1775, more tremendous and challenging
the heart of old aristocratic Europe.

On the 4th of February, at the suggestion of Lafayette,
ouis XVI went down to the Assembly and declared that
and the Queen accepted the new order without mental
ervations and wished all Frenchmen to follow their ex-
le. Paine studied the giant events which had revolu-
zed French society, and wrote long, enthusiastic letters
x, Burke, and friends in America on the inspiring
ss and harmony of the new France. Burke, however,
a blast in the Commons against the French Revo-
d announced that he would soon publish a com-
denunciation. At this outburst, amazing and ec-
the first months of 1790, Paine promised the
rs that he would champion their cause when-
us would appear.

e leaders of the Revolution—Condorcet,
—who had previously gathered at Jeffer-
liot, had turned to Paine as the outstand-
nce. Lafayette, member of the Assem-
the National Guard, was the strong-
ment and aspired to play the rôle of
wn country. Both Lafayette and Paine
r the spectacular and symbolic, and La-
to Paine the key of the Bastille for presen-
ashington. "When he mentioned to me the

127

present he intended you," Paine reported to Washingto.
"my heart leaped with joy. . . . That the principles (
America opened the Bastille is not to be doubted, and ther
fore the Key comes to the right place."

In March Paine left Paris for England, where his bridg
was now completed. He set up the bridge in an open fiel
in the village of Paddington near London. There were n
natural abutments, and the beautiful fabric had only
speculative interest to the curious visitors from the capit
A speculative interest was growing, too, here and there
this mysterious, unattached political personage traveli
back and forth across the Channel. On the 3rd of Aug
in a letter to William Short, American Chargé d'Aff
in Paris, Paine laments the fact that English papers ar
casionally printing paragraphs "sufficiently pointing r
as a person whom it is proper to have an Eye upc
that my erecting a bridge is but a cover."

In the fall of 1790 he was once again an eage
thetic observer in Paris. There was popular
against the aristocratic henchmen of the King
pressive measures of Lafayette, and Louis had a
his suicidal policy of secret negotiations
princes. Yet the great, inspiring fact was tha
Constitution was being put into force and
the heart of France. Mixing with the lea
dorcet, Sieyès, Madame Roland, ar
sponded to their enthusiasm and j
social visions for France and the wo
October he attended the first meeting
founded by Nicolas de Bonneville and
to regenerate humanity through a kind of N
hood and ritual.

A business crisis brought Paine hurriedly back to England. His partner Whiteside had gone bankrupt and the creditors demanded that Paine settle an account of £620 attached to the bridge. He managed to save the bridge temporarily, the American merchants Clagett and Murdoch taking over the indebtedness. The exhibition went on, with as yet no private or governmental buyer for the bridge.

On the 31st of October Burke's long-awaited *Reflections on the Revolution in France* appeared. Paine stopped thinking of bridges and personal security and marched forth again as a revolutionary pamphleteer. In his room at The Angel in Islington, a London suburb, in the atmosphere of open fields and grazing cows, he gathered together his impressions of the French Revolution. Realizing that "it is in high challenges that high truths have the right of appearing," he would not for a moment let the memory of Burke's personal kindness stand in the way of supreme social duty. He would defend the cause of liberty from the forces of reaction. He would return thunderbolts for thunderbolts. Paine began his greatest political pamphlet, *The Rights of Man*.

CHAPTER XIII

HIGH CHALLENGES AND HIGH TRUTHS

THE debate between Burke and Paine was a turning-point in human history. The *Reflections* and *The Rights of Man* furnished the credos for the long warfare between Aristocracy and Democracy which drew into its vortex all the peoples of the western world. Through this controversy the French Revolution came home to England with a tremendous impact, and across the Atlantic the new political groupings were deeply affected by the aspirations and symbols of the European struggle.

Before the Burke-Paine controversy the French Revolution appeared to the dominant politicians in London as a promise rather than a threat. It was comforting to Whigs and Tories alike to see the ancient enemy thrown into temporary confusion and moving to strengthen by a continental example the political system that had been so profitable in England. Shrewd men like Pitt and Fox hoped to hear soon that a French King, Lords, and Commons would govern across the Channel.

The English system itself, dating from the Revolution of 1688, seemed immune to all dangers. In 1787 Paine beheld a régime with the same familiar outlines into which he had been born fifty years before. The ambition of George III to rule instead of reign had imparted vigor to the Tories, who now contested with the Whigs for the loaves and fishes of public office. The gentlemen's game between the two parties did not shake the basic alliance between the King and the landed nobility. Hereditary Lords and elected Commons were the willing instruments of the wealthy landlords, whom Bishop Wilberforce blessed as "the very nerves and ligatures of the body politic." This oligarchy of ancient vested interests fattened on rents, sinecures, pensions, and monopolies at the expense of the middle and lower classes. While improved modes of production and the growth of towns were inevitably shifting economic power and social problems, political dominance remained the special preserve of a barren aristocracy. "I do not know," declaimed Bishop Horsley in the House of Lords, "what the mass of the people in any country have to do with the laws but to obey them."

Against this social arrangement no radical protest had been made for more than a hundred years. The student of democratic origins in England finds almost a dead waste from the harangues of Lilburne and the Levelers in the New Model Army of the Commonwealth to the revolutionary message which Paine brought over from France. The perfect teamwork of the King and the landed nobility prevailed over an ignorant and superstition-ridden peasantry and a rising middle class still seeking favors instead of demanding rights. Under the impetus of the American Revolution, a moderate reform movement began in the '80's to liberalize representation in the Commons, where it was typical that a deserted spot like Old Sarum had two seats and a thriving commercial town like Manchester had none. But this reform movement had no revolutionary spirit. The liberal Society for Constitutional Information, of which Pitt himself was an early member, cast no hostile eye upon the hereditary monarch and the hereditary upper house.

The Dissenters, under the diplomatic leadership of the chemist Priestley and the economist Price, coquetted with the Whig members of Parliament for admittance into the franchise and public office. In lengthy treatises on government Price and Priestley voiced their allegiance to the general aristocratic pattern of King, Lords, and Commons.

The centenary of the Revolution of 1688 revived a mild interest in the reform of the Commons, and the temperate opening of the revolution in France quickened the hopes of the Dissenters and the middle class. There was probably slight revolutionary intent in the aged heart of Dr. Price as he mounted the pulpit of the meeting-house in the old Jewry of London on the 4th of November, 1789, to address the Society for Commemorating the Revolution in Great Britain on the anniversary of the landing of William of Orange; yet from this discourse would spring the war of words in which Burke and Paine were the chief protagonists. To his comfortable and exclusive audience of Dissenters, Churchmen, Peers, and members of the Commons, Dr. Price offered some liberal axioms on the love of country. Christ, he said, did not enjoin the duty of patriotism, and we should therefore love our country "ardently but not exclusively." The chief blessings of human nature are TRUTH, VIRTUE, and LIBERTY, which contain the seeds of all social progress. The Revolution of 1688 guaranteed "first, the right to liberty of conscience in religious matters; secondly, the right to resist power when abused; and, thirdly, the right to chuse our own governors, to cashier them for misconduct, and to frame a government for ourselves." He suggests that the English Revolution is not yet complete because of the discrimination against Dissenters and the inequality of representation in the Commons. Finally, carried away by the dramatic spectacle of the events in France, the reverend doctor pronounces a solemn warning to "all ye oppressors of the world." "You cannot now hold the world in darkness. Struggle no longer against increasing light and liberality. Restore to mankind their rights; and consent to the correction of abuses, before they and you are destroyed together."

This sermon would now be long since forgotten except by antiquarians, had it not furnished the pretext for Edmund Burke's masterpiece, *Reflections on the Revolution in France, and on the Proceedings in certain Societies in London relative to that event.* Of all great historic diatribes, none has proceeded from less provocation than Burke's *Reflections.* The French Revolution had been on the whole a peaceful development under the firm governance of liberal aristocrats and the upper middle class, and there was no revolutionary movement to fear in England. In February, 1790, Burke's closest friend, Sir Philip Francis, criticized his passages on the Queen as "pure foppery" and warned against "the mischief you are going to do yourself." But Burke went doggedly on, shaping and polishing an ingeniously constructed mass of argument eight months more, oblivious to any and all deterrents. What did it matter to him that in that same February Louis XVI had visited the Assembly and had accepted the Revolution? Or that on the 14th of July, the first anniversary of the taking of the Bastille, thousands of happy Frenchmen had stood in the rain and shouted *vive* to the King, the Queen, and the Dauphin? He would stand forth alone, a plumed knight before the gallery of the world, and would champion law and order. His pamphlet incited bloody hate against a socially just and useful movement in France and threw a mantle of blinding eloquence over the rotten aristocratic system in England.

With a flagrant disregard of the age-old injustice and rankling misery under the old régime, Burke views the French Revolution as a wild, anarchic outburst against "the elements of a Constitution very nearly as good as could be wished." What madness has come to pass "in a nation of gallant men, in a nation of men of honor, and of cavaliers," drowned by the orgiastic violence of the rabble and the delegates of the third estate, "in which was scarcely to be perceived the slightest traces of what we call the natural landed interest of the country." To Burke the only France that mattered was the finery and show of the idlers at old Versailles. He weeps for the poor Queen, once "full of life and splendor and joy" but now inconvenienced by the millions of boors who have slaughtered "that generous loyalty to rank and sex, that proud submission, that dignified obedience, that subordination of the heart, which kept alive, even in servitude itself, the spirit of an exalted freedom." In his *Speech on Conciliation* Burke had said that he did not know the method of drawing up an indictment against a whole people. Now he discovered it. "Believe me, Sir," he lectures his French correspondent, "those who attempt to level never equalize. In all societies consisting of various descriptions of citizens, some description must be uppermost. The levelers, therefore, only change and pervert the natural order of things: they load the edifice of society by setting up in the air what the solidity of the structure requires to be on the ground. The associations of tailors and carpenters, of which the republic (of Paris, for instance) is composed, cannot be equal to the situation into which, by the worst of usurpations, an usurpation on the prerogatives of Nature, you attempt to force them."

The French Revolution was not the only concern of Burke's *Reflections*. The brunt of his tirade is directed against "the gentlemen of the Society for Revolutions" who seek to "pervert the natural order of things" in England. To Burke the disposition of political power established by the Revolution of 1688—God, kings, parliaments, magistrates, priests, nobility—was "a parent of settlement, and not a nursery of future revolutions." Dr. Price's "new and hitherto un-heard-of" theory of a perpetual right in the nation is contradicted by the specific declaration of the Lords and Commons, in ousting James II and bringing in William and Mary, that they "do, in the name of all the people aforesaid, most humbly and faithfully submit *themselves, their heirs, and posterities forever*" to the new arrangement. We Englishmen, having "real hearts of flesh and blood beating in our bosoms," have signified our assent to this "condition of unchangeable constancy" by "binding up the Constitution of our country with our dearest domestic ties; adopting our fundamental laws into the bosom of our family affections; keeping inseparable, and cherishing with the warmth of all their combined and mutually reflected charities, our state, our hearths, our sepulchres, and our altars."

Do men have any rights? Yes, within limits, answers Burke. They have rights to justice, to the fruits of their industry, to the acquisitions of their parents, to "instruction in life and to consolation in death." But, on the crucial point, "As to the share of power, authority, and direction which each individual ought to have in the management of the state, that I must deny to be amongst the direct origi-

135

nal rights of man in civil society; for I have in my contemplation the civil social man, and no other. It is a thing to be settled by convention." The Lords and Commons are full of good patriots and true politicians who know how to "make the most of the existing materials" and may be trusted to decide in the best interest of the English people.

This was good doctrine to the dyed-in-the wool reactionaries in both parties, and they eagerly bought up and distributed thousands of copies. The King, who hitherto had had no great love for Burke because of his attacks on the royal prerogative and his cruel haste in calling for the Regency, now went about blathering to everybody that this was a good book, a very good book, and every gentleman should read it. But the nation recoiled with disgust. On behalf of the liberal Whigs, Fox and Sheridan denounced the doctrine. Even Pitt's organ, *The World,* assailed the "execrable sentiments" and expected to see Burke jousting about the country to rescue distressed damsels. Windham, a disciple of Burke in the Commons and an ardent admirer of the *Reflections,* had to note ruefully in his diary on the 7th of November: "The writer is a man decried, persecuted and proscribed; not being much valued, even by his own party, and by half the nation considered as little better than an inspired madman!"

It was therefore in a favorable atmosphere in the winter of 1790-91 that English liberals rushed forward to defend the French Revolution and the cause of reform in England. A flood of recriminatory pamphlets fell upon the apologist of despotism. In *Vindiciae Gallicae* the rising young Whig James Mackintosh wrote a lucid and methodical defense of the commercial class in France as against the landed gentry, and of the need for "tranquil and legal Reform" at home. On behalf of the Dissenters, Priestley's *Letters to the Right Honourable Edmund Burke* reviewed the history of Christianity, demonstrated the uselessness of an Established Church, and pleaded for toleration and equality for all sects. The bluestocking Catharine Macaulay, a learned historian, in *Observations on the Reflections of the Right Hon. Edmund Burke* lectured him on how the practical necessities of the revolutionists in 1688 dictated their compromises and declarations. The great-hearted Mary Wollstonecraft began her social crusading by the *Vindication of the Rights of Men,* with its furious tears at the sight of "the clogged wheels of corruption continually oiled by the sweat of the laborious poor." Thomas Christie, a personal acquaintance of Paine, wrote *Letters on the Revolution of France,* producing a mass of papers and documents to prove the wholesome and inevitable development of the Revolution.

None of these and other pamphlets outlived its moment. Hasty productions, they were all disjointed, except *Vindiciae Gallicae,* which was dull. They faded out of reckoning with the appearance of Paine's *The Rights of Man.*

Here was indeed the authentic answer. Against Burke's affirmations for reaction Paine hurled his affirmations for progress. The right of the Parliament of 1688 to bind posterity forever to their settlement is sweepingly and grandly denied. "Every age and generation must be as free to act for itself *in all cases* as the age and generation which preceded it. The vanity and presumption of governing beyond the grave is the most ridiculous and insolent of all tyrannies. Man has no property in man; neither has any generation a property in the generations which are to follow." Government belongs to the living, not the dead. The events in France are directed not against the mild King but against "the Augean stables of parasites and plunderers too abominably filthy to be cleansed by anything short of a complete and universal Revolution." Burke mourns for "the Quixot age of chivalry nonsense" but cannot feel for the unspectacular misery of the multitude. "He pities the plumage, but forgets the dying bird." To Burke's loose talk about unprovoked orgies and violence, Paine replies by a detailed narrative of the taking of the Bastille and the march of the women who brought the King to Paris in October, 1789. He puts these events in the light which is now commonplace among historians, as popular precautions against the threat of violent counter-revolution. The cruelties inflicted by the mob on the aristocrats were learned from the aristocratic governments, which hang, draw, and quarter petty thieves and stick their heads upon pikes to frighten the poor. And where does the mob come from? "It is by distortedly exalting some men, that others are distortedly debased, till the whole is out of nature. A vast mass of mankind are degradedly thrown into the background of the human picture, to bring forward, with greater glare, the puppet-show of state and aristocracy."

Having cleared the ground, Paine proceeds to follow Burke "through a pathless wilderness of rhapsodies." Meeting the reasoner-by-precedent on his own terms, he asks him to go back for a precedent all the way to the original Adam, who alone had the power to bind posterity and did not choose to do so. "Every generation is equal in rights to generations which preceded it, by the same rule that every individual is born equal in rights with his contemporary." Since obviously "all men are born equal," what is the sense of all the artificial barriers between man and his

Maker—kings, parliaments, magistrates, priests, nobility? "Mr. Burke has forgotten to put in 'chivalry.' He has also forgotten to put in Peter." All men have basic natural rights, a portion of which they contribute to the common stock in order to have social security. Governments by priestcraft or by conquerors cheat the multitude out of their natural and civil rights, which can be safeguarded only by a government of reason based on a written constitution.

If there has been any doubt of Paine's revolutionary intention, it now disappears. No mere reform of the Commons will satisfy him. The whole aristocratic régime in England must go. In an impressive series of paragraphs each beginning "The French Constitution says," he shows the English people the desirability of adopting French reforms—broadened franchise, uniform electoral districts, universal right of conscience, abolition of game laws, tithes, titles, and monopolies. With rough democratic vigor he rejoices that Frenchmen have stopped the childish game of vying for "blue ribbons" and "new garters" from the King. "The punyism of a senseless word like *Duke, Count,* or *Earl* has ceased to please. Even those who possessed them have disowned the gibberish, and as they outgrew the rickets, have despised the rattle." When he turns to celebrate religious liberty in France, Paine reaches his highest level of eloquence and liberal sentiment. "Toleration is not the *opposite* of Intolerance, but is the *counterfeit* of it. Both are despotism. The one assumes to itself the right of withholding Liberty of Conscience, and the other of granting it. The one is the Pope armed with fire and faggot, and the other is the Pope selling or granting indulgences." There is the the voice of a Thetford Quaker, the tone of Fox and Barclay, in his cry: "Who then art thou, vain dust and ashes!

by whatever name thou art called, whether a King, a Bishop, a Church, or a State, a Parliament, or anything else, that obtrudest thine insignificance between the soul of man and its Maker? Mind thine own concerns. If he believes not as thou believest, it is a proof that thou believest not as he believes, and there is no earthly power can determine between you."

The tremendous achievements in France, Paine continues, did not happen overnight. Burke's astonishment is the proof of his ignorance. Under the despotism of the French monarchy, a liberal spirit had been finding expression in the writings of men like Montesquieu, Voltaire, Rousseau, Raynal, Quesnay, and Turgot. French volunteers had gone to "the school of Freedom" in the American Revolution and had brought back copies of the various state constitutions which "were to liberty what a grammer is to language; they define its parts of speech, and practically construct them into syntax." The financial crisis precipitated a train of events in which the King, "a man of good heart," was victimized by the "Nobles or Nobility, or rather No-ability," and the third estate moved inexorably forward to establish the liberties of the people. Paine quotes in full the seventeen democratic guarantees of the Declaration of the Rights of Man. This epochal document "is of more value to the world, and will do more good, than all the laws and statutes that have yet been promulgated." The promise of world regeneration is implicit in the triumphal progress in France. "What are the present governments of Europe but a scene of iniquity and oppression? What is that of England? Do not its own inhabitants say it is a market where every man has his price, and where corruption is common traffic at the expense of a deluded people? No wonder, then, that the French Revolution is traduced. Had it confined itself merely to the destruction of flagrant despotism perhaps Mr. Burke and some others had been silent. Their cry now is, 'It has gone too far'—that is, it has gone too far for them. It stares corruption in the face, and the venal tribe are all alarmed. Their fear discovers itself in their outrage, and they are but publishing the groans of a wounded vice."

In a Miscellaneous Chapter riddling Burke's "mob of ideas," Paine denounces the hereditary principle, the legitimizing of ancient robberies. "Wrongs cannot have a legal descent." He strikes fiercely at the anointed heads of kings. "It is easy to conceive that a band of interested men, such as Placemen, Pensioners, Lords of the bed-chamber, Lords of the kitchen, Lords of the necessary house, and the Lord knows what besides, can find as many reasons for monarchy as their salaries, paid at the expense of the country, amount to; but if I ask the farmer, the manufacturer, the merchant, the tradesman, and down through all the occupations of life to the common laborer, what service monarchy is to him? he can give me no answer." He exposes the conspiracy of Whigs and Tories against the common interests of the English people, and sees in this game the universal practise of aristocratic Europe. The humbug will collapse before the march of reason and enlightenment. "From what we now see," he concludes with militant optimism, "nothing of reform in the political world ought to be held improbable. It is an age of Revolutions, in which everything may be looked for."

Thus the logician of the new democratic era met the casuist of the decadent aristocratic régime. By what strange perversity do some modern historians who cherish the democratic liberties that Paine's followers won for them, shower encomiums on Burke for his *Reflections?* There is room for a reasoned advocacy of the real wisdom at the core of conservatism, but the *Reflections* is not that book. It is not to Burke's credit—least of all is it original with him—that he appreciated the deeply ingrained network of habit and prejudice that makes men cling to their miseries. From the beginning of social existence, for better or worse, every conservative politician has exploited those automatic impulses, while the radical has based his argument on reason and the vital interests of men. By the end of the eighteenth century, in western Europe generally, the aristocratic régime had outlived whatever social usefulness it may have had, and the unprivileged multitudes were asserting their undeniable claim to political power. Burke wanted to freeze the British Government forever into the form of a narrow self-perpetuating oligarchy, while Paine urged the democratic step forward. Yet repeatedly Burke is credited with a sense for the historic flow of things, and Paine is derided as an impractical utopian!

Paine's reply to Burke awakened new enthusiasm among the genteel reformers of England. "There have been several answers to Burke since you left us," writes Sir Samuel Romilly to a French correspondent on the 5th of April, "but none that have much merit, except one by Paine, the author of the famous American *Common Sense*. It is written in his own wild but forcible style; inaccurate in point of grammar, flat where he attempts wit, and often ridiculous when he indulges himself in metaphors; but, with all that, full of spirit and energy, and likely to produce a very great effect. It has done that, indeed, already; in the course of a fortnight it has gone through three editions; and, what I own has a great deal surprised me, has made converts of many persons who were before enemies to the revolution." The moribund Society for Constitutional Information, of which Paine had become a member, revived. It published in the newspapers a resolution adopted on the 23rd of March, thanking Paine for his "most masterly book," which exposes "the malevolent sophistries of hireling scribblers," states "the most important and beneficial political truths," and rings in the doom of "usurping borough-sellers and profligate borough-buyers."

The Tory government did not know what to do with this French Revolutionist sprung up on its own soil. So it did nothing. Since *The Rights of Man* was issued at first in the same expensive three-shilling format as the *Reflections,* Pitt hoped that it would have a narrow and harmless circulation.

The extreme reactionaries quivered with outraged righteousness. "Here is started up another corsair," shrieked the foppish Horace Walpole on the 5th of April; "one Paine, from America, who has published an answer to Mr. Burke that deserves a putrid fever." The Earl of Mornington turned from taking the baths to complain to the Foreign Secretary Lord Grenville on the 3rd of July: "I wonder you did not hang that scoundrel Paine for his blackguard libel on King, Lords, and Commons. I suppose the extreme scurrility of the pamphlet, or the villainy of those who wish to disperse it among the common people, has carried it through so many editions. For it appears to me to have no merit whatever; but it may do mischief in ale-houses in England, and still more in whisky-houses in Ireland. I

143

think it is by far the most treasonable book that ever went unpunished within my knowledge; so, pray, hang the fellow, if you can catch him."

A crew of ecclesiastics, university dons, peers of the realm, broken-down American loyalists, and nameless hacks scrambled to the profitable sport of defending law and order from the new vandalism. In the wide sweep of his fusillade Paine had left himself open at various points. His glorification of a non-existent paradise in America and his rigid insistence on a written constitution were vulnerable; the earthy phrases of his richly impatient disgust were offensive to refined readers; and his advocacy of extreme political democracy could easily be distorted as a crazy plan to wipe out all distinctions and divide the wealth. But the decadent aristocratic system could not be rationally defended, and this pamphleteering ruck is mostly devoted to throwing mud at the upstart critic Paine.

An anonymous pamphlet, *Defence of the Rights of Man* —a tricky title, catering to Paine's disciples—assailed the "advocate of perjury as well as of robbery and murder." In *Letters to Thomas Paine* A Member of the University of Cambridge smugly declared, "The names of Dukes, Earls, and Barons, which are so disgusting to your ear, give me no more offense than those of a Justice of the Peace, or a Constable," flung at Paine Latin phrases, referred him to his Parisian friends for their meaning, and advised a better use of the uncommon talents "which, if properly directed, would amply atone for, and even dignify, the obscurity of your birth, and defectiveness of your education." In *Rights of Englishmen,* sub-titled *An Antidote to the Poison now vending by the transatlantic republican Thomas Paine,* Isaac

Hunt (father of the liberal poet Leigh Hunt), whom Paine may have seen carted ignominiously as a Tory through the streets of Philadelphia in 1775, screamed in all seriousness to his readers about "the rancorous temper of this sovereign-deposing, bishop-kicking, title-leveling, American independent, who has brought over from Pennsylvania his tremendous bloody tomahawk, to scalp the Government, and murder the Constitution of Great Britain. In this glass, Englishmen, you will see all the prominent, dismal features, the scowling brow, the hard and brazen front of this dingy, ugly, voracious, boasted monster from America. You will be able to remark the length and strength, the sharpness of his *nails* and *teeth,* and be guarded against his baneful, abominable, infectious, and corrupting breath, enemy to life and matter, and every institution and character, wise, sacred, and illustrious." Using the pseudonym Francis Oldys, M.A. of the University of Pennsylvania, a government official named George Chalmers composed a libelous *Life of Paine,* an insidious mixture of truth and error, which in many editions provided the nation with scandalous canards about the ne'er-do-well from Thetford.

While in England *The Rights of Man* smashed the peace and put the privileged order on the frantic defensive, it swung the American democratic movement into the orbit of the French Revolution. The Secretary of State, Jefferson, had become alarmed at seeing the universal equality of the Declaration of Independence perverted by the Hamiltonian brigade of merchants, manufacturers, and bankers who foisted the Constitution on the agrarian masses and regarded the national welfare as identical with their own profit. There was an undemocratic tendency in President Washington's levees and royal equipage, and in the solicitous spouting of Vice-President Adams on behalf of "the rich, the well-born, and the able." Jefferson had regretted his endorsement of Hamilton's plan to assume the state debts, which linked the national government and moneyed speculators; and he had begun quietly to round up the democratic forces. When he received a copy of *The Rights of Man,* which was dedicated to President Washington, he sent it on to the publisher with his hope that it would check "the *political heresies* which have sprung up among us" and that "our citizens will *rally* a second time around the standard of *Common Sense.*" The publisher printed this letter without authorization, and in the wake of Paine and Jefferson the popular press blazed with tirades against the political theories of Vice-President Adams. In defense of his father, the young John Quincy Adams wrote the anonymous *Letters of Publicola* in the Boston *Columbian Centinel* during June and July.

Jefferson was embarrassed by the whole affair. An astute politician, he valued his democratic adherents as the base of his projected party, but he was not ready to come out openly against the all-powerful clique who had made Washington their figurehead. To his lieutenants, Monroe and Madison, Jefferson reaffirmed his political creed. To his English friend Benjamin Vaughan he wrote that Paine's pamphlet was "a refreshing shower," and to Paine he declared, "Indeed I am glad you did not come away till you had written your Rights of Man." But to Washington and Adams he explained that the rumpus was not of his seeking. Adams answered like an undeservedly hurt child that he knew of no political differences between him and Jefferson and that he valued their mutual friendship most highly. All was smooth again, except that the public had chosen the two rival champions who would fight the battle of English aristocracy and French democracy in the United States.

CHAPTER XIV

The Apostle of Republicanism

IN THE spring of 1791, leaving *The Rights of Man* to work its own way in England, Paine went over to Paris. Affairs in France were verging to a new crisis. The doom of Louis XVI was written in the stars. He had neither the sense nor the heart to yield to the inevitable. Behind his open professions of "accepting" the Revolution, he had engaged in shoddy obstructive stratagems in the face of increasing democratic sentiment in the sections, clubs, and newspapers of Paris. As a last desperate resort against the new order, Louis hit upon the supreme treason of negotiating for the armed support of foreign powers against his own people. Suspicious rumors beginning to float about the city, the Assembly strengthened the guard at the Tuileries in order to keep Louis as a hostage for the good conduct of European monarchs. But Louis escaped from the guard, leaving a manifesto categorically denouncing the whole course of the Revolution and appealing to loyal Frenchmen for their support.

When Lafayette dashed into Paine's bedroom on the morning of the 21st of June to announce that the royal family had fled to the border, Paine cried, "It is well. I hope there will be no attempt to recall them." Going into the streets, Paine was engulfed by frantic roving mobs, a city in turbulent alarm. The King had escaped, Lafayette had let him go, the King would return with an army and drown the Revolution in blood! The people blotted out with mud and paint the word *Royal* from public signs, tore down royal statues, and carried aloft on pikes wooden straw-stuffed heads representing the King and the Queen.

The royal carriage was stopped at Varennes. On the 24th of June Paine was in the vast crowd that stood silent, ominous, keeping their hats on, as the royal carriage and the nervous convoy rode by to the Tuileries. Paine was dressed in the conventional breeches and long hose of a European gentleman, and had forgotten to put a tri-colored cockade in his hat. It was enough. What business had such a person in a crowd of long-trousered Parisian workmen and small shopkeepers, the sansculottes? They fell upon the quiet stranger with the hanging cry *"Aristocrat! à la lanterne!"* and he had some difficult moments before being rescued by an English-speaking Frenchman. It was not the last time that Paine's life was threatened by the oppression-maddened Parisian masses, whom he loved as a humanitarian but whose language he could never learn to speak.

In the liberal salons Paine essayed the organization of a republican movement. "There has been formed a republican society," writes Madame Roland to the philosopher Bancal on the 1st of July; "Payne is at the head." This society—whose program, sensational in 1791, became the accomplished fact in the France of 1792—consisted of only five members, Paine, Condorcet, Duchâtelet, and two others of uncertain identity. Paine got up a republican proclamation in English, and Duchâtelet, young noble turned libertarian, went about seeking a translator. The Abbé Sieyès and Dumont, the late Mirabeau's secretary, shied off, but a translator was found. On the 1st of July every section of Paris blazed with Paine's placards. He tells his readers,

who are now his "brethren and fellow citizens," that the
King's flight constituted an abdication. There can be no
excuses, he bluntly argues, whether the King acted as "fool
or hypocrite, idiot or traitor." "The nation can never give
back its confidence to a man who, false to his trust, per-
jured to his oath, conspires a clandestine flight, obtains a
fraudulent passport, conceals a King of France under the
disguise of a valet, directs his course towards a frontier
covered with traitors and deserters, and evidently medi-
tates a return into our country, with a force capable of
imposing his own despotic laws." Since France has now
"arrived at the age of reason," she has no further use for
the expensive services of Louis Capet and his clan. The
placard was posted even on the door and in the corridors
of the National Assembly. The royalist deputies called for
the author's arrest, but the moderates refused to press the
issue and moved to the order of the day.

The Abbé Sieyès, who had achieved great prominence in
1789 with his progressive pamphlet *What is the Third
Estate?*, was vexed to find himself associated in general
opinion with the new republican movement. In a letter to
the *Moniteur,* July 6, he declared his preference for monarchy as permitting more liberty to the individual, and invited sincere republicans to dignified debate. On the 8th,
accepting the offer, Paine expressed his "highest esteem"
for Sieyès, defined republicanism as representative government, and poured forth his passion against despotism in
a powerful pulsating sentence: "I am the avowed, open and
intrepid enemy of what is called Monarchy; and I am such
by principles which nothing can either alter or corrupt—
by my attachment to humanity; by the anxiety which I feel
within myself, for the dignity and the honour of the human

150

race; by the disgust which I experience, when I observe men directed by children, and governed by brutes; by the horror which all the evils that Monarchy has spread over the earth excite within my breast; and by those sentiments which make me shudder at the calamities, the exactions, the wars, and the massacres with which Monarchy has crushed mankind: in short, it is against all the hell of Monarchy that I have declared war." Sieyès' reply in the same issue is thick with compliments for Paine, "his ardent love for humanity, his hate for every kind of tyranny." "Who is the French patriot," Sieyès writes, "who has not already, from the bottom of his heart, thanked this stranger for having fortified our cause with all the strength of his reason and his reputation!" He then gives a metaphysical distinction between republic and monarchy as plural versus single executive and states that he has no leisure to duel with "republican polycrats." So bizarre and unconvincing was Sieyès' argument that it was rumored the debate was a comedy concerted by Paine, Condorcet, and Sieyès to prepare the public mind for republicanism.

Paine had headed his letter "at the moment of my departure for England." On the same day the dutiful British Ambassador Earl Gower sent a warning to his Foreign Secretary, Lord Grenville: "I have to announce to you the departure of Mr. Paine, who is on his road for England, where he piously intends, if possible, to make confusions."

Paine went to London to attend the celebration at the Crown and Anchor Tavern of the second anniversary of the fall of the Bastille. Government newspapers, however, had been busy for weeks stirring up bad will against the celebrants and warning that the responsibility for any disturbances would fall upon their heads. The presence of

151

Paine would have precipitated a riot. He stayed away, as did also Fox, Sheridan, and Stanhope. The meeting was held as scheduled, and adjourned just before a gang of rowdies burst upon the scene. On the 26th of July Horace Walpole relates the news of London. "The villain Paine came over for the Crown and Anchor; but, finding that his pamphlet had not set a straw on fire, and that the 14th of July was as little in fashion as the ancient Gunpowder-Plot, he dined at another tavern with a few quaking conspirators; and probably is returned to Paris, where he is engaged in a controversy with the Abbé Sieyès about the *plus* and *minus* of the rebellion."

Walpole was wrong about Paine's mettle and intentions. Paine had dug in for a siege. The Church-and-King mobs, who enjoyed such dirty work as smashing the home and laboratory of Priestley in Birmingham, could not dismay this veteran of revolution. "The ardour of Seventy-six is capable of renewing itself," he writes to Washington on the 21st of July.

The London radicals planned a meeting at the Crown and Anchor for the 4th of August to celebrate the second anniversary of the decree abolishing the feudal system in France, but the landlord, intimidated by government agents, refused the use of the hall at the last moment. On the 20th, assembled at the Thatched House under the chairmanship of Horne Tooke, a radical group adopted for publication an Address and Declaration written by Paine, a fighting program toned down to the condition of England. Not revolution, not even a fundamental change in the form of government is advocated, though "we profess and claim it as our principle that every nation has at all times an inherent and indefeasible right to constitute and establish such government for itself as best accords with its disposition, interest, and happiness." Antiquity and other men's authority cannot stand in the way of reason, which "is given at all times, and is for the purpose of being used at all times." It is evident that feudal vestiges in England—"game laws, borough tenures, and tyrannical monopolies of numerous kinds"—must be eradicated, and that the government must reckon with "the moral obligation of providing for old age, helpless infancy, and poverty." "These are our objects, and we will pursue them."

Paine was becoming an institution to be conjured with in England. Jefferson's political organ in Philadelphia, *The National Gazette,* which followed Paine's activities closely and with admiration, quoted a letter written from Hackney, England, on the 2nd of September, 1791: "In this country the spirit of reformation is spreading very impetuously. Nor has Mr. Paine, the renowned author of *Common Sense,* contributed a small portion of fuel to the flame that has been kindled. His answer to Mr. Burke is in all hands; it is read in all circles; it makes converts among all parties." The emissaries of reaction dressed him up as a grotesque bugbear, called common footpads "disciples of Paine," and blamed on him the terrible new democratic fashion of short hair-cuts for men.

Meanwhile, at the home of his friend Rickman in London, Paine lived the quiet life of a gentleman writer accustomed to a regular afternoon nap. In his eulogistic biography of Paine, Rickman has given various sidelights on his distinguished boarder—tall, broad-shouldered, with his remarkable eyes, "full, brilliant, and singularly piercing," "generally very cleanly," wearing his hair powdered and in a queue, with side curls. Rickman tells that, while the

153

Whig members of Parliament no longer cared to be seen with Paine, unshackled radicals and enlightened middle-class leaders gathered around him—the young Irishman Lord Edward Fitzgerald, the French and American ambassadors, the artists Sharp and Romney, the cynical clergyman Horne Tooke, Joel Barlow, Thomas Christie, Dr. Priestley.

It was at a dinner given by the publisher Johnson that Paine met two of the most prodigious parlor radicals of the age. Mary Wollstonecraft and William Godwin were complete strangers to each other, and had come on purpose to see Paine. The conversation turned to monarchy, religion, and the moral integrity of celebrated persons like Horne Tooke, Dr. Johnson and Voltaire. Mrs. Wollstonecraft and Godwin fell into ill-natured argument, Godwin finding her too conventional in religious views and unduly derogatory of the persons under discussion. In this dialogue the guest of honor became a mere outsider. Describing the incident, Godwin records that Paine was "no great talker," though he threw in "some shrewd and striking remarks." "The conversation," says Godwin, "lay principally between me and Mary. I, of consequence, heard her, very frequently when I wished to hear Paine." Apparently it did not occur to Godwin that Mary probably heard him when she, too, wished to hear Paine. At any rate, Paine had provided the occasion for that marvelous union of pure heart and more or less pure reason.

With his political preoccupation Paine had been obliged to put his bridge project out of mind. After standing on the Paddington green for about a year, the bridge broke through the makeshift abutments and had to be taken apart and stored away. Paine intended another vigorous assault on the British citadel of privilege and corruption, after which he would return to America in the spring. In this mood he wrote to Short on the 2nd of November, 1791: "I have but one way to be secure in my next work, which is, to go further than in my first. I see that *great* rogues escape by the excess of their crimes, and, perhaps, it may be the same in honest cases." And in this mood he accepted the compliments of the London Revolution Society at their annual November 4th celebration, when they sang:

> The joyful tidings spread around,
> Monarchs tremble at the sound!
> Freedom, freedom, freedom, freedom,
> Rights of Man, and Paine resound!

CHAPTER XV

THE REVOLUTIONARY CAUSE IN ENGLAND

IN THE year 1792 the history of Thomas Paine is the history of England. From the issuance of Part Two of *The Rights of Man* in February until his outlawry in December and the subsequent hanging and burning of his effigy in almost every town and village, Paine shook the country in a Titan's grasp. His revolutionary message created a dangerous radical movement, split the Whig party in two, and stiffened the reactionary forces for their expensive and impermanent victory.

Burke, surprised but undismayed at having estranged the great bulk of his fellow-Whigs by the *Reflections,* had reaffirmed his own conception of pure Whiggism in the *Appeal from the New to the Old Whigs.* Closing his eyes to the fact that Paine had transformed the central issue into the universal right of revolution, Burke devoted many tedious pages to proving that his notion of the Revolution in 1688 harmonized with the historic record. He scoured the vocabulary of abuse to express his abhorrence for the "foul, impious, monstrous" doings in France, and frenziedly declared his "warm opposition to the spirit of leveling, to the spirit of impiety, to the spirit of proscription, plunder, murder, and cannibalism" that menaced England. Quoting extensively from the "insolence" of Paine's pamphlet (without naming it), he did not even attempt an answer, but contented himself with suggesting "criminal justice" for the author. Finally, invoking the Almighty to support the social inequities of 1791, he solemnly averred his belief that "the awful Author of our being is the Author of our place in the order of existence—and that, having disposed and marshalled us by a divine tactic, not according to our will, but according to His, He has in and by that disposition virtually subjected us to act the part which belongs to the place assigned us." Despotic theory had reached its perfect limit.

To continue the debate with Burke was no major part of Paine's purpose. At all hazards he had to take the next forward step and present the English people with a full-bodied revolutionary program. When Paine let it be known that a second part of *The Rights of Man* was on the way, newspapers generally predicted that he would not escape the arm of the law this time. The publisher Chapman, who first undertook the printing, later testified at Paine's trial that he offered Paine for complete rights to the manuscript successively one hundred, five hundred, and a thousand guineas. Paine refused, and Chapman threw up the enterprise in January because of its "dangerous tendency." Chapman's offer was obviously part of a conspiracy by His Majesty's Government to suppress a book which it could not answer in kind. Paine entrusted the manuscript to Jordan, whose growing uneasiness at the venture he allayed by a written statement on the 16th of February: "Sir, should any person, under the sanction of any kind of authority, inquire of you respecting the author and publisher of *The Rights of Man* you will please to mention me as the author and publisher of that work, and show to such person this letter. I will, as soon as I am acquainted with it, appear and answer for the work personally." Immediately *The Rights of Man, Part Second,* was issued for general sale.

Less brilliant and spectacular than Part One, Part Two is more compact and cogent, both more theoretical and more concrete—a veritable textbook of revolution written under the shadow of prosecution. After taunting Burke for his desertion of the debate on principles and his appeal to "a set of childish thinkers and half-way politicians born in the last century," Paine asserts the universal right of free public discussion. Governments and laws, whether good or bad, should be obeyed, but the sovereign people may discuss and change them. The revolution in America has spread to France and will irresistibly triumph in the rest of the world, because men will not tolerate much longer "the greedy hand of government thrusting itself into every corner and crevice of industry, and grasping the spoil of the multitude. Reason, like time, will make its own way, and prejudice will fall in a combat with interest."

Condemning the parasitic and stifling aristocratic régime, Paine voices the progressive demand for lessening the scope and expense of government. As evidenced by the untrammeled democratic system in America, where "the poor are not oppressed, the rich are not privileged," the great mass of useful citizens in any country regulate their social intercourse by common and familiar principles of society and civilization which are easily enforced because they are generally accepted. The present old governments of Europe were founded on force and plunder, and kings, courts, and cabinets waste the essence of the people in order to satisfy their own selfish appetites. Simply, with rising eloquence, Paine drives the point home: "What inducement has the farmer, while following the plough, to lay aside his peaceful pursuit, and go to war with the farmer of another country? or what inducement has the manufacturer? What is dominion to them, or to any class of men in a nation? Does it add an acre to any man's estate, or raise its value? Are not conquest and defeat each of the same price, and taxes the never-failing consequence?—Though this reasoning may be good to a nation, it is not so to a government. War is the Pharo-table of governments, and nations the dupes of the game."

Against the old order and the principle of seizing power for self-aggrandizement, a new champion has arisen—the democratic order, which delegates authority for the common benefit of all. This is a selective, not a leveling, system. The actual leveler is hereditary government, which subjects men indiscriminately to the dominance of the wise and the foolish and "appears under all the various characters of childhood, decrepitude, dotage, a thing at nurse, in leading-strings, or in crutches." The representative system, having "society and civilization for its basis" and "nature, reason, and experience, for its guide," avoids civil and foreign wars and creates a government really in the public interest—that is, a republican government.

No government, says Paine, has a sound foundation except upon a written constitution to which the people have given their assent. American experience in the working-out of constitutions is "the real volume, not of history but of facts," showing the way to Europe. England has no constitution. The highly celebrated Bill of Rights, passed after the Revolution of 1688, was merely a division of spoils by the ruling oligarchy and left the people only the right of petitioning. It "is more properly a bill of wrongs, and of insult." The English people will soon throw off "the stilts and crutches of precedents" and will establish their own constitution. To start right, they must bear in mind that "Every man wishes to pursue his occupation, and to enjoy the fruits of his labours and the produce of his prosperity in peace and safety, and with the least possible expence. When these things are accomplished, all the objects for which government ought to be established are answered." The legislature may be constituted on any one of various rational principles; the executive must not be superstitiously entrusted to an hereditary monarch. "There is a morning of reason rising upon man on the subject of government." National prejudices are falling away, Frenchmen and Englishmen are fraternizing, expensive and quarrelsome governments will soon be abolished everywhere. "For what we can foresee, all Europe may form but one great Republic, and man be free of the whole."

Paine interprets the wide-spread poverty and wretchedness in Europe as resulting from vicious political arrangements. "The barbarism of government" drains wealth and throttles "the internal civilization of a country." The purpose of revolutions is therefore to bring "the moral condition" of governments into harmony with the people. The special privileges of courts and courtiers stand in the way of human progress. In England, the landed interest monopolizes the House of Lords and buys up the House of Commons. Hence the tax on land has actually decreased in the past hundred years, and is now far outdistanced by taxes on the common necessities of the poor. There is no more reason to favor the landed interest than any other branch of enterprise. The natural importance of plowing, sowing, and reaping will not be impaired by the loss of parliamentary majorities, for "The aristocracy are not the farmers who work the land, and raise the produce, but are the mere consumers of the rent; and when compared with the active world are the drones, a seraglio of males, who neither collect the honey nor form the hive, but exist only for lazy enjoyment."

The idealism of the revolutionary epoch was in the last analysis the individualistic idealism of an aggressive middle class seeking to wrest freedom and political power from a stagnant aristocracy. But Paine was a proletarian by origin. He appreciated the immediate demand for bread as well as for freedom. He could not forget the hungry days of his youth, the desperate wandering and job-hunting, the wretched hovels of mean streets. The details of his practical program are completely collectivistic and look forward to the revolutionary idealism of the nineteenth and the twentieth centuries. With the shrewd practicality that never quite deserted him and was in fact the prime cause for the popularity of his pamphlets, Paine adds and subtracts English governmental statistics and arrives at some startling conclusions. Of the £17,000,000 annual revenue £8,500,000 goes to the public creditors and £7,500,000 to current expenses. As a matter of fact, only £1,500,000 is necessary for all the honest expenses of government. While gradually scaling down the taxes, the Government should abolish the parish poor rates, which viciously tax the poor to support the poor, and should institute instead with the remaining £6,000,000 what we would call even to-day an advanced social security plan—public support of poor children, old-age pensions ("not as a matter of grace and favour, but of right"), free education, maternity benefits, marriage bonuses, decent funerals for the poor and homeless at public expense, a public works program for the unemployed ("Hunger is not among the postponable wants"). If any more funds are needed, they can be obtained from a progressive income tax, which would have the additional advantage of reducing the monstrous landed fortunes.

On the dynamics of his proposed change Paine is vague, perhaps intentionally. As a bridge-builder he knew the difference between a sound and a rotten structure. "It signifies not who is the minister. The defect lies in the system. The foundation and the superstructure of the government is bad. Prop it as you please, it continually sinks into court government, and ever will." Nothing of basic reform is to be expected from the established government. The people themselves must change the system by means of a national convention. Guardedly he warns that when the people have seen the light, "the danger will be, as in America and France, to those who oppose." He expresses his faith in the power of reason, given full sway, to accomplish "a passive, rational, and costless revolution."

Though the road might be hard and hazardous, countless thousands were ready to follow the inspiration of Paine. To the moderate, middle-class reformers who found the vision of a humbled aristocracy and unfettered trade congenial, came new adherents from the workers and shopkeepers, inflamed by Paine's practical program and the new proletarian stirrings in France. In April the London cobbler, Thomas Hardy, got together a group of his friends at a humble tavern and received an overwhelming affirmative to the question, "Have we, who are tradesmen, shopkeepers, and mechanics, any right to seek to obtain a parliamentary reform?" Thus, alongside the Society for Constitutional Information was launched the London Corresponding Society, which was soon in touch with kindred organizations in the manufacturing and industrial districts —the Sheffield cutlers, the Manchester weavers, the Staffordshire potters, the Tyne stevedores, the Cornwall miners. In the first turbulent birth-pangs of modern industrialism, forward-looking workers and employers, recruited from the same undistinguished multitude, made common cause against monarchy and aristocracy and swore by *The Rights of Man*. The avidity with which these classes nourished themselves on Paine's pamphlet, even in the expensive edition, was described by the *Annual Register* for 1792 as "incredible." Paine's close identity with the revolutionary movement in England is illustrated in the following bit of badgering of the witness Edward Smith by the prosecutor Garrow at Hardy's trial for treason in 1794:

"You were a cutler?"—"Yes."

"Then of course, you had a cheap copy of Tom Paine's *Rights of Man,* had not you?"—"I have read Paine."

"That is not an answer; you know every cutler in Sheffield had one; you had a cheap copy, had you?"—"I have seen one of the others."

"I dare say you have seen the best edition; have you one of the cheap copies?"—"I have seen both."

"I am sorry to be so troublesome, but I must have an answer."—"I appeal to the court, whether I am to answer that."

"I do not ask you whether you read it to any human creature but yourself; do you happen to have one?"—"Yes, I have read one."

"A cheap copy; was it made a present of to you, or how did you get it?"—"I obtained it by a subscription."

"A subscription of the society?"—"No; my own, and a few friends."

"Upon your oath, to the amount of how many thousand of your townsmen were there, that had this cheap edition of *The Rights of Man?*"—"I cannot tell that."

"Do you not believe that of the cutlers alone, in the town of Sheffield, there were many thousand?"—"There were many."

"I take for granted, that you have read that book, considered it very much as a sensible, well-written book?"—"Yes, I thought well of it."

Part Two of *The Rights of Man* threw the Government into the same quandary which had been caused by Part One. Pitt feared that a prosecution of Paine might strengthen rather than check the radical spirit. Would the Whigs rally to the Tory leadership, or would they raise the issue of a free press? For a while the Government did nothing, or almost nothing. Paine walked the streets of London a free man, and occasionally of a Friday afternoon engaged in warm political talk with Daer, Mackintosh, Barlow, Tooke, and the other members of the Constitutional Society around the dinner-table at the Crown and Anchor. On the 13th of April, however, in the name of Paine's bridge creditors, the constables pounced upon him at the London Tavern and hustled him off without his hat to the King's Head Spunging House. The publisher Johnson bailed him out within the hour, but the only full-length bridge that Paine ever built went into other people's hands.

Free, and with the Government apparently afraid of him, Paine's spirit expanded with the swelling tide of the social revolution. At London gatherings he offered as a toast, "The Republic of the World." He began to mix with the common folk beyond the metropolis. Early in May Fanny Burney writes in her Diary: "There are innumerable democrats assembled in Suffolk; among them the famous Tom Paine, who herds with all the farmers that will receive him, and there propagates his pernicious doctrines." Being warned at Bromley in Kent that the Government was preparing some action against his printer Jordan, Paine immediately returned to London. On the 14th of May Jordan revealed that he had been cited to appear at the Court of King's Bench as the publisher of the criminal *Rights of Man,* and furthermore that he did not want Paine's assistance and would plead guilty. Paine refused to have his book proscribed after such a hollow judicial hearing. On the 18th he wrote an open letter to the Constitutional Society, saying that he had "the pleasure" to inform them that he would soon publish a cheap edition of his pamphlet to be scattered broadcast among the poor. Thus, instead of running to cover while he had the chance, Paine flung the gage pointblank into the face of the Government. The response was prompt. On the 21st Paine received a court summons for libeling the British Constitution. On the same day George III issued in behalf of Pitt a Proclamation for the Preventing of Tumultuous Meetings and Seditious Writings. The proclamation urged all "faithful and loving subjects" to discountenance and to report to officers of the law all publications and societies "tending to excite tumult and disorder, by endeavoring to raise groundless jealousies and discontents."

The wheels of Pitt's Juggernaut were now in motion to stamp out "groundless jealousies and discontents." Quailing and breaking before the sudden onslaught, most of the Whigs hastened to disown not only Paine but even a moderate reform of the Commons, and went over to the Tory camp. In the parliamentary debate on the 25th of May a mere handful of liberal Whigs—Grey, Francis, Fox, and one or two others—assailed the administration for exaggerating the revolutionary issue and inquired whether it was necessary to foment riots in order to preserve the peace. The Home Secretary Dundas retorted for the administration that Part One of Paine's revolutionary critique was too "wild, extravagant, and visionary" to be troublesome, but "Gentlemen would recollect, that it was from his last publication that the principles had been drawn, which had been adopted by various bodies of men, and inculcated in a variety of shapes throughout the kingdom." On the 1st of June the obeisant Parliament made an address to their "most gracious sovereign," conveying "our warm and grateful sense of this fresh proof of His Majesty's constant solicitude for the welfare and happiness of his people." Soon a ramified stream of loyal addresses, gotten up by the provincial gentry among their devoted or brow-beaten neighbors and carefully doctored by the Home Secretary and his associates, poured into the capital to warm the cockles of King George's heart.

The staunch radicals took advantage of all this hubbub as an Advertisement by Authority for *The Rights of Man,* which had not yet been formally proscribed in a court of law. "Far from preventing it from being read," the *Annual Register* for 1792 recorded, "the sale became more extensive and rapid than ever. It was circulated with the utmost speed and success through every part of the three kingdoms, and made an incredible number of proselytes to the maxims which it contained." In the most remote hamlets of Scotland booksellers plied a rush-order business dispensing cheap and expensive editions of *The Rights of Man,* and "the book that was forbidden to be sold" achieved a wider current popularity than *Pilgrim's Progress.* In Ireland, where the patriot Wolf Tone had already called Part One "the Koran of Blefescu [Belfast]," *The Rights of Man* became the scriptural text of the desperate United Irishmen, and British agents reported that the schoolboys were engrossed in Paine's pamphlet while neglecting the psalter and the prayer book.

The trial being postponed from June to December, Paine made use of every opportunity in this period of grace to publicize his doctrines. In public letters to the Attorney General and the Home Secretary and to law-and-order meetings in Surrey and Sussex, he restated the chief tenets of *The Rights of Man* and flayed "those imaginary beings called Kings and Lords, and all the fraudulent trumpery of Court." These letters were printed by the radical societies, and, being distributed gratis in thousands of copies, brought Paine's ideas to that wide stratum of readers and listeners who could afford neither three-guinea nor sixpence editions. Finding a thousand pounds to his credit from the sale of his pamphlet, Paine offered the sum to the Constitutional Society, fittingly on the 4th of July. The Society deliberated and finally refused the self-sacrificing offer, with compliments to "the consciousness which you must possess of having contributed, by your writings, to the illumination of so many millions of human beings, in this country, America, and in other nations, on subjects of the highest importance to the universal freedom and happiness of mankind."

While Paine was leading the radical forces in England, his French friends, the philosopher-politicians gathered under Brissot, were precariously riding the waves of popular patriotic fervor into a dominant position in the Legislative Assembly. Rhapsodic with mixed visions of personal power and universal freedom, these middle-class oracles spurned the warnings of Marat and Robespierre and in April plunged the country into war with Francis II, King of Austria, who protected the émigré camps on the border. The French armies fared badly, prominent generals like Lafayette playing into the hands of the enemy and the ill-trained volunteers taking to their heels at the first sign of battle. Adding to the national distress, the suicidally devious Louis vetoed necessary war measures, summoned and dismissed ministers with chaotic frequency, and maintained a secret correspondence with the Austrians, their Prussian allies, and the émigrés. In a bloodless demonstration on the 20th of June the aroused Parisian masses asserted their vigilance for a united France and their impatience with all obstructers. The arrogant manifesto of the Austrian commander, the Duke of Brunswick, on the 25th of July, threatening the complete destruction of Paris if the royal family were molested, touched off the pent-up reservoir of revolutionary resentment. On the 10th of August the Parisian proletariat became the real French government. The mob stormed the Tuileries and slaughtered the Swiss guards after a fierce battle, while the royal family cowered at the Assembly in a small box behind the president's seat. The frightened deputies, pretending to lead, took orders from Paris. They suspended the King and countenanced his imprisonment in the Temple, and they made plans for yielding power to a National Convention which would reorganize the Government on democratic lines.

On the 26th of August the Assembly decreed that France could not regard as strangers the illustrious champions of the cause of peoples against the despotism of kings, and that France welcomed these luminaries to the National Convention, which would determine the destiny of France and perhaps of the human race. The Assembly conferred the honor of French citizenship upon eighteen renowned foreigners—a strangely assorted company including Paine, Priestley, Anacharsis Clootz, Washington, Wilberforce, Pestalozzi, and Kosciusko. In the elections to the Convention Priestley was chosen by Rhône-et-Loire and de l'Orne, Clootz by Saône-et-Loire and l'Oise, and Paine by l'Aisne, l'Oise, le Puy-de-Dôme, and le Pas-de-Calais. Pitt's organ, *The London Sun,* indulged in the following raucous *Prophecy* on October 9:

> In Seventeen Hundred Ninety-two
> (A Year which many a Frank shall rue),
> Three mighty Chiefs shall rise of free-born roots,
> Nam'd PRIESTLY, PAINE and ANACHARSIS CLOOTS;
> The first shall pare *Religion to the bone;*
> The next *wage War 'gainst every Regal Throne;*
> Whilst ANACHARSIS, wond'rous to relate,
> Shall, *Sans Culotte,* re-edify the State.
> Thus without *Priests, Religion, Kings,* or *Breeches,*
> *Gallia* shall *bare*—rise in fame and riches.

The judicious Priestley pleaded ignorance and declined. More ardent, Paine and the bushy-haired Prussian Clootz snatched the historic opportunity.

Paine had intended to stay in England, fighting against the privileged orders through the autumn and propagandizing for liberty at a sensational trial in December. The French National Convention, however, to which he was now a deputy from four departments, would begin its sessions in September. Achille Audibert, a special envoy from Calais, was waiting to convey him across the Channel. Paine knew what to expect in England. If he was not lynched by a law-and-order mob, he would be imprisoned and perhaps put in the pillory for libeling the Constitution. How could he best serve the Revolution? By martyrdom in England, or by membership in the French Convention? Paine accepted the invitation of France.

The story is told in Gilchrist's *Life of William Blake* that Paine hastily decided to leave England after a radical meeting where the visionary poet touched him on the shoulder and said, "You must not go home, or you are a dead man." The truth of the story is questionable. No such information by Paine has come to light. If His Majesty's Government had wanted to detain him, it could easily have done so. An official spy watched him at Rickman's, a suspicious post-chaise followed his roundabout route to Dover, an official spy went aboard the same packet to Calais. The simple fact is that Pitt was afraid of making a *cause célèbre* out of the prosecution of Paine and was glad to see him go. *The London Sun* declared on the 3rd of October: "We cannot think it was very judicious in those who really wish well to the country, to obstruct Mr. PAINE on *his leaving it*. If he should ever attempt *to return,* we should be much less surprised at any such obstruction."

Paine left London with Audibert and a young English attorney, John Frost, early on the 13th of September. Arriving at Dover at half-past ten that morning, they went to the York Hotel for a brief rest. The customs officials kept the party confined to the room for more than an hour, in order to search their pockets and rummage through their papers. Finally, being permitted to go on the packet, the dangerous trio made their way through a jeering, hissing mob of loiterers at the wharves. "Personally he is a very mean looking man," reported the British agent Mason, respectably sneering at Paine. "He is the very picture of a journeyman tailor who has been drunk and playing at nine-pins for the three first days of the week, and is returning to his work on Thursday."

Though Paine was destined never again to set foot on English soil, the English ruling class was not rid of him. From Calais he wrote a public reprimand to the Home Secretary, Dundas, about the Dover indignities, and in a few days he shot from Paris a new attack at the English system, the revised proofs of his *Letter Addressed to the Addressers on the Late Proclamation*. The *Address to the Addressers* shows Paine at his polemic best, heartened rather than dejected by the frown of government, and magnificently derisive of the British "locusts" with their "heart-and-pocket-felt" devotions to the established order. He indulges in lavish and stinging parodies on the loyal speeches in Parliament by both Whigs and Tories, "this Lord" and "t'other Lord." The government and the aristocracy stand self-condemned by hysterically striking back at *The Rights of Man* with Proclamation, Prosecution, and Addresses. "The plans, principles, and arguments, contained in that work, are placed before the eyes of the nation, and of the world, in a fair, open, and manly manner, and nothing more is necessary than to refute them." He thanks the Government for unwittingly advertising his book, where countless new readers may now discover "plans for the increase of commerce and manufacturers—for the extinction of war—for the education of the children of the poor—for the comfortable support of the aged and decayed persons of both sexes—for the relief of the army and navy, and, in short, for the promotion of every thing that can benefit the moral, civil, and political conditions of Man." Against this program stands "hoary-headed error," embodied in the so-called British constitution, "a farrago of imposition and absurdity." The impending trial is a conspiracy by the magistrates and the prosecutors not merely against him but against the liberties of the people. From such a government no reform can be expected, and a nation come of age ought to stop humbly petitioning for its rights. A national convention (as in France), elected by universal manhood suffrage, should be called to lay the basis for a truly representative government. Let the nation "DECLARE ITS OWN REFORMS."

The English radical societies circulated the *Address to the Addressers* among their members and warmed to its impatient spirit. His Majesty's Government was obviously unable to banish the new virus along with Paine. Hence the politicians in power adopted the common device of publicly minimizing the danger while privately panic-ridden at its steady growth. *The London Sun* tried to flimflam the public with such wishful thinking on the 1st of October: "The Doctrines of Mr. THOMAS PAINE, which, from their novelty, the boldness with which they were delivered, the flattery they offered to the weak; and the hopes they presented to the wicked, gained a temporary consideration which they did not deserve—are now sinking rapidly to oblivion, or will only be remembered to furnish matter of future ridicule, contempt, or astonishment." But on the 26th the British agent, Storer, wrote to Lord Auckland: "Everywhere in the country people are out of humour with crowned heads. I am very much afraid that Paine's rascally book has done much mischief."

No half-way measures would exorcise Tom Paine, the demon of discord. Every propaganda device at hand, and new ones for the occasion, were invoked to tar and feather him—prosecution, sermons, law-and-order associations, loyal addresses, newspaper canards, treatises, penny broadsides, street ballads, caricature cartoons, souvenir coins and knick-knacks. Paine's name became as familiar as the Devil's, and his strong features, distorted by the artist Gillray into those of a rat-faced, drunken staymaker, frightened little children from countless shop windows and bill-boards. In October the Association against Republicans and Levelers, organized by the high Tory John Reeves, set a new tone of political "debate." In an unceasing torrent of broadside songs, dialogues, and letters "Price only ONE HALF PENNY; Or 3s. per Hundred to such as give them away," the Association made the appeal of undiluted Toryism to the ancient habits and phobias of the multitude. Do you love your beer, your roast beef, your plum pudding? Down with Paine! Do you respect your curate? Down with Paine! Do you hate the French? Down with Paine! Would you resist the division of your property with the shiftless and the idle? Down with Paine!

> Tom Paine's Rights of Man! what are those Rights to me?
> To do what is right, I am sure I am free;
> I want to hurt no man, no man can hurt me,
>   Neighbors, mind this, and be quiet.

The shameless contempt with which the privileged element rode roughshod over the possibility of intelligence and self-respect in the masses may be seen in the Association's *Dialogue between A Labourer and A Gentleman*. Summarily talking down the inquisitive Labourer, the Gentleman philosophically observes, "There are poor people happy, as well as rich people happy; poor people miserable, and rich people miserable," and warns against the riotous trouble-makers with their deceitful books "written by one Tom Paine, a staymaker (a pretty fellow to understand politics)."

The swinish multitude, however, were beginning here and there to throw off their swinishness and to aspire to human dignity. Paine had shown the way to political independence, which is the essential basis of social freedom. In clubs and taverns all over the land the vanguard of workers and shopkeepers were reasoning through to a sense of their political rights and to an understanding of the political strategy that would refute slanderous charges and win converts. On the 19th of October the editor of the Sheffield *Patriot* enjoined on the London Corresponding Society "great coolness, moderation, and patience" in giving forth "the bright and sacred energies of truth" and in repelling the palpable lies about a division-of-wealth program with which "vile ministerial prints" tried to frighten off men of property from supporting a fundamental political reform. The radicals had courage, intelligence, and money. They tore down loyal posters and put up their own. They scattered by the thousands burlesque encomiums on the excellence of the British Constitution. The most torpid peasant, if he read or listened at all, might begin to bestir himself at being told, "You have no rights but the rights of horses and beasts of burden," or at being shown the sad, sad plight of Edmund Burke, "This poor man, who strains his lungs at the risque of his health, and tears his throat for the King, has only 1,500 *l*. a year!" The logical formulas of the French Revolution, voicing the awakened appetite of ninety percent of King George's subjects, were pulsating with rising momentum throughout England.

In this dangerous atmosphere of storm and stress came the day of Paine's trial for libeling the British Constitution,

December 18. Though the "wicked, malicious, seditious, and ill-disposed person" named in the indictment was absent in France, the Government sought an easy verdict with which to bludgeon down his English followers. The celebrated advocate, Erskine, represented Paine in spite of tremendous pressure, including a personal request by the Prince of Wales, to quit the case. In the crowded chamber of the Court of King's Bench the Attorney-General Macdonald quoted some of Paine's violent phrases on the absurdities of the British system, and replied with pious exclamations of horror. "Then, gentlemen," he said, "we have been insane for these seven or eight hundred years; and I shall just dismiss this with this observation, that this insanity having subsisted so long, I trust in God that it is incurable." He introduced into evidence a letter addressed to him a month before, in which Paine charged that the jury was packed and that the British government was a "perfection of fraud and corruption," and ridiculed obedience to "Mr. Guelph, or any of his profligate sons." This open defiance of the whole procedure made the task of defending Paine a hopeless one. Yet in a beautiful and impassioned speech that belongs with the classic liberal utterances of Milton and Mill, Erskine rang the changes on his theme "that OPINION is free, and that CONDUCT alone is amenable to the law." He held that Burke's theory of despotic privilege was more dangerous to the established order than Paine's theory of public consent. There is universal aptness in Erskine's social vision: "When men can freely communicate their thoughts and their sufferings, real or imaginary, their passions spend themselves in air, like gunpowder scattering upon the surface; but, pent up by terrors, they work unseen, burst forth in a moment, and destroy everything in their course. Let reason be opposed to reason, and argument to argument, and every good government will be safe." But Erskine was not speaking to a good government. He had to pause frequently to beg a little attention from the obviously impatient jury. When he finished, the foreman of the jury stood up in his place and told the Attorney-General that it was not necessary to answer. The verdict was immediately announced—Guilty. The defendant being absent, he was outlawed. A few persons hissing the verdict were taken into custody. As the audience filed out of the court, copies of a handbill, *Confession of Tom Paine,* were thrust into their hands. "I have been Sailor, Staymaker, Schoolmaster, and Exciseman," the condemned agitator is made to babble; "but find at last I am only fit for Blood."

The Tory government now threw off all pretense of moderation and launched a merciless inquisition against the French menace and the devotees of Paine. Appalled by the sudden armed fury of the Government and law-and-order associations and unable to insert advertisements in hitherto friendly newspapers, many faint-hearted adherents of the radical cause ran to cover. In 1792 the radical movement in England had not matured sufficiently for a life-and-death struggle with the aristocratic régime, supported by "old Custom, legal Crime, and bloody Faith" and reenforced by the mailed fist of the Government. Furthermore, the English radicals had been unable to avoid the continual weakening of their cause by being associated with the bloody coups of the Parisian proletariat, which alienated the bulk of the middle class—the very class which could benefit most from political reform. Now the radicals bent, lest they be broken. "The tide here is completely changed," rejoices the Home Secretary, Dundas, on the 23rd of December; "all levelers are drooping their heads, and"—he adds unctuously—"my only fear now is that they may proceed to any excesses on the other side." Throughout the land the Christmas season was observed by the devout and law-abiding, fortified by hogsheads of ale and *God Save the King,* in hanging and burning effigies of the man who had tried to bring them a new gospel of freedom. In Leeds the mob jeered at the chief works of Paine flopping from one side of the effigy, and a pair of old stays flopping from the other; in Worcestershire they plunged daggers into the effigy and huzzahed when sheep's blood spurted out. Even in far-away Barbados in the West Indies this patriotic game was played. 1793 was a black year for the venturesome publishers and booksellers who continued to deal in the illicit works of Paine. The prison sentences fell thick and fast—three months, six months, eighteen months, four years. With France and England officially at war in that year, reform became quickly synonymous with treason in the English language. Pitt fought the French Revolution in England and in Europe at the same time.

Paine's dream of a revolution in England did not come true, but his principles had a life beyond his own and would eventually triumph. In the short space of five years Paine had worked his way in a descending spiral through the united Whigs, the liberal Whigs, and middle-class reformers, down to an ultimate base in the affections of enlightened leaders among the poor and disinherited millions. In the gathering twilight, as late as January, 1794, the London Corresponding Society drained their glasses to such brave toasts as "The Rights of Man; and may Britons never want spirit to assert them" and "Citizen Thomas Paine—May his virtue rise superior to calumny and his name still be dear to Britons." Even after the societies were suppressed and the leaders were haled into court for high treason, the stalwart radicals kept the faith in the long desolate years of reaction. Thomas Paine is the unacknowledged Rousseau of the "passive, rational, and costless revolution" of 1832 and the subsequent Reform Bills which have made England a political democracy. In spite of lip service to King, Lords, and Established Church, the English people to-day, so far as political rights are concerned, live in the full exercise of the democratic system which Paine offered them in 1792 with *The Rights of Man*. Modern England owes its democracy to Thomas Paine more than to any other one man.

CHAPTER XVI

Deputy from Calais

FOR the rough send-off which England gave him at Dover in the morning of September 14, Paine was more than compensated by the gala welcome three hours later in Calais. Official France opened her arms wide to the great world-liberator who had come to enrich the new Republic with his own idealism. Regardless of the rain, a company of soldiers stood at attention, the officer on guard embraced him, a pretty girl put the national cockade in his hat. He walked to Dessein's famous hostelry through a holiday crowd of men, women, and children shouting *"Vive Thomas Paine!"*

The trip to Paris was a triumphal progress, with elaborate ceremonies at Abbéville, Amiens, and Clermont. Arriving at Paris in the evening of the 19th, Frost and Paine engaged rooms at White's *Hôtel Philadelphie* in the Passage des Petits Pères, and went to one of the closing sessions of the Legislative Assembly. Paine's entry created a sensation on the floor and in the galleries, and the financial expert Cambon hastened for the honor of being the first deputy to embrace him. On the 20th Frost reported in a letter to John Horne Tooke: "Mr. Paine is in good spirits, and indeed the flattering reception he has met with all through France could not fail of it. It is more than I describe. I believe he is rather fatigued with the kissing." They dined that night with Petion, the mayor of Paris.

On the eve of the National Convention, a deceptive quiet hung over the city. The September Massacres had taken place three weeks before, and the sansculottes had not laid their pikes and fire-arms out of reach at the sound of the tocsin. Nor would the National Convention long offer the exhilarating spectacle of a unified republican power in arms against the aristocratic system. The Convention was destined to be torn by bitter class alignments which could be resolved only by the shedding of blood. In general, men of property found their desires championed by the dominant party in the Convention, the Girondins, led by Brissot, Condorcet, and Roland, who believed in curbing the illegal outbursts of the Parisian mob and in maintaining the internal status quo —complete freedom of trade and governmental financing by paper assignats. The poorer classes looked to the men who came to dominate the Jacobin Club at Paris—figures like the tempestuous Marat and the adroit Robespierre, who favored burdening the rich with the war expenses and raising wages to meet the new high assignat prices. Between the Jacobins and the Girondins were the neutral members of the Plain, ready to jump either way at the call of passion or expedience.

Paine's ignorance of the French language and the swiftly shifting political current doomed him to a tragic rôle in the Convention. In Paine's view there was only one enemy—the aristocratic system. It was natural for him in the turbulent confusion of French affairs to come to regard the Jacobin leaders as noisy but unimportant hindrances to the common struggle of all useful citizens against the privilege of birth. Not perceiving that the Girondins were the mere agents of a minority class, he turned to them. They were his old friends. He had known them at earlier stages of the Revolution, when they had fearlessly led the battle for reform against the aristocrats in power. The Girondins spoke the language of philosophy, the slogans of universal freedom. They had invited him to the Convention and they took him into their homes and hearts. A year later, he almost shared their fate under the guillotine.

Whatever the future might bring, Paine threw himself into the work of the Convention with high and jubilant seriousness, to bring swiftly into existence the golden epoch of an unshackled humanity. With the other deputies from Calais, for which department he had chosen to sit, he went through the ceremonies attending the verification of credentials. At the opening session, on the 21st of September, the Convention voted the abolition of royalty. This decree was to Paine a personal triumph, a united France having caught up with his republican manifesto of the preceding year. But the storm cloud came up quickly. On the 22nd a deputation of citizens from Orléans announced that the people of that city were out of sympathy with their local officials, who refused to resign. Following a denunciation of the officials by Danton, it was moved that all minor administrative bodies be purged and particularly that law-courts be conducted by arbitrators trained only in the laws of reason. Debate broke out, and terrible thunderous words filled the air of the Convention Hall and roused the gallery—*sang, glaive des lois, Que la loi soit terrible, gangrené de royalisme, des trahisons, l'anarchie*. Catching the drift of the furious give-and-take, Paine suggested through the Girondin Goupilleau that a radical change of the judicial system would disturb the whole government and would make thorough-going constitutional reform all the more difficult. Yes, said Danton, of course he agreed with Citizen Thomas Paine; yet he pro-

181

ceeded to insist on altering the judiciary. The Jacobins and the gallery frightened the neutral deputies and carried their point. In the *Patriote Français* the next morning Brissot inveighed against the Jacobins as the party of disorder; and in the Convention Roland and Buzot enraged the Parisian deputies by calling for an armed guard against the people of the city.

Paine's magnificent hopes for the new France were too deep-seated to be suddenly dashed by factional bickering. He issued on the 25th a formal *Address to the People of France,* in which he congratulates them for extending the example of the American Revolution and laying the foundation for "the great Republic of Man." "It is to the peculiar honour of France, that she now raises the standard of liberty for all nations; and in fighting her own battles, contends for the rights of all mankind." And he appeals to the French nation for calm, union, "greatness of friendship."

The basic differences between the factions could not be talked away by the beautiful words of the imported philosopher. The Jacobin-Girondin war in the Convention went on with accelerated vigor. The Girondins harangued against the dominant position of Paris, and the Jacobins declaimed against the weakening influence of disunion and federalism. The Girondins took the offensive and accused Robespierre of aspiring to a dictatorship, Marat of inciting to riots, Danton of pocketing the public funds. Among those 750 furiously excited Frenchmen Paine was bound to sit silent and ineffectual, to seem, as the British agent, Miles, phrased it, "an owl in a room filled with monkeys and jackdaws." On October 11 the Convention appointed a committee of nine to bring in a new Constitution for republican France. The members were Paine, Brissot, Petion, Vergniaud, Gensonné,

Barère, Condorcet, Sieyès, Danton—all, except the equivocal Sieyès and the Jacobin Danton, frequenters of the
semi-weekly salons at the Rolands, where the Girondins
concerted their most important maneuvers. The next day at
the Jacobin Club the impressive paralytic deputy Couthon
declared war on the "clever, subtle, scheming, and, above
all, extremely ambitious men." "Look at the appointments,"
he cried; "they are all filled from among this faction. Look
at the composition of the Constitution Committee; that is
what did most to open my eyes. It is this faction, which
wants liberty only for itself, that we must combat with all
our might." What Paine had gladly accepted as an honor
from the French people was branded by the uncompromising Jacobins as a Girondin badge.

Outside of the Convention itself there were expansive out-
lets for Paine's revolutionary energies. He met with his
friend, the philosopher Condorcet, to draft the new constitution, and he wrote republican articles for Condorcet's
Chronique du Mois and Brissot's *Patriote Français*. At
White's Hotel he was the center of a group of British expatriates who soon organized themselves for Sunday and
Thursday meetings as the Friends of the Rights of Man.
The British agent, Munro, affected contempt for "the party
of conspirators," "such a wretched society" led by "such a
fellow," but he sent careful and specific reports about their
doings to Foreign Secretary Grenville. In October "the party
of conspirators" was supplemented by the arrival of Lord
Edward Fitzgerald, the young Irish patriot and future martyr. In a letter to his mother, Fitzgerald wrote enthusiastically, "I lodge with my friend Paine; we breakfast, dine and
sup together; the more I see of his interior the more I like
and respect him. I cannot express how kind he is to me;

there is a simplicity of manner, a goodness of heart and a strength of mind in him that I never knew a man before possess."

The Girondins in power imprudently felt that they could be highhanded to all opposition, because their war policy, which had been carried in 1791 over the dissent of two or three Jacobins, was at last being vindicated by a succession of spectacular victories—"the torment and despair of the agitators," according to Brissot. The battle at Valmy on the 20th of September stopped the Duke of Brunswick's leisurely promenade to Paris, and caused the sudden withdrawal of the foreign armies from France. With the stirring slogan "war to the castles, peace to the cottages," the French troops under Dumouriez swept into the Netherlands and routed the Austrians at Jemappes on the 6th of November. The local peasantry and middle classes hailed the French as deliverers, and gladly organized republican societies and accepted French propagandistic tracts including the works of "docteur Payne." The national struggle for existence was being transformed into the militant liberation of all the oppressed peoples in Europe.

In Paris liberty-loving hearts were inflamed by the prospects of international freedom. Paine attended the celebration of recent French successes held by the British residents at White's Hotel on the 19th of November. The drawing rooms, decorated with civic and military trophies, were filled with renowned foreigners, deputies of the Convention, and officers of the army. Two military bands played, and the company sang the vibrant songs of the Revolution— *Ça Ira,* the *Marseillaise,* the *Carmagnole.* Toast followed toast: "The Republic of France, founded on the Rights of Man"; "The armies of France, and may the example of its

184

citizen soldiers be followed by all enslaved countries, till tyrants and tyranny be extinct"; "Thomas Paine, and the new mode of advertising good books by Proclamation and the Court of King's Bench."

While the Girondins were concerning themselves with the mission of world liberation, a vital problem was clamoring for attention at home. What should the Republic do with the prisoner at the Temple, Louis Capet, formerly Louis XVI? The Parisian masses, who had engaged in many a bloody street fight with Louis' adherents, could not see why the arch-traitor was permitted to live so long after the deposition in August. The Girondins shied away from the issue as long as they could. They feared that the anger of the people, having once tasted the execution of Louis, might turn against them; they feared the alienation of moderate sympathizers in foreign countries; they feared a sudden extension of the war with which they could not cope. So they tacked and wavered, achieved nothing and lost prestige.

Paine would not go along with his Girondin associates in their twistings and turnings. He had a clear and honest program of action, based on the view that it was futile and unwise to resist the overwhelming desire of the people for a prompt and speedy trial—that, in fact, a public exposé of Louis' machinations would have great psychological value both in France and abroad. The fallen monarch should of course be tried and officially condemned; but his life should be spared.

In early November, while the Jacobin deputies clamored for Louis' head, the timorous Girondin leaders kept to the background. One or two of their braver subordinates argued against turning the Convention into a court and vainly parried St. Just's impassioned contention that the King was a barbarian, a foreign enemy liable to the laws of war. The discovery on the 20th of November of the King's secret cupboard in the Tuileries, containing correspondence with counter-revolutionists and the émigrés, infuriated the sections of Paris and hastened action by the Convention. The next morning the Convention listened to a communication from Deputy Paine. "I think it necessary that Louis XVI should be tried," he bluntly began. A conspiracy exists among the "crowned brigands" of Europe (Mr. Guelph of England and the rest) against the liberties of the people. The facts should be brought to light. Louis is not important in himself but as a partner in this conspiracy against all Europe. The Republic of France cannot remain free as long as she is surrounded by armed, hostile despots. "It is therefore her immediate interest that all nations shall be as free as herself; that revolutions shall be universal; and since the trial of Louis XVI can serve to prove to the world the flagitiousness of governments in general, and the necessity of revolutions, she ought not to let slip so precious an opportunity."

The Girondins now affected to lead where they could not repress. Barbaroux proposed on the 3rd of December that Louis should be brought to trial, and other Girondins posed as extreme revolutionists by demanding that all advocates of royalty should be put to death, all the Bourbons (including the King) should be banished, and the primary assemblies should review the conduct of the deputies. On the other side, the Jacobins stuck relentlessly to their purpose of taking Louis' life. Robespierre urged that the infant Republic could be best consolidated by the execution of Louis, which would stamp on French hearts a contempt for royalty and would paralyze the partizans of the King. The Girondins, not daring to confess any fear of the public, allowed Marat's

186

motion for open debate and vote by roll-call to pass without opposition. Louis' fate would be decided under the probing eyes, the hisses and hurrahs of the ragged gallery spectators, thirsting for royal blood. These were the people who had dashed out of their shops and hovels into all the Parisian broils from the taking of the Bastille to the September Massacres. It would call for the courage of epic heroes to say No to them.

The trial began on the 10th of December and dragged along for more than a month, the Girondins interrupting frequently for the consideration of other business. Just before Louis was brought into the Convention Hall on the 11th, Paine began his efforts for clemency. He recommended through Bancal that a distinction should be made between the crimes committed before the Constitution of 1791 and the crimes committed after the Constitution of 1791—the crimes of the absolute king, which were due to monarchy in general, and the crimes of the sworn servant of the people, the man himself. The Convention refused any such distinction and proceeded to question Louis, who blandly denied everything.

Paine was now at the zenith of his French renown in the reflected glory of his own trial and the nationwide burning of his effigies across the Channel. Though vilified in England as the scheming apostle of murder and riot, in France Paine devoted his energies and risked his reputation and his life in order to save Louis Capet. In December the American ambassador, Gouverneur Morris, and the British agent, Munro, knew that Paine would make a forthright appeal for mercy. The Girondin Genet records a meeting at the home of Lebrun, the Minister of Foreign Affairs, on the evening of January 14. Paine, Brissot, Guadet, Fauchet, and other Girondin leaders were there. Paine took no part in the conversation but sat quietly sipping his claret. At Brissot's suggestion Genet asked Paine what effect the execution of Louis might have in the United States. "Bad, very bad," Paine answered. Lebrun expressed a hope that Genet might go to the United States and take Louis with him. But, though Lebrun appointed Genet ambassador on the 15th, the other Girondins lacked the courage to fight for their own plan. Paine, however, presented the Convention a calm, reasoned plea to spare the prisoner's life.

Reminding the Convention of his own unquestionable hatred for "the perfidy, corruption, and abomination" of monarchy, he argues that the execution of Louis would parallel the horrible practises of monarchy and would only give new ambitions to Louis' two brothers in foreign lands. Also, it should be remembered that Louis served the cause of freedom by aiding the American revolution. Let him pass the rest of his life in exile in the United States. "In relating this circumstance, and in submitting this proposition, I consider myself as a citizen of both countries. I submit it as a citizen of America, who feels the debt of gratitude which he owes to every Frenchman. I submit it also as a man, who, although the enemy of kings, cannot forget that they are subject to human frailties. I support my proposition as a citizen of the French republic, because it appears to me the best, the most politic measure that can be adopted."

Paine's argument brought forth no debate. The Convention was tired of the prolonged discussion. Voting took place from the evening of the 15th to the morning of the 20th. Three questions confronted the deputies: Was the King guilty? Should the decision be referred to the people? What should the penalty be? On the first question the 707

188

deputies present declared themselves unanimously in the affirmative. On the Girondin proposal that the decision should be referred to the people—a measure involving infinite possibilities of corruption and chaos—Paine voted in the negative. The motion was rejected, 424 to 287. The question of penalty occupied a continuous and memorable session from 10 o'clock in the morning of the 16th to 10 o'clock in the evening of the 17th—all day, all night, all the next day and evening. In that long Convention Hall, close-packed, stuffy, dimly lighted, while the viragoes in the gallery hissed or cheered and scratched down the votes on scorecards, deputy followed deputy in the tribune and gave his verdict and, if he wished, his reasons. The Abbé Sieyès, staunch advocate for monarchy against Paine in 1791, bent to the gallery and voted for death "without fancy talk [*sans phrases*]." The theatrical Prussian, Clootz, who took his international character with grotesque seriousness, declaimed, "Louis is guilty of lèse-majesté. What punishment have his crimes merited? I answer, in the name of the human race, death." Paine simply said in French, "I vote for the imprisonment of Louis until the end of the war, and for his perpetual banishment after the war." And Paine's brave and comparatively obscure admirers gloried in the dangerous honor of standing beside him. There was Christiani: "I rely on the opinion of Thomas Payne, and I vote like him for imprisonment." There was Duval: "By the example of Thomas Payne, whose vote is not suspect; by the example of that illustrious stranger, friend of the people, enemy of kings and royalty, and zealous defender of republican liberty, I vote for imprisonment during the war, and banishment at the peace." The philosopher Bancal supported the same view in a compact series of arguments climaxing with a grand flourish: "I think that this judgment will be that not of kings, who prefer a dead king to a humbled king, but the judgment of the nations and of posterity, because it is that of Thomas Payne, the most deadly enemy of kings and royalty, whose vote is for me the anticipation of posterity." All to no avail. The Parisians wanted a verdict of death, and the majority in the Convention decreed it—387 to 334.

On the 19th, as a last stratagem, Buzot, Brissot, and Condorcet urged a reprieve in view of the delicate external situation. Taking the floor, Daunou warned against hasty judgment. "One of your members, Thomas Payne," he said, "has an important opinion to communicate to you. Perhaps it will not be useless to learn from him what in England—" Angry shouts cut him short. To hell with England! And there had been too much delay already. Paine, however, ascended the tribune and stood there quietly as his friend Bancal began to read a translation of his speech. Though recognized technically on the motion for a reprieve, Paine really wanted a commutation of sentence and he spoke for the American people, not the English. "Very sincerely," he began, "do I regret the Convention's vote of yesterday for death." At this Marat broke out, "I submit that Thomas Paine is incompetent to vote on this question; being a Quaker his religious principles are opposed to capital punishment." A hot free-for-all argument followed, Paine standing beautifully unafraid in the midst of that wild alien jabber, until shouts for freedom of speech prevailed. Bancal resumed the reading of the deep, eloquent phrases in which Paine begged for mercy on the fallen king. With quiet passion Paine reminds the Convention of his almost twenty years in the service of "liberty *and* humanity," and warns against an act which may appear as justice to-day but as vengeance in the future. A convention brought together to establish a Constitution should not take an irrevocable step which will increase the nation's enemies. France needs the help of America, and the Americans regard Louis as their friend. "Could I speak the French language," Bancal read, "I would descend to your bar, and in their name become your petitioner to respite the execution of the sentence on Louis." Marat and Thuriot now created another disturbance, asserting that Paine had been falsely translated, but Paine and Bancal stood their ground and were allowed to proceed. "Ah, citizens," the plea ends, "give not the tyrant of England the triumph of seeing the man perish on the scaffold who has aided my much-loved America to break his chains!" Marat again shouted that Paine voted against the punishment of death because he was a Quaker. Paine replied, "I voted against it from both moral motives and motives of public policy." In a debate between Paine and Marat, no group assembled in the heart of Paris could long hesitate as to a decision. The motion for a reprieve was rejected, 380 to 310.

On the 21st of January, 1793, the doomed Louis was trundled off to the Place de la Révolution to square his accounts with the French people at the guillotine. As Robespierre predicted, his execution strengthened patriot sentiments among the masses; but the theater of the war was appallingly expanded. The Girondins—philosophers, humanitarians, middle-class apologists—stood condemned in the popular mind for the same devious type of politics that had brought Louis to disaster. And their foreign associates, like Paine, were definitely under suspicion.

CHAPTER XVII

THE GIRONDIN DEBACLE

THE first half of the terrible year 1793 witnessed the life-and-death struggle of the factions and its final resolution with the complete victory of the Jacobins. Though Paine was not one of the chief gladiators, he was generally on the side of the Girondins and their downfall was his.

The Girondins had been, and fatally continued to be, narrow middle-class politicians. Backbiting and hollow threats against the Jacobins and the suppression of hungry mobs by legal violence constituted their domestic policy. The plain people, from whom the mass army was recruited, was gradually to lose all confidence in them.

The execution of Louis had furnished the aristocratic governments of Europe a pretext for waging war against the revolutionary system which threatened their own foundations. There was no room in Europe for both a comfortable aristocracy and a militant republicanism. Pitt gave the French agent at London his papers on the 24th of January, and on the 1st of February France and England were officially at war. The Convention appointed Paine, Barère, Condorcet, and Fabre to formulate an Address to the English People. In a few weeks France was at war with all the other countries of Europe except Switzerland, Denmark, and Sweden. Great masses of the French people steeled themselves for Liberty, Fraternity, and Equality against the onslaughts of the common enemy. Wasting no tears for the dead Louis, Deputy Paine made the French enthusiasm his own. "The first characters in Europe are in arms" (he writes to an American acquaintance on the 17th of February); "some with the bayonet, some with the pen, and some with the two-edged sword of Declamation, in favour of Liberty. The tyrants of the earth are leagued against France; but with little effect. Altho' single-handed and alone, she still stands unshaken, unsubdued, unsubdueable, and undaunted: for our brave men fight not, as the troops of other nations, like Slaves chained to the oar of compulsory power. They fight freely, and for conscience' sake. The nation will perish to a man, or be free." On the 20th of February the Convention decreed the levy in mass, drafting 300,000 able-bodied and unmarried men between the ages of 18 and 40 into the armed forces of *la patrie*.

In spite of the fine Girondin proclamations difficulties piled on difficulties in February and March in a headlong flight to chaos and anarchy until the Jacobins forced the adoption of energetic remedies. The attempt at a nation-wide conscription of soldiers provoked a formidable civil war in the Vendée, where aristocrats and fanatically religious peasants raised the banners of the Catholic and Royal Army. The leading French general, Dumouriez, deserted to the Austrians and began a march on Paris to restore the monarchy and the Constitution of 1791. The accelerated flow of printing-press money boosted prices and caused food shortages and bread riots in the principal cities. The Girondins, with governmental responsibility in their hands, affected to believe that the revolt in the Vendée was some sort of Jacobin subterfuge; and it was inharmonious with the Girondin free-trade ideals to do anything about lifting the wages of the unorganized laborers to a parity with the soar-

193

ing prices. Parisian workmen began to gather in dangerous groups, and the Jacobin deputies stormed against the administrative inactivity which was imperiling the Revolution. As the popular discontent in Paris was about to crystallize into an armed march against the Convention, the Girondins made a temporary surrender. In March and April the Convention passed a set of emergency decrees which organized a new revolutionary tribunal, proclaimed the death penalty for all rebels, and inaugurated special tax burdens upon the rich. A chief executive power superior to that of the ministers was established in the Committee of Public Safety, dominated by the Jacobin Danton.

In forcing the adoption of a strong terroristic central government, the Jacobins defeated a pet Girondin project—the Paine-Condorcet Constitution. The Girondin constitutional committee, of which Paine and Condorcet were the main figures, had presented their draft on the 15th of February. Even if the proposed constitution had had no defects, the Jacobins would have found some; and Paine and Condorcet had not worked out the most extremely democratic constitution. Though the Paine-Condorcet system was based on universal manhood suffrage, it stipulated for the indirect election of deputies and for an executive council independent of the Assembly. And suspicious sansculottes found sinister undertones in what seemed the special concern for property in the proposed Declaration of Rights. The Jacobins pounced upon the "rolandist, brissotin, girondin" scheme and intermittently during the next two months poured unmeasured hate and scorn upon it. "Know this, Condorcet, Thomas Payne, Duchâtelet," the *Journal des Amis* raged on the 25th of February, "our republic is not a fruit of your coterie-copulation" and will not be "the arid negation of royalty." "Our republic, ours, Parisian magistrates," must be based upon "the revolution of the poor," and "that is why we declare: the first of properties is existence." In summarizing the sporadic debates of the Convention, the priest Thirion told the Jacobin Club in April: "Citizens will not be able to eat or dress except at the pleasure of the greedy men of fortune; that's the constitution which the statesmen want to give us." The Girondin deputy Gorsas, in his paper *Le Courrier des Départemens* for the 24th of April, fiercely hit back at the "cruel perfidy" and "crafty art" of Thirion. "Whom will you persuade, cowardly calumniator," Gorsas sneered, "that Thomas Payne, Condorcet and Petion, whose writings and whose lives equally honor humanity, have neglected the well-being of the wretched? Go, continue to calumniate the philosophers, that's the business of priests." The Jacobins, however, had the ear of the all-powerful "Parisian magistrates," and the Girondins finally gave up the futile task of defending a constitution, which, if adopted, could not be put into effect during the revolutionary crisis.

Practically all Europe was waging war against the French Revolution, yet the chief revolutionists themselves were mainly occupied in hurling epithets at one another and plotting revolutionary coups. Sadly Paine wrote to Jefferson on the 20th of April: "Had this revolution been conducted consistently with its principles, there was once a good prospect of extending liberty through the greatest part of Europe; but I now relinquish that hope. Should the Enemy by venturing into France put themselves again in a condition of being captured, the hope will revive; but this is a risk that I do not wish to see tried, lest it should fail."

Like every one else in the storm-ridden capital Paine was

195

liable to lunge out under the impulse of political hatred. There was nothing sadistic or merely personal about Paine's hatred. When the British agent Munro compromised himself by lingering in Paris after the declaration of war, it was Deputy Paine who interceded for him; and when the British Captain Grimstone struck Paine in the face and called him a traitor to his country, it was Deputy Paine himself who got the reckless patriot safe conduct out of France. Paine fixed his hatred squarely on the most Jacobin of the Jacobins, the idol of the Parisian proletariat, Marat. Like the Girondin leaders but with more excuse (for as a stranger Paine could not be intimately acquainted with French affairs) Paine looked upon the Friend of the People as a bloodthirsy madman and an enemy of the Revolution. Certainly Marat was an enemy of the Girondin Revolution. He believed that no man was entitled to superfluities while others lacked the necessities of life. "I am the anger, the just anger of the people," Marat explained to Robespierre, "and that is why they listen to me and believe in me." In challenging Marat, Paine and the Girondins brought on a disastrous fight with unconquerable Paris.

Marat gave the Girondins their opening. On the 5th of April, as presiding officer of the Jacobin Club, he put his signature to a circular letter demanding the recall of the deputies who had voted to refer the late King's punishment to the people. Thereupon the Girondins under the leadership of Petion attacked Marat in the Convention and, recklessly setting aside the inviolability of deputies, obtained the passage of a decree for his arrest on the charge of inciting to riot and anarchy. Paine became involved in the affair. A few days before the accusation a young Englishman named Johnson, a friend of Paine, had attempted to commit suicide. Before stabbing himself, Johnson had left a statement blaming his act on Marat, the assassin of liberty. Paine showed Johnson's note to Brissot, who quoted it in his *Patriote Français* on the 16th with a preface implying that Johnson was dead and the "anarchists" were responsible. Paine and Brissot's editor, Girey-Dupré, were summoned to Marat's trial to testify briefly as to the facts. In the presence of a rapturous gallery Marat denounced all the charges as atrocious calumnies, and the circumspect revolutionary tribunal acquitted him. The mob carried their hero in triumph from the court into the Convention Hall and marched through and around the deputies, shouting *"Vive Marat! Vive le peuple!"* and throwing red caps into the air. Two days later Gorsas' *Courrier* lauded the "respectable Englishman," "docteur Payne," for the "candor" and "energy" with which he had stood up for Johnson and Brissot against Marat. By thus airing his views all over the city, poor Gorsas was putting his own head under the guillotine and graciously trying to drag Paine along with him.

Had Paine been a wary politician, it was high time for him to be quiet. But still hoping for peace among the factions and for the preservation of democratic government, he wrote on the 6th of May a high-minded appeal for unity to Danton, the dominant figure in the Committee of Public Safety. Paine speaks as a disinterested friend, "exceedingly disturbed by the distractions, jealousies, discontents and uneasiness that reign among us, and which, if they continue, will bring ruin and disgrace upon the Republic." He pleads for some regulations against the rampant libels which undermine public confidence in the officials, particularly in the Girondin deputies. "Most of the acquaintances that I have in the Convention," he tells his Jacobin correspondent, "are

197

among those who are in that list, and I know there are not better men nor better patriots than what they are." Danton, kindly disposed though he was, had no intention of risking himself for the Girondins, whose unremitting personal attacks had made him in self-defense a confirmed Jacobin. He must have pocketed the letter with a grim smile at the naïveté of Citizen Paine.

In his letter to Danton, Paine says that he has also written a letter to Marat and "He may show it to you if he chuse." This letter has not come to light, but it would seem to indicate that at least once Paine considered Marat as a reasonable human being with whom it was possible to co-operate. The letter failed to bring peace between the two—or, rather, Paine did not cease trying by legal means to silence Marat. To Marat Paine was a pathetic bewildered philosopher, worth watching but not particularly dangerous; while to Paine Marat was the chief internal trouble-maker whose continued inflammatory outbursts might bring the Revolution down in ruins.

The Commission of Twelve, which had been appointed by the Convention to investigate illegal political activity in Paris, shared Paine's politics but lacked his courage. The Friend of the People was not to be molested. What the Commission did, however, in the charged atmosphere of Paris was enough to set in motion a swift sequence of events concluding with the dramatic debacle of their own faction. They banned secret meetings, called for the registers of radical groups in the sections, and arrested several popular leaders including the journalist Hébert. Since Hébert was assistant procurator of the Commune, the Girondin Commission was aligning against itself not only the insurrectionary elements but also the legal government of Paris.

The Parisian proletariat were on the march, and theirs was the sovereign power. A revolutionary committee from the sections combined with the legal Commune to declare Paris in a state of insurrection. While the tocsin rang and the alarm cannon boomed incessantly and 30,000 armed volunteers stood in readiness throughout the city, delegation after delegation marched into the Convention Hall and demanded the arrest of twenty-two leading Girondins and the enactment of relief measures for the poor. The frightened Convention yielded slowly, dissolving the Commission of Twelve and on the 1st of June referring the fate of the Girondin leaders to the Committee of Public Safety. That night the city blazed with the illegal meetings of impatient rebels, and Brissot, Vergniaud, Gensonné, and Guadet did not go to bed at home but sat around until sunrise at the house of a friend, discussing the relative merits of suicide and death on the scaffold. On the 2nd, the National Guard of the city, led by the Jacobin Henriot and swelled by volunteers into a mass army of 80,000, surrounded the Convention and announced that no deputy could leave until the Girondins were formally expelled. The Parisians rejected a mere suspension of the Girondins and pushed a few bolder deputies back into the hall. There, in a dead silence, the cripple Couthon lifted himself to propose that the Girondin leaders, including the Commission of Twelve, be expelled and arrested under surveillance at their homes. The Convention so decreeing, the temporarily sated Parisians made way for the deputies.

Paine stood aghast at the Parisian masses and their triumphant uprising, which far exceeded his worst fears. And with what incredible speed had his own stock fallen! As recently as the 12th of January, three days before he came out for clemency to Louis Capet, the Jacobin *Révolutions de Paris* had paid Paine the most exalted compliment at its disposal. It had opposed any restrictions on the freedom of the press even against the most unprincipled defamers of the Revolution, because "If we silence today the Vilettes and the Gauthiers, tomorrow silence will be imposed on the Th. Paynes, the J. J. Rousseaus; for a policy which begins by closing the mouths of servile and cowardly pamphleteers because they can do harm, will end by depriving of utterance the generous defenders of the rights of man, because they do not know how to flatter or to compromise with principles." Now, on the 30th of June, an Englishwoman living in France writes, "No person can entrust a letter to the post, but at the risk of having it opened; nor could Mr. Thomas Paine himself venture to express the slightest disapprobation of the measures of government, without hazarding his freedom, and, in the end, perhaps his life."

But it was not for himself personally that Paine agonized. From the Estates General in 1789 to the National Convention in 1792 the French people had marched inexorably away from the hierarchical system, from the dual despotism of monarchy and aristocracy, to the social freedom of republicanism. Now that march was violently deflected into an alien course. Whatever might be said for the revolutionary coup of June 2d as the inevitable and legitimate response by the sansculottes to the narrow middle-class policy of the Girondins, it could mean to Paine only this: the Republic was dead. The nascent democracy of all useful citizens had been abolished by the special dictatorship of one class. Some of Paine's Girondin associates, bitter-enders like Petion, Buzot, and Barbaroux, fled the city to stir up a war of the provinces against Paris. Paine did not sympathize with such a venture. The war of class against class might open a path for the old monarchical and aristocratic despots who were no closer to his heart than the Jacobins. He took no part in Girondin intrigues against Paris after June 2d. Yes, the Republic of his inexhaustible hopes and labors, the Republic that would emancipate the world, was dead. Only a miracle could revive it. And Paine did not believe in miracles.

He escaped—by way of the liquor bottle. Drunkenness was the asylum of the revolutionary idealist whom the hungry Parisians condemned as an agent of traitorous conservatism. He got drunk and stayed drunk most of June, blotting out the flashes of horrible truth by more and more liquor. It is not a pretty picture, the great social enthusiast now dead to the world, drinking until the glass drops to the floor from his palsied hand. Later Paine confessed this indulgence to Rickman, and Rickman recorded it. Such is the basic fact out of which the myths about Paine the drunkard have been elaborated.

Slowly Paine's vision cleared. He returned to the world of living men. He found himself still a member of the Convention, his personal reputation shaken but not destroyed. In a comprehensive denunciation of the Girondins on the 9th of July, St. Just brought forth evidence tending to link Paine with a Royalist-Girondin conspiracy that would blame all the ills of France on republicanism; but this charge against the chief republican of the world was so wild and ridiculous that St. Just did not press it. "Respect a pillar of liberty from the other hemisphere," he recommended; "do not condemn him, for he has been deceived."

The Jacobins accepted Paine warily, and he gradually became almost reconciled to the fact that, for better or worse, the fate of France was in their hands. Perhaps out of this transitory dictatorship might yet emerge a social order harmonious with a rational and humane philosophy. There were hopeful signs. The Parisian censors dispersing to their shops and hovels, Danton's Committee of Public Safety shrank from launching a ruthless campaign against the rebellious Girondins in the provinces, and the Convention played with the idea of sending Jacobin hostages to the disaffected departments. On the 13th of July the fanatical Norman girl, Charlotte Corday, inflamed by the stories of Girondin fugitives, assassinated Marat in the act of drawing up a new proscription list; no more blood-cries would be heard from the Friend of the People.

When the Committee of Public Safety was reorganized in mid-July, the equivocal Danton was dropped, but a new important member was soon added—the bespectacled, almost dandyish Robespierre, whose demand for Louis' death had not impaired his reputation as a philosopher and humanitarian. Robespierre had pushed through the Convention late in June a Jacobin Constitution which differed from the Paine-Condorcet system only in slight details; while it recognized the right of the poor to subsistence, it guaranteed the middle classes their property. Had the French Revolution at last found a Jacobin leader sobered by responsibility into a savior around whom all the enemies of the aristocratic régime could rally?

This hope, if Paine indulged in it, died quickly. Robespierre was indeed the savior of revolutionary France, but the universal and undifferentiated ideals of *The Rights of Man* had ceased being serviceable to the Revolution in 1793. The martyred Marat, his heart enshrined in an urn at the Cordeliers Club, was a greater force among the Pari-

sians than Marat living. Robespierre accepted the mandate
of June 2 as a call for uncompromising terror against every
shade of opposition, domestic as well as foreign; when he
moved too slowly, the Parisians pushed him along. The
crisis was enough to break any leader except a man of iron:
Prussian, Austrian, Sardinian, Spanish armies pressing on
the land frontiers; British warships blockading the coast;
peasant rebels in the Vendée; counter-revolutionary Girondins in every department except central France; food
scarcity, high prices, sansculotte discontent. When the delegates from the provinces came into Paris in August bearing
the popular endorsement of the Jacobin Constitution, little
argument was needed to persuade them that the entire
nation must be organized indefinitely on a war-time basis
under the dictatorship of the Jacobin Convention and the
grand comité headed by Robespierre. In this terroristic atmosphere Deputy Paine was a harmless bit of flotsam from
the outmoded democratic past. He attended the Convention
seldom, and then only to be recorded as present.

He had moved his residence from White's Hotel in the
turbulent center of Paris to a farmhouse in an outlying
section, the Faubourg St. Dénis. Here—as he has recorded
in the essay *Forgetfulness*—with a few English fellow boarders, young Johnson, Mr. and Mrs. Christie, a Mr. Choppin,
and one or two others, he found a soothing rural haven.
A high wall and a gateway secluded the old house from
the street. The courtyard was divertingly alive with ducks,
turkeys, geese, rabbit-hutches, two pigs in a sty. Behind the
house was an acre of garden, where the trees were laden
with oranges, apricots, and green-gage plums, and cucum-
bers grew wild. The enforced idlers tried to lighten the
nervous tension of 1793 by a simple routine, playing at cards,

walking in the garden, throwing crumbs to the fowl, telling stories of the adventurous past and projecting hopeful reveries into the future. Sometimes, after dinner, the recluses might be visited by Joel Barlow or Mrs. Wollstonecraft and her Captain Imlay; less frequently, they might venture out themselves to visit the Girondin leaders in arrestation at their homes.

Of an evening, after brooding alone in his apartment, Paine would go out to the balcony and down a vine-covered staircase into the garden, there to stalk sorrowfully about, cursing in his helplessness the terroristic rulers in Paris. He did little writing that summer in the Faubourg St. Dénis. "Pen and ink were then of no use to me," he says; "no good could be done by writing, and no printer dared to print; and whatever I might have written, for my private amusement, as anecdotes of the times, would have been continually exposed to be examined, and tortured into any meaning that the rage of party might fix upon it. And as to softer subjects, my heart was in distress at the fate of my friends, and my harp hung upon the weeping willows."

Paine could not become a zealous champion for the domestic terror of the Jacobins; nor could he take a cue from the embattled Girondins who preferred chaos if they could not govern. His knowledge of practical affairs was, within limits, at the service of the Committee of Public Safety, which was heroically endeavoring to keep a distracted and beleaguered nation together. Barère notes in his *Memoirs,* concerning the receipt of corn and flour from America: "Thomas Paine, an American member of the Convention, had given us great help in this matter; he showed us the way to go to work, he aided in the correspondence, and worked hard in the Foreign Office to bring about this extensive purchase of food, all the more necessary as without its help our armies and the provinces were threatened with terrible famine."

Paine continued exercising his privilege as a deputy to write vouchers in behalf of minor suspected persons and to get them safe conduct out of the country. He also hoped that through his work for the Committee of Public Safety he might gain a mild dispensation for the arrested Girondin leaders, against whom the Committee was not inclined to proceed anyhow. As for himself personally, it seemed absurd to fear. Things were bad, but they were not as bad as they might be. His mission in France was over, and he was ready to return to America. In a cordial note to Barère on the 5th of September, Paine expresses his intention to leave in October.

What happened to make that voyage impossible, to bring the Girondins to the guillotine, and to throw Paine into prison in imminent danger of the same fate? Mainly the intensification of the crisis and the Parisian clamor for scapegoats. And, specifically for Paine, the fact that to silence him forever suited the strangest pair of political bedfellows in history—Gouverneur Morris and Maximilien Robespierre.

Gouverneur Morris had been sojourning in Europe since the fall of 1789. This American aristocrat, with his credo that the property and luxury of a privileged caste were the pillars of society, had only cynical contempt for the democratic aspirations of revolutionary France. Occasionally he met Paine. The two had crossed swords in 1779 in the Deane affair, and though the basic needs of the American Revolution had thrown them together after 1779, there was no love lost between them. They recognized each other in

Europe without joy. Morris's Diary has a few scattered sneers at the supremely confident and unshakeable Paine propagandizing for the Republic of the World on both sides of the Channel.

After Jefferson left France in the fall of 1789, William Short continued as Chargé d'Affaires in cautious but genuine sympathy with the progress of French politics and hourly expecting his appointment as ambassador. Then, in February, 1792, came the news that Washington had appointed Gouverneur Morris to that position. It was as if Hamilton Fish were made ambassador to the Soviet Union.

The appointment had been bitterly contested. The Senate debated the nomination over a period of eighteen days and confirmed it by the narrow vote of 16 to 11. Lafayette, no great radical himself, sent a sorrowful protest to Washington, appealing for an ambassador sympathetic with American and French principles; and Paine wrote to the Secretary of State, Jefferson, on the 13th of February that the appointment was *"most unfortunate."* But Washington and his chief adviser Hamilton knew what they were doing. To France Americans owed an immeasurable debt of gratitude and the fraternal attachment for a people struggling to be free. England, however, was the best customer and the most profitable source of imports to the cabal of merchants and bankers who dominated the Washington administration. Moreover, the new American government felt helpless before the British forts illegitimately strung within the confines of American western territory at Detroit, Niagara, Oswego, and the shores of Lake Champlain. Washington's deliberate policy was peace with England at any price, and the first payment was the appointment of the Anglophile Gouverneur Morris as ambassador to France.

Whatever could be said against Morris, at least he did not disguise his real sympathies. The American embassy became the rallying-point of the most reactionary nobles, who plotted a new flight for the royal family. After the deposition of the King in August, 1792, the American ambassador refused to deal with the Girondin government until he received specific instructions from his "court." This attitude and language incensed the Girondins. Lebrun, the Minister of Foreign Affairs, protested to Ternant, the French minister at Philadelphia, that America should be represented by an envoy so hostile to the democratic ideals of the two nations; but Morris was not recalled. The Girondins and the American ambassador settled down to a loveless union.

Occasionally in the winter of 1792-93 Paine and Morris worked together—at arm's length, so to speak—in matters where they desired the same outcome. Paine confided to Morris his plans for saving the life of Louis XVI, and the two Americans discussed the Girondin project of seizing the Louisiana territory under the rule of Spain, with whom war was imminent. It was Paine rather than Lebrun who introduced Edmond Genet to Morris as the new French minister to the United States—an irregular procedure which did not add to Morris's love for the revolutionary government or the deputy Paine, who seemed to regard himself as an unofficial American ambassador.

The coup of June 2 ousted the Girondins and put the Jacobins in complete control of the French government. Had there been a likelihood that Genet would succeed in revolutionizing the American people in spite of the American government, the Jacobins would have taken him into their fold and given him their full support. But he was failing, and he was a Girondin. The Jacobins hastened to disown him and to mollify the Washington administration. It was necessary, too, to be more cautious and compliant with Gouverneur Morris, whom Washington kept in Paris in spite of the strong protests by Ternant and Genet. Robespierre was on his knees before the American ambassador whom he hated with all his heart.

Morris wanted of course only one thing—to break the Franco-American alliance beyond repair. To this objective he clung tenaciously regardless of any changes in French policy. He bought a large estate in Sainport about twenty miles out of Paris, and entertained aristocratic friends (even one or two against whom the Committee of General Security had issued warrants of arrest) to the neglect of his diplomatic duties. Deputy Paine persisted in spoiling Morris's plan. When in the summer of 1793 ninety-two American vessels were seized by the French Government at Bordeaux lest their cargoes fall into the hands of the British fleet, the American captains appealed to their ambassador for liberation. They had come to the wrong man. The continued embargo would serve his purpose of breaking the alliance, the liberation would not. Morris dawdling, the indignant captains appealed to Deputy Paine, who went out to Sainport and scolded the ambassador for taking the money of Americans and doing nothing for them. On the 20th of August Morris wrote the Foreign Office an unvigorous protest, in which he said: "I do not pretend to interfere in the internal concerns of the French Republic [Morris had a fine sense of humor], and I am persuaded that the Convention has had weighty reasons for laying upon Americans the restriction of which the American captains complain. The result will nevertheless be that this prohibition will severely aggrieve the parties interested, and put an end to the commerce between France and the United States." The Foreign Office, uncertain whether Morris genuinely wanted the release of the American ships, hesitated. At Paine's suggestion the captains petitioned the Convention itself on the 22nd and were promptly liberated. Morris had lost his pretext. And now, with no remuneration beyond the eighteen francs per day of a deputy, Paine was helping the Foreign Office to negotiate shipments of corn and flour from the United States.

What a topsy-turvy state of affairs—the American deputy doing everything to strengthen Franco-American friendship, the American ambassador doing everything to destroy it, and the French Government, desperately in need of it, eager to please the ambassador even if it involved sacrificing the deputy!

Paine was swept into the danger zone by a new surge of the Parisian masses in September of 1793. The Jacobins had not yet proved their capacity to meet the crisis. Famine confronted Paris, and the revolutionary army had not yet begun to push back the invaders. When the report came on the 4th of September that the city of Toulon had surrendered to the British, the Parisians went wild with fear. A delegation marched into the Convention Hall to demand bread and swift punishment to traitors. On the 5th a compliant Convention decreed that terror should be the order of the day. The revolutionary tribunal was reorganized and speeded up, and a steady stream of victims was provided by the comprehensive Law of Suspects passed on the 17th. The Convention overrode the plea of the Dantonists for moderation and gave Robespierre and the Committee of Public Safety *carte blanche* to carry out the relentless program of the sansculottes. On the 27th the Law of the Maximum fixed prices at 30 percent and wages at 50 percent above the 1790 level. In October the heads began to fall. The journalist Gorsas, having violated his domiciliary arrest and subsequently returned to Paris, was taken up and summarily guillotined on the 9th of October. Marie Antoinette ascended the scaffold on the 16th. The turn of the twenty-two Girondin leaders came next. The Convention cut short their trial, and on the 30th they were carted to the guillotine, singing the *Marseillaise* while the Parisians jeered. Pathetic figures—Brissot, Vergniaud, Fauchet, Gensonné. Even the body of Valazé, who had stabbed himself to death in the courtroom, was decapitated by the executioner. The Terror pursued all the other leaders of counterrevolutionary Girondism. Within a few months they were dead from suicide, starvation, or the guillotine—Roland, Madame Roland, Condorcet, Buzot, Petion, Guadet, Barbaroux, Lebrun. Robespierre and the Committee rallied the sansculottes by this display of revolutionary justice, and the emboldened citizen-soldiers began to fling back the Prussians from the northern frontiers and to exterminate the rebellious peasants in the Vendée.

The October fury assailed Paine but did not destroy him in a common fate with his colleagues. Though he absented himself entirely from the Convention after the first week of September, his reputation as a cosmopolitan radical and a well-wisher to the revolutionary French people was not entirely gone. In calling on the 3rd of October for a trial of the Girondins, Amar declared that Paine "dishonored himself" by associating with Brissot and by arguing that the Americans loved the French tyrant Louis; but Paine was not put in the prisoners' dock with the Girondin defendants. At the trial of Marie Antoinette, when the president of the tribunal asked the witness Manuel why he had abandoned the honorable post of deputy, Manuel pleaded in extenuation: "I trusted in the morality of Thomas Payne, master in republicanism; I desired like him to see the reign of liberty and equality established on fixed and durable bases; I may have varied in the means that I proposed, but my intentions were pure." But Paine's cloak was not large enough to cover Manuel. Within the month he was guillotined.

All the Girondins who had made history were dead or in their last flight—except Paine. How glad would the lone survivor have been to be back in America now! But the American ambassador and the French committeeman had other designs for him. If Paine returned to America, he would tell some dangerous truths about both Morris and Robespierre, the aristocrat and the terrorist. And great sections of the American people would accept the indictment of Common Sense. The wishes of Morris and Robespierre dovetailed perfectly. Sometime in October Robespierre jotted down in his notebook a memorandum: "Demand that Thomas Payne be decreed of accusation for the interests of America as much as of France."

Life was now desolate for Paine. His ideals had been killed in June, his dearest friends had been killed in October. His fellow boarders in the Faubourg St. Dénis were fleeing before the storm. One morning before four o'clock the Englishmen Johnson and Choppin, having obtained passports through Paine, left for Switzerland. Two days later in the dead of night a file of soldiers with fixed bayonets came up the gateway. Paine thought that they had come for him, the only lodger, but they were looking for the enemy subjects who had gone. A month later they came again and took away the landlord, Georgeit. Paine was alone in a big house, haunted with ghosts and memories.

When the shadow of death lay upon them, the leading Girondins used the precious moments in characteristic ways. Brissot and Madame Roland, self-conscious actors on the stage of history, composed their *Memoirs.* Condorcet, the philosopher fallen among politicians, wrote his *Outline of the Progress of the Human Mind,* looking dreamily forward to the day when the human race would be freed from its chains and would march with giant strides in the path of happiness. Paine, the fighting idealist, worked over a manuscript on religion which he had written early in the year. He wanted to commune with his God—and to attack the atheistic movement which symbolized a France gone mad. Away from the murderous revolutionary capital, in a big farmhouse quiet in the late autumn, sits a man fifty-six years old, prematurely aged, his strong face deeply lined by tragic experience, writing a book, *The Age of Reason.*

CHAPTER XVIII

A Rational Creed

WHAT was the religious situation of the eighteenth century in general and of Jacobin France in particular, into which Paine projected *The Age of Reason?*

The Christian creed of the eighteenth century was a set of theological certainties which had been essentially unchanged since the days of the twelve apostles. It was the profession of faith which has endured intact into our own time as Fundamentalism. The Protestant Reformers had not laid hands upon the basic dogmas. Christians continued to believe that God had created Adam in His Own image; that Adam had sinned, and that the burden of his guilt had been entailed to all his descendants; that a supernatural redemption had been necessary to free the human race from the burden of Adam; that this redemption had been wrought by God's only begotten son, Jesus Christ, who had been born of a virgin, had suffered and died and risen from the dead; that repentance and faith in Christ were obligatory to attain salvation and avoid eternal hell-fire; and that the Bible was the inerrant revelation and word of God. Further, the Holy Book taught that God revealed Himself by mysteries, miracles, and the fulfilment of prophecies; that He had ordained and sanctioned the cruelties of His chosen people on the march; and that He had created a snug little universe especially for the human drama, a flat earth under sun, moon, and stars swinging

213

in the hands of angels, heaven somewhere near above, hell somewhere near below.

From the Renaissance onward secular philosophers and men of science had been unintentionally but inevitably coming into conflict with the Christian world-view. Men were acquiring a progressive mastery over the forces of nature by observation and experiment, not by scholastic deductions spun out of the declarations in the Bible. Building on the researches of Copernicus, Kepler, and Galileo, Newton charted the regular movements of the planets around the sun according to the invariable law of universal gravitation. Where, now, was the jealous God and the earth, his footstool? Human reason, confident of its own powers, began to inquire whether the whole system of Christianity evinced the clarity and consistency which ruled in the universe at large.

Out of the attempt to reevaluate the Christian religion in the light of reason developed the system of religious concepts known as Deism. This is mainly an English contribution, in a long series of rationalistic inquiries, from Herbert's *De Veritate* in 1642 to Annet's *The History of the Man After God's Own Heart* in 1766. Each deist emphasized only one or two phases of the argument, but the total indictment and revision were comprehensive and substantial. Against the Christian system the deists contended that the obscure and self-contradictory Bible could not be the word of God; that the Bible taught low morality; that the Biblical cosmology was false; that Christian dogmas and legends were derived from pagan myths; and that mysteries, miracles, and prophecies were incredible. Affirmatively they argued for the existence of one God, the law-giver of the natural universe, and for "virtue and piety" as the chief parts of divine worship. The deists, however, did not wage war on Christianity as such. They called themselves Christians, and the titles of their books—Toland's *Christianity Not Mysterious,* Tindal's *Christianity as Old as the Creation,* Chubb's *The True Gospel of Jesus Christ Asserted*—announced their intention to retrieve pure original Christianity, uncontaminated by the rites and ordinances of priestcraft. Before Paine, English deism was an aristocratic system, with converts in the intellectual circles and even in the clergy of the Established Church but without influence upon the common people or the nation as a whole.

In France the impact of social revolution rather than of free-thinking treatises brought the Christian belief into mortal danger. Deists like Voltaire and Rousseau and atheists like Diderot and Holbach had sought in Catholic France only a measure of toleration similar to the state of affairs in Protestant England. In 1789 no one dreamed of de-Christianizing France; in 1793 that was almost accomplished. The whole Gallican Church—which in France was equivalent with Christianity—stood condemned from top to bottom as the arch-agent of counter-revolution. In October, 1793, the Convention adopted a revolutionary calendar ending the Christian Sabbath; in November the tricolor-garbed girls from the Opera enshrined the Goddess of Reason in the Cathedral of Notre Dame. Paris was in the grip of atheistic left-wing Jacobins headed by Hébert, Chaumette, and the Prussian Clootz, who ordered the closing of all the churches and led recanting bishops to the Convention to lay down their miters and croziers at the altar of liberty. Not only Christianity but all religion, including deism, seemed about to be consumed in the fires of the Jacobin Republic of Virtue.

215

The atheistic rampage of the French radicals, with their complete negations and intolerant spirit, grated on the ears of the lone exile in the Faubourg St. Dénis. Jacobin Paris was throwing Paine's religion into the discard along with his politics. In common with most of the advanced thinking of the age Paine had accepted the deistic view of the universe. The foundation of his deism had been laid in his native Quakerism, which in its democratic and humane spirit, its exaltation of the inner light above the scriptural pronouncement, and its rejection of the sacraments and "great lumps of earth" speaking for pay from the pulpit, was already within the Christian fold a living criticism of rigid dogmas and fat priests. In his studies at the Royal Society and in his own scientific experimentation, Paine had developed a comprehension of natural processes and the scientist's impatience with a religion of mystery and obscurantism. In 1792, in Part Two of *The Rights of Man,* he said: "Independence is my happiness and I view things as they are, without regard to place or person; my country is the world, and my religion is to do good." Although he declares in *The Age of Reason* that he had long thought of publishing his religious views, it is doubtful that he would ever have gone beyond the simple statement in *The Rights of Man* if practical urgencies had not impelled him. It seemed a moral obligation to put up some sort of barrier against atheism, and in the enforced leisure of the old farmhouse there was no mental exercise more congenial to a political outcast in the shadow of death.

Paine's equipment for religious writing was no better and no worse than his equipment for political writing. He had only a thin smattering of study in the political philosophers before he voiced the dreams and created the slogans of revolutions on both sides of the Atlantic; and he had no first-hand acquaintance with deistic treatises before writing Part One of *The Age of Reason*. Not only was he ignorant of Hebrew and Greek and therefore unable to make sure and thorough statements about the textual difficulties in the Old and New Testaments. He did not even have an English Bible to work with in the Faubourg St. Dénis! But in the poverty and limited resources of his youth he had read the Bible over and over, and he had preeminently the type of genius that draws into itself all the vital thinking in the social atmosphere and forges new weapons out of old thoughts. In spite and partly because of his handicaps Paine wrote a pamphlet which was a synthetic treasury of deistic arguments and an historic event.

If the attack on atheism was to be effective, the attack on Christianity must be distinct and unhesitant. Pure deism alone must be offered to the spiritual appetite of revolutionary France. Though Paine belongs intellectually in the company of eighteenth-century English deists, his attitude is on the whole new and revolutionary. Where the older deists were timidly critical—questioning, re-arranging, allegorizing, "accommodating," interpreting, and so forth—Paine was bluntly hostile. He was no Christian and he said so. His intention was conservative, to save France from atheism; and he expressed this conservatism in the most radical and militant of anti-Christian deistic pamphlets.

At the outset he states his creed:

"I believe in one God, and no more; and I hope for happiness beyond this life.

"I believe [in] the equality of man, and I believe that religious duties consist in doing justice, loving mercy, and endeavouring to make our fellow-creatures happy.

"But, lest it should be supposed that I believe many other things in addition to these, I shall, in the progress of this work, declare the things I do not believe, and my reasons for not believing them.

"I do not believe in the creed professed by the Jewish church, by the Roman church, by the Greek church, by the Turkish church, by the Protestant church, nor by any church that I know of. My own mind is my own church.

"All national institutions of churches, whether Jewish, Christian, or Turkish, appear to me no other than human inventions set up to terrify and enslave mankind, and monopolize power and profit.

"I do not mean by this declaration to condemn those who believe otherwise; they have the same right to their belief as I have to mine. But it is necessary to the happiness of man, that he be mentally faithful to himself. Infidelity does not consist in believing, or in disbelieving; it consists in professing to believe what he does not believe."

Imbued with the spirit of science, Paine insists that a religion deserving the allegiance of intelligent men shall harmonize with the highest concept of God and the most exacting demands of human intelligence. He proceeds to analyze and demolish by logical reasoning the common basis of all the established supernatural religions—divine revelation. Of course, he says, the Almighty can reveal Himself directly to his human creatures; but such a revelation is convincing only to those with whom God has been in direct communication; other men have only the testimony of fallible human beings that the revelation really did take place. No man should give up his spiritual independence merely on other men's authority. Paine refuses to accept on hearsay the miraculous legends about Moses or Mahomet. These are human stories, otherwise unsupported, and they may or may not be true. "When also I am told that a woman, called the Virgin Mary, said, or gave out, that she was with child without any cohabitation with a man, and that her betrothed husband, Joseph, said that an angel told him so, I have a right to believe them or not: such a circumstance required a much stronger evidence than their bare word for it: but we have not even this; for neither Joseph nor Mary wrote any such matter themselves. It is only reported by others that *they said so*. It is hearsay upon hearsay, and I do not chuse to rest my belief upon such evidence."

This is no disrespect for Jesus Christ, for whom Paine feels the affection due to a "virtuous reformer and revolutionist." Spurious "revelations" hide the real greatness of this moral teacher. Since the miraculous conception could hardly be publicly performed, the truth of that story can neither be proved nor denied with certainty; but the story of the miraculous resurrection stretches credence far beyond the breaking point. "The resurrection and ascension, supposing them to have taken place, admitted of public and ocular demonstration, like that of the ascension of a balloon, or the sun at noon day, to all Jerusalem at least. A thing which everybody is required to believe, requires that the proof and evidence of it should be equal to all, and universal; and as the public visibility of this last related act was the only evidence that could give sanction to the former part, the whole of it falls to the ground, because that evidence never was given. Instead of this, a small number of persons, not more than eight or nine, are introduced as proxies for the whole world, to say they saw it, and all the rest of the world are called upon to believe it. But it appears that Thomas did not believe the resurrection; and, as they say, would not believe without having ocular and manual demonstration himself. *So neither will I;* and the reason is equally as good for me, and for every other person, as Thomas."

To the fabulous part of the Christ story the Christian mythologists have added the fable of Satan, which is copied from the legendary war on Olympus between Jupiter and the Giants. The absurdity of the Satan myth is self-evident. After the fall of Satan, says Paine, "He is then introduced into the garden of Eden in the shape of a snake, or a serpent, and in that shape he enters into familiar conversation with Eve, who is no ways surprised to hear a snake talk; and the issue of this tête-à-tête is, that he persuades her to eat an apple, and the eating of that apple damns all mankind." The church mythologists, bringing together the two ends of the story, "represent this virtuous and amiable man, Jesus Christ, to be at once both God and man, and also the Son of God, celestially begotten, on purpose to be sacrificed, because they say that Eve in her longing had eaten an apple." Such a doctrine, Paine argues, cannot be reconciled with a rational view of the power and wisdom of God. It gives to Satan really divine or superdivine power. It represents Satan as forcing upon the Almighty a terrible alternative—either to surrender His dominance over the earth or to come down in a human form and be crucified. "Had the inventors of this story told it the contrary way, that is, had they represented the Almighty as compelling Satan to exhibit *himself* on a cross in the shape of a snake, as a punishment for his new transgression, the story would have been less absurd, less contradictory. But, instead of this they make the transgressor triumph, and the Almighty fall."

Having thus disposed of the basic Christian formula,

Paine examines the claims of the Old and the New Testaments to divine inspiration. With no copy of the Bible at hand or obtainable he relies on his memory and therefore produces in this section a brief and disjointed statement of ideas which were to be more fully developed a year later in Part Two.

The dogma that the Old Testament is the word of God cannot be rationally maintained, Paine says. It is based upon the mere testimony of human beings, not upon a universally convincing sign by the Almighty Himself. The church mythologists picked up some miscellaneous writings and voted by majority in council which were and which were not the word of God. "Had they voted otherwise, all the people since calling themselves Christians had believed otherwise; for the belief of the one comes from the vote of the other." Secular histories and anecdotes, such as the accounts of Samson's fox-hunting and love-making, have nothing of divinity in them. The Mosaic story of the Creation reads like a Hebrew legend and could hardly have been written by Moses, who as one educated among the Egyptians must have known better. But, after all, that story may be tolerated as belonging to the small number in the Old Testament which are morally harmless. "Whenever we read the obscene stories, the voluptuous debaucheries, the cruel and torturous executions, the unrelenting vindictiveness, with which more than half the Bible [Old Testament] is filled, it would be more consistent that we called it the word of a demon, than the Word of God. It is a history of wickedness, that has served to corrupt and brutalize mankind; and, for my own part, I sincerely detest it, as I detest everything that is cruel." The Psalms and the Book of Job have much elevated sentiment on the power and goodness of God but are no more valuable than many similar compositions which claim no divine inspiration. The Proverbs are less keen than the proverbs of the Spaniards and not more wise than those of Benjamin Franklin. The word *prophet* did not originally mean a divine soothsayer, but a poet or musician, for the Biblical prophets usually appear with harps, psalteries, and cymbals, and sometimes whole companies of them join in concerts. The corruption of this word's meaning makes all the labored commentaries on the so-called prophecies not worth disputing about, and points the folly of trusting to such treacherous guides as words and books for direct messages from the Almighty. "If we permit ourselves to conceive ideas of things, we must necessarily affix the idea, not only of unchangeableness, but of the utter impossibility of any change taking place, by any means or accident whatever, in that which we would honour with the name of the Word of God; and therefore the Word of God cannot exist in any written or human language."

By the same reasoning, Paine continues, the New Testament must be rejected. It bears no proofs of divine authorship, and the chief character does not perform what human reason can accept as a truly divine rôle. The New Testament was not written by Jesus Christ or authenticated by him. We know very little about Christ except that he was the son of God in the same way that every other man is, and that he preached morality and the belief in one God. The legend that Christ lay in concealment and was detected only through the betrayal by Judas, reveals not a divine but a pusillanimous nature. If Jesus Christ was the divine being pictured by the mythologists, he suffered on earth in living, not in dying, for death restored him to

222

heaven. The New Testament is full of equivocal and contradictory statements, showing confusion rather than divine clarity. One thing, however, is plain about the Christian church: "It has set up a religion of pomp and of revenue in pretended imitation of a person whose life was humility and poverty." Out of the original redemption the church has built up an institution of secondary redemptions and has driven a profitable trade in pardons, dispensations, and indulgences. Paine looks upon the vicarious atonement, the cardinal dogma of Christianity, and finds it morally contemptible. "Moral justice cannot take the innocent for the guilty even if the innocent would offer itself. To suppose justice to do this, is to destroy the principle of its existence, which is the thing itself. It is then no longer justice. It is indiscriminate revenge."

There is, Paine proclaims, a religion and a revelation equal to the demands of the Age of Reason. "THE WORD OF GOD IS THE CREATION WE BEHOLD." "It is always necessary," he says, resuming the logical criterion which he had applied to the miraculous resurrection, "that the means that are to accomplish any end be equal to the accomplishment of that end, or the end cannot be accomplished." Practical difficulties made it impossible for Christ to publish any glad tidings to all the nations. But the heavens and the earth speak a universal and unmistakable language which cannot be forged, counterfeited, altered, or suppressed. Every man everywhere can read this true word of God. "Do we want to contemplate his power? We see it in the immensity of the creation. Do we want to contemplate his wisdom? We see it in the unchangeable order by which the incomprehensible Whole is governed. Do we want to contemplate his munificence? We see it in the abundance with which he fills the earth. Do we want to contemplate his mercy? We see it in his not with-holding that abundance even from the unthankful. In fine, do we want to know what God is? Search not the book called the scripture, which any human hand might make, but the scripture called the Creation."

Only in deism does Paine find a system of faith provid-ing for the moral dignity and creative intelligence of which the human race is capable. For the existence of God he gives the familiar argument from First Cause. Since noth-ing that we behold made itself, we must rationally deduce the eternal existence of a transcendent nature, God, by whose power all things are created. The 19th Psalm and some verses in Job give hints of the superhuman, supreme God, but the Scriptures generally vulgarize Him. By intro-ducing a spurious redeemer between man and his Maker, Christianity "has put the whole orbit of reason into shade." Christianity reverses the positions of true theology, which is the study of the works of God, and false theology, which is empty speculation concerning God. Natural science, the true theology, is no mere human invention but the dis-covery, according to God's will, of the divine plan of the universe. The lever and the triangle are His inventions, not ours, and the Almighty lecturer has instructed us in their use. "Man had no more to do in the formation of those properties or principles, than he had to do in making the laws by which the heavenly bodies move, and therefore the one must have the same divine origin as the other." It is not to be wondered at that the Christian church has always opposed the march of science, has persecuted the great sci-entists, and has cultivated a disproportionate emphasis for the sterile study of dead languages. "What is called the Christian system of faith, including in it the whimsical account of the creation—the strange story of Eve, the snake, and the apple—the amphibious idea of a man-god—the corporeal idea of the death of a god—the mythological idea of a family of gods, and the Christian system of arithmetic, that three are one, and one is three, are all irreconcilable, not only to the divine gift of reason, that God has given to man, but to the knowledge that man gains of the power and wisdom of God by the aid of the sciences, and by studying the structure of the universe that God has made."

Paine argues that the findings of astronomical research make the pretensions of Christianity ridiculous. He gives, "not for the sake of those that already know, but for those who do not," a simple exposition of the solar system— the planets, their millions of miles from each other and the sun, their orbits—an exposition attested by the accuracy of science in foretelling eclipses. And beyond our solar systems are other solar systems in the infinity of space. "From whence then could arise the solitary and strange conceit that the Almighty, who had millions of worlds equally dependent on his protection, should quit the care of all the rest, and come to die in our world, because, they say, one man and one woman had eaten an apple! And, on the other hand, are we to suppose that every world in the boundless creation had an Eve, an apple, a serpent, and a redeemer? In this case, the person who is irreverently called the Son of God, and sometimes God himself, would have nothing else to do than to travel from world to world, in an endless succession of death, with scarcely a momentary interval of life."

Paine considers the methods whereby false ideas of God have been imposed upon mankind—mystery, miracle, and prophecy. No such arguments and stories can stand up before the clear and self-respecting intelligence. The roots of all things are mysteries hidden in the mind of the Creator, but there is no room for mystery in religion. "The God in whom we believe is a God of moral truth, and not a God of mystery or obscurity." No phenomenon can be truly called a miracle until we know the whole extent of natural laws. The ascension of balloons, magnetic attraction, and sleight-of-hand tricks would appear miraculous if we did not know their natural principles. God would not speak to us in such an equivocal manner as miracles, for it would be impossible to distinguish between His true revelations and those of impostors and liars. "Suppose I were to say, that when I sat down to write this book, a hand presented itself in the air, took up the pen and wrote every word that is herein written; would anybody believe me? Certainly they would not. Would they believe me a whit the more if the thing had been a fact? Certainly they would not. Since then a real miracle, were it to happen, would be subject to the same fate as the falsehood, the inconsistency becomes the greater of supposing the Almighty would make use of means that would not answer the purpose for which they were intended, even if they were real." The credibility of a miracle depends in the last analysis upon the integrity of the person reporting it. Since we have never known nature to go out of her course, "it is, therefore, at least millions to one, that the reporter of a miracle tells a lie." As to prophecies, not only has the meaning of the word *prophet* been corrupted, but the language of the prophecies is too loose and obscure to be attributed to the Almighty. We cannot be certain that a self-styled prophet is not a liar, and "if the thing that he prophesied, or pretended to prophesy, should happen, or something like it, among the multitude of things that are daily happening, nobody could again

226

know whether he foreknew it, or guessed at it, or whether it was accidental."

In conclusion Paine summarizes his doctrines: "first, that the idea or belief of a word of God existing in print, or in writing, or in speech, is inconsistent in itself; . . . secondly, that the Creation we behold is the real and ever existing word of God, in which we cannot be deceived; . . . thirdly, that the moral duty of man consists in imitating the moral goodness and beneficence of God manifested in the creation towards all his creatures."

Unlike other proclaimers of new religions Paine is no bigot. His last paragraph asserts the possibility of universal agreement or at least universal freedom. "It is certain that, in one point, all nations of the earth and all religions agree. All believe in a God. The things in which they disagree are the redundancies annexed to that belief; and therefore, if ever an universal religion should prevail, it will not be anything new, but in getting rid of redundancies, and believing as man believed at first. Adam, if ever there was such a man, was created a Deist; but in the meantime, let every man follow, as he has a right to do, the religion and worship he prefers."

Those who regard Paine the deist as a shameless mud-slinger at sacred things are lacking in historic-minded intelligence. Not only because, when he first composed his religious views, Christianity was a dead faith in Jacobin France and the real fight was between atheism and deism; but because the historic intelligence recognizes that there may be more religions than one. *The Age of Reason* must be considered as a religious book by a religious man. Paine deserves respect if not gratitude from religious-minded persons for trying to construct in perfect seriousness a workable religious system in harmony with the best knowledge of his time.

Paine put the last touches to his deistic pamphlet in the Christmas season of 1793. He had done his share towards liberating the human race from obsolete forms of government and obsolete forms of religion. He had waged war against the hereditary despotism of kings and nobles, and he had written a spiritual declaration of independence from other men's superstitious testimonies and pretended intercessions with the Author of the Universe. If revolutionary France preferred dictatorship and atheism to democracy and deism—well, though his heart might be sad and tired, his conscience was clear.

Paine did not finish *The Age of Reason* too soon. On Christmas Day (5th Nivose, Year Two) Barère made a motion excluding foreigners from membership in the Convention. It was passed without protest. Two foreigners had seats in the Convention—Paine and Clootz. Both were objectionable to Robespierre. Clootz was in the leadership of the left-wing Jacobins plotting new insurrections by the Parisian proletariat, and, besides, he was a violent atheist in opposition to Robespierre's deistic program. Paine was the most distinguished survivor among the Girondins. Clootz was a Prussian, and Paine could be regarded, from the place of his birth, as an Englishman. Having no longer the immunity of deputies, they were liable to arrest as the subjects of enemy countries. On the 27th of December the warrants were issued.

Paine had a hint of what was coming and he went to meet it almost eagerly, as if he could no longer endure precarious freedom. On the night of the 27th he went into town and took a room at White's Hotel in the Passage des

228

Petits Pères, his official residence and the scene of his former triumphs. There the two agents of the Committee of General Security, reenforced by four privates and a corporal, found the culprit in bed the next morning. Paine declaring that his papers were at the Britain House, Rue Jacob, they took him to that address, where they discovered that he had tricked them in order to get the companionship of his American friend, Joel Barlow. Proceeding to the Faubourg St. Dénis, the guards spent a busy afternoon piling up all of Paine's manuscripts and letters in the sitting-room and searching for incriminatory evidence. Since they found nothing suspicious, they decided not to affix any seals on Paine's personal papers. With permission, Paine entrusted the manuscript of *The Age of Reason* to Barlow. Then the guards took the ex-deputy to the Luxembourg prison.

On the way the guards picked up the other ex-deputy, Anacharsis Clootz. The atheist and the deist, unmindful of their extremely variant political views, got into an argument as to the relative merits of their cosmic systems. Even after the door of the Luxembourg closed behind them, they continued the debate. During the imprisonment, the bushy-haired Clootz, genius or madman, one of the most amazing prodigies of the Revolution, maintained that The People is the only Supreme Being and the universe an accidental collocation of atoms, until he was carted off to the guillotine and the final answer on the 24th of March. For more than ten long months, amid hope and despair and constant misery in a chamber of horrors wrought by man, Paine stood by his reasoned belief in "the moral goodness and beneficence of God."

CHAPTER XIX

In the Luxembourg Prison

IN THE spacious old Luxembourg Palace, now transformed into a *maison d'arrêt,* containing sometimes as
many as a thousand prisoners, the prospect of sudden death
crowded out the ordinary cares of life. The jailer Benoît assigned newcomers to congenial room-mates and tried to keep
everybody comfortable and busy. In the morning the inmates of an apartment took turns at sweeping the floor,
arranging the beds, making the fire, fetching water. In the
afternoon they might go into the common anteroom to
play games or hold concerts; or they might enjoy a wintry
walk around the courtyard and look out upon the magnificent trees of the famous garden and the convent-spires
and white hills beyond, until the evening bell summoned
them indoors. All were on a level in the common calamity
of being suspects. If Madame La Duchesse and Monsieur
Le Comte still found pleasure in addressing each other by
their outlawed titles, Madame wielded a housemaid's broom
and Monsieur contributed to the expenses of his fellow
prisoners, formerly shopkeepers and scullions, with a generosity all too rare in the old régime. And the difference
between English and French heads lost all meaning in
the shadow of the impartial guillotine. In prison Paine discovered a fine camaraderie of classes and nationalities, a real
Republic of the World.

Sociability, however, was helpless before the great horror.

Almost every day at midnight came the municipal police with a new list of "winners in the lottery of the blessed guillotine." The prison resounded with nerve-racking fare-wells and the swooning and screaming of human beings at bay. Up and into the cart, for a brief trial and a swift execution in the morning! No one slept well in the Luxem-bourg, except the smooth-tongued spies and provocateurs—the *moutons*—who infested the place.

If Paine had been guilty of counter-revolutionary plots against the Republic of Virtue, he could have looked for-ward to the guillotine with philosophic dignity, as one who had gambled greatly and lost. But, being innocent of all crimes except magnanimity, he was in no mood for dying. Joel Barlow and the other Americans in Paris assured him of their support. They looked to Ambassador Morris for an official protest, but Morris played the deep game of try-ing to get Paine guillotined, after which he would denounce the Jacobins for that very deed. He refused to make an appeal. On the 21st of January, 1794, in a long report on French politics and commerce to Jefferson (whom he sup-posed to be still Secretary of State, though Jefferson had already resigned) he inserted midway a contemptuous and studiedly nonchalant parenthesis about Paine's imprison-ment: "I cut short these observations, to give you a sketch of the state of parties. Previous to which, however, lest I should forget it, I must mention, that Thomas Paine is in prison, where he amuses himself with publishing a pam-phlet against Jesus Christ. I do not recollect whether I men-tioned to you, that he would have been executed along with the rest of the Brissotines, if the adverse party had not viewed him with contempt. I incline to think that, if he is quiet in prison, he may have the good luck to be forgotten. Whereas, should he be brought much into notice, the long suspended axe might fall on him. I believe he thinks, that I ought to claim him as an American citizen; but, considering his birth, his naturalization in this country, and the place he filled, I doubt much the right, and I am sure that the claim would be, for the present at least, inexpedient and ineffectual."

Rebuffed by their ambassador, the Americans turned to the Convention on the 27th of January. Major William Jackson, just arrived from Philadelphia, had a letter of introduction from Jefferson to Morris, but he brushed angrily by the ambassador and offered his letter to the Convention as the credentials for the eighteen Americans who came to the bar on Paine's behalf. The petition, from its opening—"Citizens Legislators!"—to the signatures at the end, is a beautiful testimony to the love and concern of the Americans for the imprisoned Paine. "We come in the name of our country," they said; "we come to you, Legislators, to reclaim our friend, our countryman, that he may sail with us for America, where he will be received with open arms." They implore the Convention not to give joy to the allied tyrants of Europe, especially the British government, by any cruelties to "this courageous and virtuous defender of Liberty." If Paine has erred, he deserves indulgence for the rectitude of his heart; there is nothing criminal in his papers. President Vadier, a senile terrorist, responded, "Thomas Paine is a native of England; this is undoubtedly enough to apply to him the measures of security prescribed by the revolutionary laws. It may be added, citizens, that if Thomas Paine has been the apostle of liberty, if he has powerfully co-operated with the American Revolution, his genius has not understood that which has regenerated France; he has regarded the system only in accordance with the illusions with which the false friends of our revolution have invested it. You must with us deplore an error little reconcilable with the principles admired in the justly esteemed works of this republican author." This sinister mixture of homage and reproof, coupled with a vague promise that the Convention would take the petition into consideration, made the Americans turn immediately to another authority, the Committee of Public Safety. That committee took refuge in diplomatic forms and refused to discuss the prisoner Paine with a group having no official status. The Americans in Paris could not liberate Paine; but this united appeal checked the homicidal tendency of the Jacobins towards a man whose warm friends were citizens of the only important country with which the French republic was at peace.

So the matter was thrown back to the official spokesman of America, the lord of the Sainport mansion, the accredited ambassador. In the ghastly Luxembourg, Paine could not believe that Morris would shirk the solemn official duty of interceding for the rights of a countryman. In February he appealed to Morris to reclaim him as an American citizen. Under the hostile eyes of the other Americans in Paris, who knew of Paine's appeal, Morris could no longer do nothing. No, but he could do worse. He went into Paris for a fraternal confab with Foreign Minister Deforgues. Together they hatched out a reclamation and a reply which would have warmed the heart of Machiavelli. Morris wrote: "Thomas Paine has just applied to me to claim him as a Citizen of the United States. These (I believe) are the facts which relate to him. He was born in England. Having become a citizen of the United States, he acquired great celebrity there through his revolutionary writings. In consequence

233

he was adopted as French Citizen, and then elected Member of the Convention. His behaviour since that epoch is out of my jurisdiction. I am ignorant of the reason for his present detention in the Luxembourg prison, but I beg you, Sir, if there be reasons which prevent his liberation, and which are unknown to me, be so good as to inform me of them so that I may communicate them to the Government of the United States." It is obvious that this deliberately indifferent letter makes no claim for Paine and declares him out of the jurisdiction of the American ambassador. Yet five days later Deforgues replied as follows: "In your letter of the 26th of last month [26th Pluviose, February 14] you reclaim the liberty of Thomas Payne, as an American Citizen. Born in England, this ex-deputy has become successively an American and a French citizen. In accepting this last title, and in occupying a place in the Legislative Corps, he submitted himself to the laws of the Republic, and has *de fait* renounced the protection which the right of the people and treaties concluded with the United States could have assured him. I am ignorant of the motive of his detention, but I must presume they are well founded. I shall nevertheless submit the demand you have addressed me to the Committee of Public Safety, and I shall lose no time in letting you know its decision." Morris suppressed his own reclamation which was no reclamation, and sent a copy of Deforgues' letter to the American administration. By all appearances Morris had appealed for Paine, and what could be done was being done. Meanwhile, Paine was in the toils deeper than ever.

Morris also sent a copy of Deforgues' letter to Paine. The prisoner gladly assumed that in spite of profound political differences he was dealing with a man of honor and a con-

234

scientious ambassador. Deforgues' arguments could be easily met. Writing to Morris on the 24th of February, Paine shows and urges the next step: "Though you and I are not on terms of the best harmony, I apply to you as the Minister of America, and you may add to that service whatever you think my integrity deserves. At any rate I expect you to make Congress acquainted with my situation, and to send to them copies of the letters that have passed on the subject. A reply to the Minister's letter is absolutely necessary, were it only to continue the reclamation. Otherwise your silence will be a sort of consent to his observations."

Morris did not choose to believe that he was under obligation to communicate with Congress about Paine or to go through any further motions for him in Paris. To the man who brought Paine's letter, Morris said that he agreed with Deforgues (it would have been nearer to truth to say that Deforgues agreed with him). If, Morris continued, he should change his mind, he would take up the claim again. A week later he wrote to Jefferson as Secretary of State, "I have heard no more of the affair since." Naturally, since he had done no more about it.

There was nothing left for Paine but to accept the Luxembourg as his home, perhaps his last home before the grave. The Terror tightening and suspicious of plots between the prisoners and their sympathizers, all contacts with the outside world were cut off. For six months he heard from nobody in freedom, while horror swelled as the victims of the Terror poured into the Luxembourg and out to the tribunal, the guillotine, the executioner's basket. Robespierre, playing the middle of the Convention against both ends, was getting rid of radical and reactionary elements equally antagonistic to the Republic of Virtue. Early in March came

235

the radicals, the *ultras*—Hébert, Momoro, Ronsin, Chaumette—to embrace their old comrade Clootz, then to move on with him to condemnation and death for inciting to anarchy; later in the month, the conservatives, the *citras*—Danton, Fabre, Desmoulins, Chabot, and others—under the cloud of Robespierre as conspirators for a monarchist restoration. Danton hailed Paine, wished him good morning, and said, "What you did for the happiness and liberty of your country, I tried in vain to do for mine; I was less fortunate but not more to blame. They will send me to the scaffold; very well, my friends, I shall go gaily." Each in his way in the Luxembourg prepared for the final agony—Hébert motionless, head sunk upon his chest; Chaumette asking the inmates and the wall who there was who never made a mistake; Chabot taking poison, screaming for a doctor, and after the cure being carried out to the death-cart by two guards; Danton laughing mightily at the stupidity of the human race.

To the pageant of human misery Paine responded like the thoroughly social-minded man that he was, a man who never turned his back on his fellows when he could help them. After a while he almost envied each night the ten, twenty, thirty, forty, or fifty of his companions who passed out of the Luxembourg and into eternity. They, at least, hearing their doom, could say, "Now, thank heaven! hope is gone." Month after month Paine waited even for that release and did not obtain it. But he did not break. Miss Helen Williams, an English poet living in Paris and for a time an inmate of the Luxembourg, tells in her *Letters Containing a Sketch of the Politics of France* about the prison behavior of "Monsieur P——," "a friend of mine, who is well known in the literary world as a man of distinguished talents, but whose name I am not at liberty to mention." "His cheerful philosophy under the certain expectation of death, his sensibility of heart, his brilliant powers of conversation, and his sportive vein of wit, rendered him a very general favourite with his companions of misfortune, who found a refuge from evil in the charms of his society. He was the confidant of the unhappy, the counsellor of the perplexed; and to his sympathizing friendship many a devoted victim in the hour of death confided the last cares of humanity, and the last wishes of tenderness." If the spirit of Christ walked in the Luxembourg in the year 1794, it was in the tall, bent figure of this plain American democrat (the author of "a pamphlet against Jesus Christ").

Late in the spring the pathetic amenities of prison life were abolished. Benoît was removed, and a ferocious custodian called Guiard took over the Luxembourg. The prisoners could no longer walk in the courtyard. They were not even permitted to get close to the window for a breath of air, two inmates having thrown themselves out to death on the pavement. Continually through the night the halls resounded with the noise of the guards marching with drawn swords and shouting to one another, *"Sentinelles, prenez garde à vous!"*

One day the prisoners awoke to great commotion in the courtyard and strange systematic movements in the halls. In every apartment, as they rushed to the door, they ran into a guard who pushed them back. They could glimpse outside the soldiers maneuvering cannon in the courtyard and cavalry driving away promenaders from the public gardens and closing the outer gates. Had the last hour come for all? Was this to be a new and more terrible September

237

Massacre? In due time the moderate intention behind the show was revealed. The soldiers had come only to ransack the cells for money and jewels and to carry off the metal knives, forks, and spoons, which would be replaced by wooden ones. In Paine's belongings they found nothing valuable. He had hidden in the lock of the apartment an English banknote and some coins. He was later able to give two hundred pounds to the English prisoner General O'Hara, whom the soldiers had left penniless.

Paine was spared the worst of the Terror. He fell sick with a fever. In his ground-floor cell, with the prison-physician and physician-prisoners attending and his room-mates—Joseph Vanhuele of Bruges and Michael Rubyns and Charles Bastini of Louvain—fluttering helplessly about, he lay in impervious delirium while the Terror surged forward to the breaking-point.

When, after a month, Paine was able to sit up in bed, he heard from his comrade Vanhuele the great news—Robespierre was no more. The two ends of the Convention, the terrorists and the moderates, the firebrands and the cowards, had put their strength together and destroyed the middle on the 28th of July (the 10th of Thermidor). The leaders of the Republic of Virtue—Robespierre, his brother, Couthon, Le Bas, St. Just—were dead. Before the completion of the Thermidorian coup the prisoners at the Luxembourg had been thrown into panic by the clangor of the tocsin and the riots in the neighborhood. Now they breathed easily for once, and with new hopes Paine convalesced rapidly.

The prison rigors relaxed. The prisoners were again permitted to correspond with the outside world and to stroll about in the courtyard, from which they could make affectionate signs to their friends in the public gardens. The Luxembourg lost its inmates in batches every day, not to the guillotine but to freedom.

Robespierre being out of the way, Paine could not believe that he would be buried much longer in the Luxembourg. With pleasure he embraced his innocent prison-companions now being liberated; he was glad to see them go and was sure that he would soon join them. His French friends at last dared to speak up for him. Lanthenas and Audibert wrote to members of the Convention and the Committee of Public Safety to "re-examine the motives of Thomas Paine's imprisonment." On the 8th of August Paine confidently wrote out an appeal to the Convention and the Committee. The voice from the prison is poignantly sad and noble. "Ah, my friends," he cries, "eight months' loss of Liberty seems almost a lifetime to a man who has been, as I have been, the unceasing defender of Liberty for twenty years."

No answer, not a word. Morris was still the American ambassador, and terrorists still dominated the important committees. With sinking heart in the long days the American prisoner watched the continual exodus of the liberated, and pondered on the complex web in which he seemed hopelessly enmeshed.

A new path to liberation soon presented itself, a path destined after three months of tortuous and tantalizing negotiation finally to set him free. Almost as wonderful as the fall of Robespierre was the fact that Morris's ministry was actually coming to an end. The deep, unfriendly motives of the Washington administration were not yet apparent. On the surface it seemed that Washington had magnanimously bent to the wishes of France and her American sympathizers by removing the notorious aristocrat Morris and substituting the democratic James Monroe. When Paine heard the news, his hopes flared up. During the month of August he wrote excited letters to Monroe setting forth his joy at the new appointment, the injustice of his long imprisonment, his expectation for a quick deliverance.

Monroe could not spring to Paine's aid. He had his own difficulties. Morris refused to cooperate in the installation of his successor, and the Committee of Public Safety procrastinated. After waiting nearly a whole month, Monroe appealed to the Convention and was promptly received with the honors befitting a sympathetic envoy from the sister republic. Once installed, the new ambassador turned to the affair of Paine. Monroe told one of Paine's friends, Peter Whiteside, that he had no official instructions about Paine but would do what he could for him under the circumstances. Whiteside also reported to Paine that Americans newly arrived in Paris regarded him as a French citizen and out of the protection of the United States. Apparently, though Gouverneur Morris was no longer a power, his conspiracy with Deforgues was still blocking all efforts to liberate Paine.

On the 10th of September Paine sent Monroe a long memorial, which in the situation is surprisingly temperate and patient. He observes that the French people conferred their citizenship upon foreigners as an honor, not as a ruse to lure them from allegiance to their own country; that he came to the Convention not to become a Frenchman, but to give the French people the benefit of his political understanding and then to return to his own country, America. "I have never abandoned her in thought, word, or deed," he declares. Beginning to see the light, he traces the opinion that he is not an American citizen to a tacit or deliberate conspiracy between Morris and the old Committee of Public Safety. He says that he accepted the call to the Convention not to enjoy foppish honors but to fight for liberty in an hour of danger. "I am not an ambitious man," he protests, "but perhaps I have been an ambitious American. I have wished to see America the *Mother Church* of government, and I have done my utmost to exalt her character and her condition." He asks Monroe to reclaim him, at least provisionally, as an American citizen—a service to which he is entitled "upon every principle of Constitutional Justice and National honour."

No reply came from the ambassador immediately. Meanwhile, inconspicuous prisoners were being released by the score from the Luxembourg. Paine remained. The autumnal rains set in, making the bricks of his ground-floor cell constantly damp. Money was gone, fuel scarce, candles unobtainable. He caught cold, and an abscess began to form in his side. Through his liberated room-mate, Vanhuele, the distracted prisoner applied again to the Committee of Public Safety. There the terrorist Bourdon de l'Oise haughtily describing Paine as an old Girondin conspirator, the enraged Vanhuele almost jumped upon the sacrosanct Committeeman, though it was criminal even to hint dissatisfaction. The Committee did nothing. The prospect of another winter in the Luxembourg loomed for the American prisoner.

On the 4th of October Paine received a letter which Monroe had written the 18th of September. Probably the terrorists on the Committee had kept it so long in transit. Here at last was an American ambassador solicitous for a fellow-citizen. Monroe announces himself squarely for Paine. He

241

says that his point of view has been misrepresented. "It becomes my duty, however, to declare to you, that I consider you as an American citizen, and that you are considered universally in that character by the people of America. As such you are entitled to my attention; and so far as it can be given consistently with those obligations which are mutual between every government and even a transient passenger, you shall receive it." There was healing for the prisoner in this noble paragraph: "Is it necessary for me to tell you how much all your countrymen, I speak of the great mass of the people, are interested in your welfare? They have not forgotten the history of their own revolution and the difficult scenes through which they passed; nor do they review its several stages without reviving in their bosoms a due sensibility of the merits of those who served them in that great and arduous conflict. The crime of ingratitude has not yet stained, and I trust never will stain, our national character. You are considered by them as not only having rendered important service in our own revolution, but as being, on a more extensive scale, the friend of human rights, and a distinguished and able advocate in favour of public liberty. To the welfare of Thomas Paine, the Americans are not, nor can they be, indifferent." Monroe advises "patience and fortitude" since he finds himself "upon a difficult theatre" and must proceed carefully.

Momentarily heartened, Paine thanked Monroe cordially. But still no liberation; only assurances unrealized and heartbreaking. One day his English friend Beresford wrote him that he would be free in two or three days. More than a week later, his French friend Labonadaire sent a note advising that a letter to the Convention appealing for liberty as an American citizen would produce results. Paine dispatched such a letter, and heard nothing. Then Vanhuele told him that he would surely be liberated to-morrow—another false hope. It was a cat-and-mouse game in which the mouse was reaching the limit of "patience and fortitude." His letter to Monroe on the 13th of October is a taut and furious appeal for justice. "My patience is exhausted," he announces. "Did I reason from personal considerations only, independent of principles and the pride of having practiced those principles honourably, I should be tempted to curse the day I knew America. By contributing to her liberty I have lost my own, and yet her Government beholds my situation in silence. Wonder not, Sir, at the ideas I express or the language in which I express them. If I have a heart to feel for others I can feel also for myself, and if I have anxiety for my own honour, I have it also for a country whose suffering infancy I endeavoured to nourish and to which I have been enthusiastically attached. As to patience I have practiced it long—as long as it was honourable to do so, and when it goes beyond that point it becomes meanness." Yet the letter trails off in pathetic friendliness: "I will be obliged to you to send me for the present, three or four candles, a little sugar of any kind, and some soap for shaving; and I should be glad at the same time to receive a line from you and a memorandum of articles. Were I in your place I would order a Hogshead of Sugar, some boxes of Candles and Soap from America, for they will become more scarce. Perhaps the best method for you to procure them at present is by applying to the American Consuls at Bordeaux and Havre, and have them up by the diligence."

Monroe was perplexed. He was anxious to do the generous thing, but, after all, having no official instructions about

Paine, he could not embark upon a public controversy which the Washington administration had not authorized. He wrote to Paine that most Americans regarded him as both an American and a French citizen; no matter what his citizenship, he was liable for any violations of French law. Did he wish a formal reclamation, regardless of consequences, or would he approve a continuation of the unofficial efforts in his behalf? On the 20th of October Paine replied calmly and with penetration. Yes, he wanted a trial; he had been asking for it. He was no French citizen. Had the French intended to kidnap him when they invited him to the Convention? A reclamation must be made. The present unofficial efforts, ineffective for ten weeks, can never succeed, for the Committee of Public Safety thereby assumes that some official restriction prevents more positive appeals and that President Washington connives at Paine's prolonged imprisonment. Paine offered a model letter, using some of Monroe's own phrases, to be submitted to the Committee reclaiming him as an American citizen; first, however, there should be conversations with some of the Committeemen. Pleading for liberty or a trial, the letter concludes: "I cannot rest any longer in this state of miserable suspense, be the consequences what they may."

In accordance with the program laid down by Paine, Monroe at last threw official niceties to the wind. He met with two or three of the Committee of General Security, which had immediate supervision over such matters, and demanded definite action upon the case of the much-abused American citizen Paine. The Committeemen assured the American ambassador that his wish would be promptly granted and that Paine would be freed. Only an official letter was needed. This Monroe wrote on the 1st of No-

vember. He admits that American citizens must obey the
law wherever they may be, but they are entitled to a speedy
trial. "The citizens of the United States can never look
back to the era of their own revolution, without remember-
ing, with those of other distinguished Patriots, the name of
Thomas Paine. The services which he rendered them in
their struggle for liberty have made an impression of gratitude which will never be erased, whilst they continue to
merit the character of a just and generous people. He is now
in prison, languishing under a disease, and which must be
increased by his confinement. Permit me, then, to call your
attention to his situation, and to require that you will hasten
his trial in case there be any charge against him, and if
there be none, that you will cause him to be set at liberty."
The Committee of General Security held a meeting with
the Committee of Public Safety. On the 6th of November
they sent the American ambassador the order that "Citizen
Thomas Paine be set at liberty." Monroe forwarded the
order to the Luxembourg, and the prisoner was informed
that his long tenancy was over. What Morris could have
done in December and lied about doing in February, Monroe did in the following November. The American ambassador having spoken officially, the American prisoner was
free.

So Thomas Paine left the Luxembourg, not in a death
cart through the jeering streets to the tribunal and the guillotine, but in a carriage with honor and respect to the home
of James Monroe, who had belatedly saved him from a living death and America from a national dishonor.

CHAPTER XX

Back to the Wars

IN THE Thermidorian Reaction (so called from Thermidor, the month in which Robespierre and his satellites were destroyed) no social distinction was more enviable in France than that of having been victimized by the Republic of Virtue of malodorous memory. The invalid guest in the American ambassador's mansion on the Rue de Clichy returned to a semblance of his former health in an atmosphere of adulation.

In these first days of liberty Paine felt that his accounts with revolutionary France and blood-soaked Europe were settled. He wanted only to escape to his beloved America—in a spring voyage, since he was too feeble for the wintry seas. But on the 8th of December, 1794, after the Convention had decreed the recall of seventy-three formerly expelled Girondin deputies, Thibaudeau reclaimed "one of the most zealous defenders of liberty, . . . Thomas Payne, who powerfully contributed to establish liberty in a nation allied with the French Republic." The Convention adopted the motion unanimously and with great enthusiasm. Paine yielded. He returned warily, but he returned. On the 17th of December he wrote Thibaudeau: "My intention is to accept the invitation of the Assembly. For I desire that it be known to the universe that, although I have been the victim of injustice, I do not attribute my sufferings to those who had no part in them, and that I am far from using reprisals towards even those who are the authors of them. But, as it is necessary that I return to America next spring, I desire to consult you on the situation in which I find myself, in order that my acceptation of returning to the Convention may not deprive me of the right to return to America."

Paine conferred with Thibaudeau and was assured that his position as deputy would not interfere with his projected voyage. Yet when, a month later, in pursuance of this understanding Monroe applied to the Committee of Public Safety for permission to send the good-will decrees of the Convention to America by Citizen Paine, the Committee answered that Deputy Paine could not be spared. This, in spite of the fact that language disability and physical weakness made his membership in the Convention merely honorary.

If the Committee feared to trust Paine's independent voice in America, it mistook the range and quality of his political creed. There was in the whole world no better friend of a firm fraternal accord between France and America than the American deputy, the living bond and symbol of the two republics. Though denied passage to America, he proceeded to reassert his devotion to Franco-American harmony. And he became the chief adviser in the European maze to his host, the American ambassador, a plain, honest man, only thirty-seven years of age, protégé of Jefferson and ardent friend of the French Revolution.

The efforts of Paine and Monroe could not be crowned with glorious triumph. The Washington administration had stacked the cards against them. In 1793 the dismissal of Genet had shown that the American government would not enter the European fracas on the side of the French Republic. In 1794 the aristocrat John Jay was sent to England officially to demand redress of grievances, privately to obtain a treaty with England by granting extreme concessions. The democrat Monroe was given the impossible task of seeking favors from France without making reciprocal engagements. The American people, both houses of Congress, and Monroe himself were in the dark as to the exact scope of Jay's instructions. Secretary of State Randolph declared to Monroe that Jay had a limited mission and would probably fail, and that it was imperative to cultivate French good-will. Monroe took his government at its word. In his address to the Convention in August, 1794, he spoke in glowing phrases of the French aids during the American Revolution and of the "sincere attachment" of the American people to "the liberty, prosperity, and happiness of the French Republic." Meanwhile, in London, John Jay and Foreign Secretary Grenville were working out a treaty of friendship between the American Republic and the British Monarchy, the most implacable enemy of revolutionary France and the democratic ideal.

During the suspense attendant on the Jay-Grenville negotiations Monroe could not expect uniformly smooth sailing in France. Disquieting rumors were being received from the French spies at London to the effect that Jay was intriguing against the interests of France. On the 27th of December, 1794, the Committee of Public Safety asked Monroe for definite information about Jay. Monroe had just heard from Jay that a treaty had been concluded bearing a specific declaration that previous treaties were not to be thereby affected. Monroe reported this to the Committee with assurances that Jay's activity had been misinterpreted. He wrote to Jay for more details. Jay replied that he would be glad to furnish them if Monroe would not inform the

French government, but Monroe refused to accept the information on Jay's terms. He wrote to the Committee that he knew no more about the affair than they did, and he added that Jay's treaty could not possibly be injurious to France. Had not Secretary Randolph so assured him?

Paine did not share Monroe's naïveté. For a long time the American deputy had been nursing suspicions of the Washington administration. Why had Morris been appointed and retained so long as the ambassador to France? Why had Genet been so bruskly treated? Why had the author of *The Rights of Man* (dedicated to President Washington) been left to languish in prison for eleven months, without official inquiries or instructions in his behalf? This conduct was in Paine's mind part of a conspiracy to repudiate the ideals of the American Revolution. On the 22nd of February, 1795 (Washington's sixty-third birthday), Paine composed a bitter letter to the President, but at Monroe's entreaty he did not send it. On the 6th of March, writing in the same vein to Samuel Adams, Paine declares: "What Mr. Jay is about in England I know not; but is it possible that any man who has contributed to the Independence of America, and to free her from the tyranny of the British Government, can read without shame and indignation the note of Jay to Grenville? That the *United States has no other resource than in the justice and magnanimity of his Majesty,* is a satire upon the Declaration of Independence, and exhibits [such] a spirit of meanness on the part of America, that, were it true, I should be ashamed of her. Such a declaration may suit the spaniel character of Aristocracy, but it cannot agree with [the] manly character of a Republican."

When, a few days later, the Jay Treaty became publicly

known, France and her friends discovered that their fears had been only too well founded. The American administration had gone out of her way to give aid and comfort to England. The British government got a fine return for a promise that cost nothing to make—to evacuate the western forts by the 1st of June, 1796. Under the treaty American traders could not enter a British West Indian port in a ship of more than seventy tons; they could not enter at all the ports of Canada, Nova Scotia, or New Brunswick. Yet British vessels had unlimited access to all the ports and rivers of the United States. England did not renounce the right of search. Her captains could board American vessels and seize the cargoes, compensation to be adjusted at a later date. The British fleet had free range to choke off American commerce with the French Republic. The American government, while professing neutrality in the European conflict, was actually helping aristocratic England against democratic France, in violation of the spirit of the Franco-American alliance of 1778. Monroe looked ridiculous, if not worse. Writing to his uncle, Judge Jones, about the Jay Treaty, the duped American ambassador to France cries: "It is the most shameful transaction I have ever known of the kind."

The French Committees blazed with anger. A few of the hotheads demanded that the name of America be officially inscribed on the list of enemy belligerents. If Monroe had been a conscious partner in the intrigue against France, it might have gone very hard with him. But he was innocent, and Deputy Paine vouched for him. Wait, pleaded Paine and Monroe, don't be rash; don't plunge the two republics into a shameful war. Look at America—Hamilton stoned for defending the treaty, Jay burned in effigy. The American people do not approve the strange conduct of the American government. Our friends Jefferson and Madison will turn the Anglo-men out at the next election and will scrap the Jay Treaty. Under this line of argument the passion against America subsided for a time.

Though Paine had demonstrated his devotion to the French Republic in its international affairs, he found much to disturb him in the domestic policy of the Thermidorians. No democrat or humanitarian could endorse the ruthless betrayal of democracy by the Convention. After the first general sigh of relief from Jacobin terrorism, the Thermidorian Reaction led to renewed conflict between the haves and the have-nots in which executions and riots were the only weapons. Restored Girondins, reactionaries, and secret royalists broke down the protections which the Jacobins had set up around the poorer classes. The Law of the Maximum being repealed, monopolists and speculators reaped huge profits out of artificial scarcity and high prices. The starving Parisians, their municipal government suppressed, their clubs closed, their leaders dead, broke out in violent demonstrations against a Convention in which they were no longer represented. On the 1st of April, 1795, a mob stormed into the Convention Hall shouting for "Bread and the Constitution of 1793"; they were dispersed by the National Guard. On the 20th of May they returned, better organized and in larger numbers, and killed and beheaded one of the deputies as a warning to the rest. For three days the Convention was terror-stricken, until a hastily recruited army made the rioters lay down their guns. Deputies who had sympathized with the people were summarily guillotined, and the popular movement was crushed.

The Commission of Eleven, which had been appointed by the Convention ostensibly to revise the democratic Constitution of 1793, now had no proletarian opposition to fear. Soon it became known that the Commission would reject the Constitution of 1793 entirely. In the new charter of government being manufactured by the bourgeois Thermidorians, universal suffrage was to be supplanted by property qualifications. France was to be thrown back to the political inequities of 1791.

The Thermidorian betrayal of democracy was grievous to Paine. It challenged his idealism. Government by the people —all the people—and abolition of privilege were the central tenets of his political faith from *Common Sense* to the day of his death. As he had opposed the Jacobins for corrupting democracy by mob rule and terrorism, so he opposed the flagrant usurpation by the undemocratic Thermidorians. Ten months in the Luxembourg had not taught him skepticism or prudence. The Thermidorian Constitution being unholy, he spoke out against it.

In the first week of July, having at last found a courageous translator, Paine issued his *Dissertation on First Principles of Government*. In this brief treatise, without mentioning the proposed Constitution specifically, he brings the whole influence of his political theorizing into focus against the reactionary movement. He repeats the arguments and some of the phrases of *The Rights of Man* on the irrationality and illegitimacy of hereditary government. "The present war," he declares, "is a conflict between the representative system founded on the rights of the people, and the hereditary system founded on usurpation." The only government that has a right to exist is representative government, and its only true basis is complete equality of rights. "Every man has a right to one vote, and no more, in the choice of representatives. The rich have no more right to exclude the poor from the right of voting, or of electing and being elected, than the poor have to exclude the rich; and wherever it is attempted, or proposed, on either side, it is a question of force and not of right. Who is he that would exclude another? That other has a right to exclude him." The warning is ominous but pertinent, penetrating. "In a political view of the case, the strength and permanent security of government is in proportion to the number of people interested in supporting it. The true policy therefore is to interest the whole by an equality of rights, for the danger arises from exclusions. It is possible to exclude men from the right of voting, but it is impossible to exclude them from the right of rebelling against the exclusion; and when all other rights are taken away, the right of rebellion is made perfect." Finally, a plea against the murderous methods of all the factions: "An avidity to punish is always dangerous to liberty. It leads men to stretch, to misinterpret, and to misapply even the best of laws. He that would make his own liberty secure, must guard even his enemy from oppression; for if he violates this duty, he establishes a precedent that will react to himself."

Three days after the July Fourth Celebration the American deputy came to the Convention to make a last stand for democracy in the house of its enemies. Tall, gaunt, immobile, he stood in the tribune facing the Thermidorian sea while a secretary read his address in translation. The effects of the fever contracted in the Luxembourg, he says, have hitherto prevented his attendance in the Convention. Only the magnitude of the present subject has now brought him there. Turning to the proposed charter of government he says: "If there be faults in the Constitution, it were better to expunge them now, than to abide the event of their

253

mischievous tendency; for certain it is, that the plan of the Constitution which has been presented to you is not consistent with the grand objects of the Revolution, nor congenial to the sentiments of the individuals who accomplished it." He points to the discrepancy between the liberal pronouncements in the Declaration of Rights and the disfranchisement of nearly half the population. To limit the franchise to taxpayers is deception, for the disfranchised consumers ultimately pay most of the taxes.

"I hope," he concludes, "you will attribute this effusion of my sentiments to my anxiety for the honor and success of the revolution. I have no interest distinct from that which has a tendency to meliorate the situation of mankind. The revolution, as far as it respects myself, has been productive of more loss and persecution than it is possible for me to describe, or for you to indemnify. But with respect to the subject under consideration, I could not refrain from declaring my sentiments."

In vain Paine looked for support from the Thermidorians. One or two agreed with him but they did not dare to face the wrath of their associates. That democracy which had never really existed in practise, died officially with only the American deputy to speak a eulogy among its assassins. The Convention muttered angrily while the speech was being read, and some of the members violently opposed the routine motion that it be printed. Though Paine got out of the hall safely, the resentment against him grew apace. It waxed so bitter that the Girondin-Thermidorian Louvet in his paper *La Sentinelle* cried shame at his vilifiers. "Refute his opinions," said Louvet, "but do not calumniate the man." A victim of Pitt and Robespierre deserves respect. "Is it difficult," he asked, "to tolerate that man who has never manifested the least degree of intolerance to any one?"

The rejected democrat was permitted to live in peace at the American embassy. His capacity for being a political ir-ritant would soon be curtailed, for as an American he could not be a member of the Directory government which would succeed the Convention in the fall. Paine himself yearned for that discharge. On the 5th of August he sent five thousand copies of *Dissertation on First Principles of Government* to Benjamin Bache, Franklin's grandson and editor of the democratic *Aurora,* in Philadelphia, for dis-tribution in the United States. In the accompanying let-ter he says, "I hope to be in America before next Spring." But the excitement of apologizing for the Jay Treaty and fighting Thermidorian reaction had been too much for a convalescent man. His condition became worse, the abscess turned malignant. He therefore hastened the completion of Part Two of *The Age of Reason,* on which he had been intermittently engaged. Like Part One it is the religious testimony of a person for whom death seemed near at hand.

In this pamphlet Paine develops an extensive structure of argument in support of a basic tenet in Part One—that the Bible is not the word of God. He proceeds upon a major premise which has a moral and an intellectual phase. First, the true God is no moral monster, no divine Robespierre. Second, if we are to believe the testimonies of supernatural truth attributed to Moses, Joshua, Samuel, and the others, we must be reasonably certain that those men wrote the testimonies, and the testimonies must be consistent and plausible. By the test of human conscience and human reason Paine used the Bible itself as the best argument against its divine authorship and inspiration. For this task he found some useful suggestions in the remarks of the Jewish critics Ben Ezra and Spinoza on Job and in the work of the Frenchman Boulanger on St. Paul. Mainly, however, he relied on his own eyes poring malevolently over the Bible itself, of which he now had a copy.

Part Two of *The Age of Reason* contains one long central argument—that the Bible is not Holy Writ—supported by a thousand and one evidences drawn from almost every book in the Old and New Testaments. No abstract can do full justice to this most detailed and close-packed of Paine's writings. In the present discussion we shall illustrate the method and spirit of his inquiry by a fairly close rendition of his first analysis, that on the Mosaic books, and a selection of his salient utterances on the rest of the Bible.

The books said to have been written by Moses—Genesis, Exodus, Leviticus, Numbers, and Deuteronomy—are spurious and were composed by "some very ignorant and stupid pretenders to authorship, several hundred years after the death of Moses." This is demonstrable from the Bible itself.

In the five books themselves there is no affirmative evidence that Moses was the author, and mental confusion abounds. The style and manner are altogether those of another person speaking about Moses. The references to him are always in the third person, such as "The Lord said unto Moses" or "Moses said unto the Lord." If it be granted that this is really Moses' peculiar autobiographical manner, Moses becomes ludicrous and absurd when he describes himself in Numbers as "very meek, above all the men which were on the face of the earth." "If Moses said this of himself, instead of being the meekest of men, he was one of the most vain and arrogant coxcombs." Likewise with

256

Deuteronomy. That book is written in the dramatic form, having Moses as one character among others, and relating the circumstances of his death and burial. The book is obscure and self-contradictory. In describing the burial, the writer uses the pronoun *he* without a definite antecedent. "If the writer meant that he (God) buried him, how should he (the writer) know it? Or why should we (the readers) believe him?" On the one hand, the writer says that no man knows "unto this day" where the sepulcher of Moses is; on the other, he declares that Moses is buried in a valley in the land of Moab. What does he really mean? In Exodus, the reason for keeping the seventh day is that God rested on that day from making the heavens and the earth; but in Deuteronomy it is that the children of Israel came out of Egypt on that day. Which are we to believe? Deuteronomy also contains "that inhuman and brutal law," not found elsewhere in the Bible, authorizing parents to have their children stoned to death for stubbornness.

Historical and chronological evidence throughout the Bible argues against the Mosaic authorship of the first five books. Consider the passage in Genesis which says that Abraham pursued the captors of Lot *unto Dan*. What does common sense make of this phrase? If, in reading an undated composition, we came upon the name of New York, we should reason that the composition was written after 1664, in which year New Amsterdam was changed to New York. A composition mentioning Havre-Marat should be dated 1793 or later, the name of that town having been previously Havre-de-Grâce. Now the Book of Judges relates that the Danites came to Laish, slaughtered the people and destroyed the dwellings, and built a new city named Dan, after Dan, their father. According to the Bible chronology, this act

257

occurred 331 years after the death of Moses, who therefore could not refer to the city as Dan. Or take the passage in Genesis about "the kings that reigned in Edom, before there reigned any king over the children of Israel." Again, if we found in an undated composition references to a Congress in America or a Convention in France, we should suppose that the composition could not have been written before there was a Congress in America or a Convention in France. The passage could therefore have been written only after the first king reigned in Israel. This fact dates the writing of Genesis at least as late as the time of Saul, if not later. We find the same passage verbatim in Chronicles, where it fits properly. Genesis must be a piece of patchwork more recent in authorship than Chronicles, the Homeric poem, or Aesop's Fables. "Take away from Genesis the belief that Moses was the author, on which only the strange belief that it is the word of God has stood, and there remains nothing of Genesis but an anonymous book of stories, fables, and traditionary or invented absurdities, or of downright lies. The story of Eve and the serpent, and of Noah and his ark, drops to a level with the Arabian Tales, without the merit of being entertaining, and the account of men living to eight and nine hundred years becomes as fabulous as the immortality of the giants of the Mythology."

Further, the character of the Biblical Moses is horrid and contemptible, quite the reverse of divinely inspired. He appears to have been the wretch who first began wars under the pretext of religion, as witness his command in Numbers, given in the name of the Lord, to "kill every male among the little ones, and kill every woman that hath known a man by lying with him; but all the women-children that have not known a man by lying with him, keep alive for yourselves." In Paine's imagination the cruelties perpetrated by Moses and the Mosaic God take on a frightful immediacy, and he lashes out with all his stormy eloquence against the Biblical prototypes of North and Pitt and their master, George Guelph, of Great Britain.

So Paine marches through the rest of the Old Testament, searching for big and little flaws to support his thesis that it is an anonymous compilation, slovenly, barbaric, superstitious. The book ascribed to Joshua, he says, has chronological absurdities like those in the books ascribed to "his predecessor in villainy and hypocrisy, Moses"; and it is equally blasphemous in covering its iniquities with "the orders of the Almighty." Kings and Chronicles are histories of "assassinations, treachery, and wars" by "a nation of ruffians and cutthroats" who have no moral claim to be regarded as the chosen people. While Kings and Chronicles deal with the same historic period, miracles narrated in one are not mentioned in the other. "Though men, in later times, have believed *all that the prophets have said unto them,* it does not appear that those prophets, or historians, believed each other; they knew each other too well." Ezra and Nehemiah make mistakes in adding lists of simple figures. "These writers may do well enough for Bible-makers, but not for anything where truth and exactness is necessary." Isaiah was a "lying prophet and imposter," who in the name of the Lord prophesied the exact contrary of what befell Ahaz. Jeremiah safeguards his prophecies by putting in the mouth of the Almighty provisoes that He may change His mind. "According to this plan of prophesying, a prophet could never be wrong, however mistaken the Almighty might be. This sort of absurd subterfuge, and this manner

259

of speaking of the Almighty, as one would speak of a man, is consistent with nothing but the stupidity of the Bible." The Book of Jonah is "a fit story for ridicule, if it was written to be believed; or of laughter, if it was intended to try what credulity could swallow; for, if it could swallow Jonah and the whale it could swallow anything."

The New Testament, "the fable of Jesus Christ," must go the way of the Old. The books falsely ascribed to Matthew, Mark, Luke, and John are confused, contradictory, and altogether unworthy of belief. The genealogy of Christ, given in Matthew, lists twenty-eight generations from David to Joseph; in Luke there are forty-three. "If they cannot be believed in their account of his natural genealogy, how are we to believe them when they tell us he was the son of God, begotten by a ghost; and that an angel announced this in secret to his mother? If they lied in one genealogy, why are we to believe them in the other? If his natural genealogy be manufactured, which it certainly is, why are we not to suppose that his celestial genealogy is manufactured also, and that the whole is fabulous?" The virgin birth is not mentioned in Mark and John and is related differently in Matthew and Luke on the testimony of Joseph and Mary. It requires much more proof than is given. "Were any girl that is now with child to say, and even to swear it, that she was gotten with child by a ghost, and that an angel told her so, would she be believed? Certainly she would not. Why then are we to believe the same thing of another girl whom we never saw, told by nobody knows who, nor where, nor when?" The four books vary even as to the wording of the inscription on the cross, and Mark, Luke, and John do not mention the miraculous signs described by Matthew as occurring at the Crucifixion. Concerning the resurrection

260

the writers differ as to the earthquake, the time of day, the angels, and other attendant circumstances. Could God have revealed Himself in this chaotic and unintelligible fashion? "Now, if the writers of these four books had gone into a court of justice to prove an *alibi* (for it is of the nature of an alibi that is here attempted to be proved, namely, the absence of a dead body by supernatural means), and had they given their evidence in the same contradictory manner as it is here given, they would have been in danger of having their ears cropt for perjury, and would have justly deserved it. Yet this is the evidence, and these are the books, that have been imposed upon the world as being given by divine inspiration, and as the unchangeable word of God." The vote of a church council three hundred and fifty years after the death of Christ could not transmute a mass of contradictions and absurdities into the word of God.

In the Conclusion Paine summarizes the destructive and constructive sides of his religious system. Roundly he declares: "Of all the systems of religion that ever were invented, there is none more derogatory to the Almighty, more unedifying to men, more repugnant to reason, and more contradictory in itself, than this thing called Christianity. Too absurd for belief, too impossible to convince, and too inconsistent for practice, it renders the heart torpid, or produces only atheists and fanatics. As an engine of power, it serves the purpose of despotism; and as means of wealth, the avarice of priests; but so far as respects the good of man in general, it leads to nothing here or hereafter." On the other hand, deism teaches all that is necessary or proper to be known. It cannot be made an instrument of despotic governments. The Bible of the Creation is inexhaustible in texts, and the method of science brings us, as it were, face to face with God. "If we consider the nature of our condition here, we must see there is no occasion for such a thing as *revealed religion*. What is it we want to know? Does not the creation, the universe we behold, preach to us the existence of an Almighty Power, that governs and regulates the whole? And is not the evidence that this creation holds out to our senses infinitely stronger than anything we can read in a book, that any imposter might make and call the word of God? As for morality, the knowledge of it exists in every man's conscience."

Paine's lucid straightforward intellect had no patience with half-lights and hesitations. He had absolutely no reverence for supernatural religion and professedly supernatural writings which in his opinion had served to corrupt and brutalize mankind. Hence, the broad sweep of his negations, even to calling the Book of Isaiah "one continued incoherent, bombastical rant, full of extravagant metaphor, without application and destitute of meaning," and the Book of Ruth "an idle, bungling story, foolishly told, nobody knows by whom, about a strolling country-girl creeping slily to bed to her cousin Boaz." Hence, too, his occasional use of the most devastating type of argument, the *reductio ad absurdum,* as in wondering whether the saints who rose from the dead after the resurrection "came out naked, and all in natural buff, he-saints and she-saints, or whether they came full dressed and where they got their dresses" and whether the Holy Ghost descended in the shape of a dove or that equally harmless creature, a goose. Sensitive persons of any or no creed may dislike such knockdown reasoning. Paine was, he said, marching through the Christian forest with an ax, which is not a delicate instrument.

Part Two ends like Part One on the liberal, humane note: "I here close the subject. I have shown in all the foregoing parts of this work that the Bible and the Testament are impositions and forgeries; and I leave the evidence I have produced in proof of it to be refuted, if any one can do it; and I leave the ideas that are suggested in the conclusion of the work to rest on the mind of the reader; certain as I am that when opinions are free, either in matters of government or religion, truth will finally and powerfully prevail."

These words, breathing the magnanimity of strength, were uttered by a man physically worn out and on the verge of death. On the 15th of September, 1795, Monroe wrote to Judge Jones that his guest could not last more than a month or two further. Paine was not completely philosophic at the prospect of dying that winter. Alone in the sickroom the fevered man brooded on his misery. The abscess burning into his side had developed during the three months in which Monroe had been trying by unofficial maneuvers to liberate him. Why had not Washington given specific instructions demanding his release? Paine felt that he—the author of *Common Sense* and *The Rights of Man,* the living symbol in Europe of the American Revolution against the Royal Brute of Great Britain—had been offered as a sacrifice to that Royal Brute by George Washington. This was not merely a personal humiliation and injustice, it was treason to the great ideals for which they had both fought. Paine had written a demand for explanation in a letter to Washington on the 22nd of February, but at Monroe's entreaty had put the letter aside. Though Monroe agreed with Paine in conversation, he did not wish to be embarrassed by any attack on the President coming from a guest of the

American embassy. But in the view of Paine (and the French Government) Monroe was really the ambassador of the democratic American people rather than the aristocratic American administration. Paine's letter would therefore serve the interests of the true sovereign of America. In February Paine had yielded to Monroe. In September, desperately sick and bitter, Paine disregarded whatever obligation he had to his host. On the 20th of September he sent Washington another letter secretly, under cover to his American literary agent Bache. He demands an explanation for the official neglect of his peril. "I cannot understand your silence upon this subject upon any other ground, than as connivance at my imprisonment; and this is the manner in which it is understood here, and will be understood in America, unless you will give me authority for contradicting it." He quotes Robespierre's curious memorandum that the American deputy be accused "for the interest of America as well as of France." Why for the interest of America? "I ought not to have suspected you of treachery; but whether I recover from the illness I now suffer, or not, I shall continue to think you treacherous, till you give me cause to think otherwise."

In spite of its bitterness the note to Washington contains a faint hope that a satisfactory explanation may be forthcoming. The long letter written four days later to Madison has no such expectation. The specific need for writing to Madison was to arrange for payment to him by Bache of a loan of two hundred and fifty crowns obtained by Paine from Monroe. That done, Paine relates his imprisonment and sickness and the neglect by the American administration, which in its "dark Chamber" acts "on the plan of European courts," with Washington "playing the

old Courtier." Though serene enough in the familiar presence of death, Paine cries out in the unnerving sorrow of
a man who finds himself betrayed by his friends. "It would
be agreeable to me to live, but if it is not to be so I can
quit life with as much tranquillity as any Man that ever
passed that scene for I have done an honest part in the
World. But it is not agreeable to me to remember that I
owe part of my present Condition to the ungrateful neglect
of a Country, at least of its Government, from which I had
a right to expect better things. Mr. Washington has not
served America with greater Zeal, nor with more disinterestedness than myself, and I know not that he has done it
with better effect. He may perhaps console himself on the
cold and callous line of office and say—that Mr. Paine was
a French Citizen and therefore he, as President, had nothing to do in the case.—But he ought to have informed himself if this was the Case or not, and had he made the en-
quiry he ought to have done, he would have found it was
not the Case, for I was imprisoned as a foreigner born in
England and that foreigner was a citizen of America, but
had it been otherwise it would not acquit him of ingratitude. He ought at least to have said to somebody—enquire
into the case of Mr. Paine and see if there is anything we
can do for him; but Mr. Washington has not so much as
done this and his not doing it has been interpreted by
Robespierre into connivance at my imprisonment and would
have been fatal to me if he had lived but a few weeks
longer. I ought not to have suspected Mr. Washington of
Treachery but he has acted towards me the part of a cold-
blooded traitor. Whether he has done this to gratify the
English Government or to let me fall into destruction in
France that he and his faction might exclaim the louder

against the French Revolution or whether he hoped by my extinction he might meet with less opposition in mounting up the American Government, I trouble not myself to know; it is sufficient to me that I know the fact, and any reason he may give will involve him in reproach he will not easily shake off."

During that fall and winter of 1795 English and American newspapers carried reports that Paine had died at the American embassy. Paine was in fact very much alive. His health began to improve, and new interests hastened his recovery. In these months, living quietly with the Monroes, he wrote one of his ablest pamphlets, *The Decline and Fall of the English System of Finance*. *The Decline and Fall* belongs with *Public Good* and the social security program in Part Two of *The Rights of Man* as examples of an important side of Paine's nature—the systematic analyst of a particular practical situation. Relying on the researches of Dr. Price and Adam Smith and the official statistics published by Eden (Lord Auckland) and Jenkinson (Lord Hawkesbury)—"these sort of folks change their names so often that it is as difficult to know them as it is to know a thief"—he demonstrates that the English system of a funded currency will inevitably have no better fate than the French assignats. Ever since the year 1697 a public debt has been piling up, increasing by one and a half after each war, until to-day the continued payment of the interest in paper money constitutes a colossal inflation which can be no longer maintained. When the oppressed English public will shift from mere meetings and societies to an organized demand for specie payment in return for government paper, what will become of the "placemen, pensioners, government contractors, Reeves' association, and the members of both houses of Parliament?" The French Government purchased a thousand copies of this pamphlet in April, 1796, and distributed them widely. Though the line of cause and effect need not be drawn, it is nevertheless a fact that a year later the Bank of England suspended specie payments and the hardpressed Pitt was ready to talk peace.

In the spring of 1796 Paine left the Monroes. He was in fair health and impatient of restraint. Besides, he planned a public denunciation of President Washington, who had made no answer to the letter of September 20. Paine wanted to return to America. He also wanted to see what the new French Government, the Directory, would bring forth. But wherever he might be, in glory or disgrace, he would speak with an independent voice for the liberation of humanity from kings and priests and their lackeys.

CHAPTER XXI

A Religio-Political Issue

THE AGE OF REASON aroused the unified opposition of all believers in revealed religion. Into the thirty-odd refutations which appeared, it is not necessary to make an extensive inquiry, since all the arguments flow together in two or three simple grooves. Almost without exception the defenders of Christianity dishonored their cause by frantic billingsgate at the antagonist—"renegado," "popinjay," "toad," "a lump of the coarsest clay that ever came of the potter's hand," a "nincompoop" with "so little conscience as to vomit such trash upon the bosom of the public."

The billingsgate went hand in hand with shoddy argument. Paine had presented an impressive list of errors, inconsistencies, and interpolations in the Bible. The Christian apologists challenged his citations, but, unable to dispose of them all, dismissed the unanswerable ones as "a few unsightly shrubs" "of little consequence"; yet this admission struck at the root of the utter infallibility of the Bible. Paine had denied the modern rational validity of ancient magical stories told by fallible human beings as the absolutely indisputable revelation of God Himself. The apologists lamely countered on the secular level by asking Paine whether he had not believed in his election to the National Convention on hearsay and whether miracles should be any more incredible to a well-informed man than the workings of electricity to an ignorant farmer, and Thomas

268

Williams argued in *The Age of Infidelity:* "May I not reveal a truth to a third person, through the medium of a second of such established veracity as to demand belief? Is this possible with men, and impossible with God?" Paine had cast a rationalistic doubt on the story of the Virgin Birth. The apologists retorted with expressions of outraged piety. In *The Divine Authority of the Bible* Robert Thomson said that he believed in that miracle for the very fact that it is recorded in the Bible, and "When Paine therefore asks,—'Were any girl that is now with child to say that she was gotten with child by a ghost, and that an angel told her so, would she be believed?' Our answer is easy, we would recommend her to bedlam, and give her The Age of Reason to amuse herself." Likewise Richard Watson, Bishop of Llandaff, who respectfully credited Paine in *An Apology for the Bible* with "acuteness of observation" and occasional "philosophical sublimity," retreated from the debate: "Who, you ask, would now believe a girl, who should say she was gotten with child by a ghost?—Who, but yourself, would ever have asked a question so abominably indecent and profane? I cannot argue with you on this subject."

One of Paine's basic and constant contentions against accepting the Scriptures was the ferocious cruelty of the Biblical God. The apologists distorted this issue—villainies attributed to the express command of God—by asserting that a book is not to be condemned merely for describing unpleasant things. Or, endorsing the barbarities of Jehovah, they abundantly exemplified Paine's thesis that belief in a cruel God makes cruel men. "Justice only was to be executed, when all hope of reformation was cut off," said Williams, in defending the law in Deuteronomy prescribing capital punishment for stubborn children. Concerning the slaughter of the Midianites the Bishop of Llandaff commented, "I see nothing in this proceeding, but good policy, combined with mercy." On the Canaanite children Thomson callously remarked, " 'But, wherein,' he asks, 'could crying or smiling infants offend?' a question certainly put to old nurse and just deserves old nurse's answer. 'Ay,' she would say, 'very true, Thomas, poor little innocents, but they are happy, and taken from a world of sin and misery.' "

There was another defense of the Biblical God and the literal Christian system—a dangerous, two-edged defense, the *tu quoque* argument which Bishop Butler had employed against Tindal. Is the God of the Bible, who inspired Moses and Joshua to their bloody deeds, morally worse than the God of Nature, who destroys the young and the old, the innocent and the guilty, by earthquake, flood, fire, famine, and pestilence? The Bishop of Llandaff made the strongest statement of this idea. "What I contend for," he said, "is shortly this—that you have no right, in fairness of reasoning, to urge any apparent deviation from moral justice, as an argument against revealed religion, because you do not urge an equally apparent deviation from it, as an argument against natural religion: you reject the former, and admit the latter, without adverting that, as to your objection, they must stand or fall together." From natural science itself, Paine's own Bible, Priestley in *An Answer to Mr. Paine's Age of Reason* made another point against deism. Paine had asserted his belief in the immortality of the soul while rejecting the miraculous doctrine of physical resurrection. Priestley demonstrated that Paine's view also implied faith in the miraculous. Rationally considered, how could the soul exist independent of the body and brain with which observation shows it to be inseparable?

270

Paine never came to grips with such moral and intellectual objections. He could not very well do so within the limits of the deistic system. The silence or weak rejoinders of the deists, however, did not mean ultimate victory for the Christians. A man whose reason has led him to reject revealed religion is not likely to recant if natural religion is proved to be not altogether reasonable. He will go further. By putting deism and Christianity in the same pattern of thought, the Christian apologists unwittingly pointed the way to agnosticism and atheism—more logical and more deadly enemies.

The Christian apologists were too frightened to essay a temperate and impersonal evaluation of *The Age of Reason,* because the conflict was more than a debate over ideas. Under the impetus of Paine deism had been transformed from an aristocratic intellectual sport into a popular movement which threatened to overthrow the consecrated altars and put the established churches out of business. Robert Hall grieved in *Modern Infidelity:* "Infidelity has lately grown condescending: bred in the speculations of a daring philosophy, immured at first in the cloisters of the learned, and afterwards nursed in the lap of voluptuousness and of courts; having at length reached its full maturity, it boldly ventures to challenge the suffrages of the people, solicits the acquaintance of peasants and mechanics, and seeks to draw whole nations to its standard." Especially was this true in England, where the London Corresponding Society, encouraged by the acquittal of Hardy and its other leaders at the treason trials of 1794, persisted in the radical field which the more genteel societies had deserted. "If the facts I am about to adduce were not well warranted," wrote William Hamilton Reid, a hostile contemporaneous recorder, "posterity would not believe, that in consequence of the publication of a rhapsody against the doctrines of Christianity, hazarded by a theoretical politician in 1794, and under favour of the French revolution, a very considerable number of our countrymen adopted his notions; and became equally as violent for the extermination of the Christian religion, as for the remedy of those *civil abuses,* for which alone their society was at first established!"

Thenceforth for the rest of the revolutionary epoch in England, though there were defections due to Paine's anti-Christianity, political and religious radicalism were united. A man was considered "a good Democrat and a Deist" and the favorite slogan at radical meetings was "May the last King be strangled in the bowels of the last Priest!" In 1797, dragging one Thomas Williams into court for publishing *The Age of Reason,* the Society for Carrying into Effect His Majesty's Proclamation against Vice and Immorality complained that the tract was being industriously circulated among the middle and lower classes in such widely separated parts of the kingdom as Cornwall, Nottingham, Leeds, and Scotland. The rationalistic virus penetrated even into the armed forces. When the sailors at the Nore staged their brief mutiny in 1797 against wormy cheese, the cat-o'-nine-tails, and a wage scale fixed in the time of Charles II, they issued a manifesto proclaiming, "The Age of Reason has at length revolved. Long have we been endeavouring to find ourselves men. We now find ourselves so. We will be treated as such." At the likelihood of a similar uprising for human rights in the army an aristocratic wit on *The Anti-Jacobin* sneeringly warned the soldiers against the "nice clever books by Tom Paine, the philanthropist," the teacher of

Reason, philosophy, "fiddledum, diddledum,"
Peace and Fraternity, "higgledy, piggledy,"
Higgledy, piggledy, "fiddledum, diddledum."

On the pretext of abating a public nuisance the government hounded the traveling agitators throughout the country, and the municipal police chased the indefatigable radicals of London from one meeting place to another and ultimately beyond the city limits—Cripplegate, Fetter-lane, Little Britain, Moorfields, Hoxton. Finally in 1799 Parliament outlawed the London Corresponding Society, thereby checking the open progress of free thought and social discontent.

In America, the stronghold of Protestantism and literal Christianity, *The Age of Reason* created a sensation more widespread than profound. The copies of Part One which had found their way across the Atlantic were powerfully supplemented in the fall of 1795 by a cargo of 15,000 copies of Part Two sent by Paine to Bache for quick distribution at a cheap rate. "What baneful success has attended this vile and insidious effort," lamented the Reverend Daniel Dana of Newburyport to his congregation in 1799, "you need not be told. That infidelity has had, for several years past, a rapid increase among us, seems a truth generally acknowledged." Deistic societies sprang up in New York and Philadelphia. College students, attracted by the luminous and exciting logic of deism, badgered their professors of philosophy with arguments out of *The Age of Reason*. "That was the day of the infidelity of the Tom Paine school," Lyman Beecher recalled of life at Yale in 1795-96. "Boys that dressed flax in the barn, as I used to, read Tom Paine and believed him." At Harvard the governing corporation acknowledged the intellectual strength of deism by providing every student with a free copy of Watson's *Apology*. But the church in strongly Protestant America was not really in danger. The poet-journalist Freneau spoke truly when he declared, "The Age of Reason would never have been much known in this country if the Clergy had suffered it to rest."

Taking advantage of the religious conservatism of the American people, the Federalists and their lieutenants in the pulpit attempted to make a political issue out of *The Age of Reason*. It became the great red herring of the day. The Federalists fumed that infidelity and Jacobinism were whelps of the same sire, and that a vote for Jefferson was a vote for the devil. "Tom Paine has kindly cured our clergy of their prejudices," wrote Fisher Ames in 1795, rejoicing at the solid Federalism of the religious profession. During the campaign of the next year, in *The Pretensions of Thomas Jefferson to the Presidency Examined* the New Englander Oliver Wolcott and the Southerner William Smith assured the electorate that "The late impious and blasphemous works of Thomas Paine . . . have been very industriously circulated in the United States, by all *that class* of people, who are friendly to Mr. Jefferson's politics." Losing the presidential election, the Jeffersonians could not help looking with mixed sentiments at their eloquent comrade-in-arms who had defied not only the aristocrats but Christ and Jehovah.

CHAPTER XXII

An American Democrat Under the Directory

WHILE *The Age of Reason* swelled Paine's international significance, he was trying to find a way of life in France under the Directory. He was unhappy at the decline of republicanism, at a Directory established on principles alien to the equality of rights—a Directory whose domestic troubles appeared to spring from that very apostasy. In November, 1796, Lord Malmesbury, Pitt's peace envoy to France, keeping a watchful eye on the author of *The Rights of Man* and *The Age of Reason,* reported him "very much distressed in circumstances," with "little or no influence in the country" and "highly discontented with the new Constitution."

As usual in moments of let-down Paine grew homesick for America. But, as he wrote on the 4th of March, 1797, in a letter to Governor Clinton of New York, "I am always intending to return to America, and something is always happening to prevent me; the case I believe is that, as I have embarked on the Revolution, I do not like to leave it till it is finished." Early in the spring, when Monroe departed for the United States in accordance with his recall, Paine prepared to go with him. At the port of Havre, however, the British frigates cruising within sight, Paine turned back. He would not exchange his restlessness in France for prison or worse in the England that had outlawed him.

On returning to Paris Paine visited the ardent young republican and free-thinking journalist Nicolas de Bonneville and his plump, good-natured wife, at their home and establishment, 4 Rue du Théâtre Français. He intended to stay as a guest for a week or two; but he lived with the Bonnevilles as a roomer for five years, until he left for America. He was assigned to a small study and bedroom on the second floor, shabbily furnished and not very tidily kept, for Madame Bonneville was not the best of housekeepers. He rose late, and after breakfast generally read through several newspapers—he could make out the gist of printed French—and discussed current affairs with Bonneville. Then he retired to his study, to read, write, or work on various mechanical inventions. He frequently visited Sir Robert and Lady Smith or the Barlows, with whom Robert Fulton was staying. He walked by preference for the exercise, a tall straight figure, dressed in the conventional fashion without French frills, carrying neither sword nor cane, hat in hand, black eyes shining and kind in his strong, large-featured face.

During the Directory the riotous living of war profiteers and their mistresses made flagrant immorality the mode in Paris, which, as one observer said, was thirty Sodoms gathered together. Paine's mode of living was pale before this lurid background. But as a conspicuous and intractable democrat he could not avoid being maligned by gossiping reactionaries bent on discrediting his ideals in the minds of decent people. Rumor, exaggerating his occasional heavy indulgence in liquor, pictured him as habitually a drunken sot, most amusing at ten o'clock at night with brandy and water before him. The Irish revolutionist Wolf Tone, after accepting and recording this legend, did not find Paine so monstrous; yet the homesick and tragic-starred Tone was not an altogether indulgent observer. "I have been lately introduced to the famous Thomas Paine," writes Tone in his diary, March 3, 1797, "and like him very well. He is vain beyond all belief, but he has reason to be vain, and for my part I forgive him. He has done wonders for the cause of liberty, both in America and Europe, and I believe him to be conscientiously an honest man. He converses extremely well; and I find him wittier in discourse than in his writings, where his humour is clumsy enough."

The true quality of Paine's life in Paris of the Directory may be seen, apart from the testimony of the Bonnevilles, in the manuscripts of Dr. John Walker, faithfully used by John Epps in his biography shortly after the doctor's death. Dr. Walker, eminent pioneer of the vaccination movement, friend of social reform though not an active reformer, lived in Paris with the revolutionary British expatriates in 1797. In Walker's view, as recorded by Epps, Paine was "a man of gigantic political genius, that made, while other men took baby steps, the strides of a giant," and "the Church and State party, when they could not meet his reasonings, attacked his character; a mode resorted to by all having a weak cause." Walker's papers give a jumble of sympathetic impressions about Paine. There was the dinner given by the British exiles, at which the stormy Irishman Napper Tandy raised his glass with a toast, "Gentlemen, may the tri-coloured flag float on the Tower of London, and on the Birmingham Tower of Dublin Castle!" Paine joined in the drink, with a laugh at the abstaining doctor, "Walker is a Quaker with all its follies; I am a Quaker without them." There was the case of Mary Wollstonecraft's young brother, who was clapped into jail after his imprudent letter praising the British navy had been intercepted. Walker urging Paine to intercede immediately, Paine remarked, "My interference, at this time, would be premature. Let them alone awhile, till their fury be somewhat dissipated in the violence of their proceedings, and then I shall not find any difficulty in obtaining his liberation." In due time Paine got Wollstonecraft off. One day Walker asked Paine how it was to be explained that he had not taken up the pen for Negro emancipation. Paine replied, "An unfitter person for such a work could hardly be found. The cause would have suffered in my hands. I could not have treated it with any chance of success; for I could never think of their condition but with feelings of indignation." Through Walker's eyes we see a fellowship of strong-fibered gamblers with destiny, who, if they drank much, held their liquor well, and paid a kind of republican court to the outstanding republican of the world.

In the spring of 1796, during his retirement at Surennes after leaving Monroe, Paine wrote his public *Letter to George Washington*. Paine was not merely venting a personal spleen. The administration which at the behest of Gouverneur Morris had not raised a finger in solicitousness for a man who had served the American Revolution greatly, was the same administration which in his view had sold out in the Jay Treaty to the old enemy. He felt that the official silence as to his fate was intended as an ingratiating gesture to the British despots who had outlawed him for challenging their despotism. In behalf of the French Revolution and the forces of American Democracy a mighty protest must be made. When, therefore, Dr. Enoch Edwards came out to Surennes with a desperate plea from Monroe that he should not publish the pamphlet, Paine bluntly refused to accommodate the ambassador. He said in effect that the people had the first claim upon his pen. Edwards thought this a vain sentiment. Others may see in it a kind of modesty.

The *Letter to George Washington* is a scathing arraignment of Washington and his administration from the viewpoint of an American democrat. "As censure is but awkwardly softened by apology," Paine begins, "I shall offer you no apology for this letter. The eventful crisis to which your double politics have conducted the affairs of your country, requires an investigation uncramped by ceremony." Paine condemns the whole tenor of the Federalist administration, its pretense to being the sole advocate of centralized government, its fostering of speculators and monopolists, its aping of European aristocracy. He instances the silence on his own imprisonment as an example of the betrayal of old ideals, "for it was the American system of government that I was endeavouring to spread in Europe." He denounces Washington's foreign policy, "a mean and servile submission to the insults of one nation; treachery and ingratitude to another," and the crowning infamy of the Jay Treaty—"there never was such a base and servile treaty of surrender since treaties began to exist." Going back to the American Revolution, Paine lays bare Washington's mistakes and shows the importance of other men and special circumstances in achieving victory. Boiling over with bitterness and wrath, he assails Washington personally, as incapable of sympathy or friendship and possessed of a "cold, hermaphrodite faculty" which makes him "serve or desert a man, or a cause, with constitutional indifference." The last sentence is one of the most devastating appraisals ever made by one public figure upon another: "As to you, Sir, treacherous in private friendship (for so you have been to me, and that in the day of danger) and a hypocrite in public life, the world will be puzzled to decide whether you are an apostate or an imposter; whether you have abandoned good principles, or whether you ever had any."

When Paine's public letter arrived in America to play its part in the Federalist-Republican struggle, Washington remained silent, except to complain to a correspondent that it contained "absolute falsehoods"—he did not specify them —and that it was being "disseminated with great industry." Washington had become habituated to abuse. After the emergence of his anti-French policy, the capstone of his aristocratic administration, he was far from being first in the hearts of all his countrymen. It is an historic fact that only one or two other Presidents have been as widely unpopular and as violently execrated as Washington was from 1793 through 1796.

In the spring of 1797 Paine published his revised pamphlet, *Agrarian Justice,* which he had written in 1796. It was now a timely contribution. The problem of alleviating poverty and hunger by something more positive than the abolition of aristocracy had been sharply emphasized by the recent abortive conspiracy of Babeuf. Carrying the theories of Marat to an extreme conclusion, the journalist Babeuf and his followers had plotted a violent coup to oust the bourgeois government of the Directory and to institute a régime of the propertyless and disfranchised. If Babeuf had succeeded, he might have established a socialistic sort of government which would probably have been drowned in its own blood by the French bourgeoisie in alliance with the foreign armies. Though Paine sympathized with the Babouvist denunciation of the Constitution of 1795 as illegal and counter-revolutionary, he did not see how democracy could be furthered by adding a new civil war to the difficulties of the Revolution. In opposition both to the so-called agrarian law (the equal dividing-up of all the land and its improvements) and the restoration of the old agrarian monopolies he offered a middle course in *Agrarian Justice*.

The pamphlet is practical and eloquent, closely reasoned and passionately argued. How can the aged, the blind, and the infirm be provided for? How can the young be given a decent start in life? Individual charity will not suffice. "It is only by organizing civilization upon such principles as to act like a system of pullies, that the whole weight of misery can be removed." The land belongs to all, and this common property should revert to all through a system of ground-rents collected by the state at the time of inheritance. Commercial wealth should also be required to contribute, for it cannot exist without society and "if we examine the case minutely, it will be found that the accumulation of personal property is, in many instances, the effect of paying too little for the labour that produced it." Paine goes beyond the social security scheme of *The Rights of Man,* which drew its funds mainly from eliminating the useless expensiveness of aristocracy, towards a solution of the social question based entirely upon taxing the rich for the benefit of the poor. Let every young man at the age of twenty-one be given fifteen pounds; let the incapacitated, including those over the age of fifty, be given an annual pension of ten pounds each. This will not revolutionize property relations, but will safeguard the rich by protecting the poor. Soberly and laboriously Paine demonstrates from governmental figures that his theories can work. With his old superlatively vibrant utterance he makes them alive and momentous. "It is not charity but a right, not bounty but justice, that I am pleading for. The present state of civilization is as odious as it is unjust. It is absolutely the opposite of what it should be, and it is necessary that a revolution should be made in it. The contrast of affluence and wretchedness continually meeting and offending the eye, is like dead and living bodies chained together." What a wonderful, irresistible attractiveness the French Revolution would exert over the whole world if it were known that France encouraged the young and took care of the old! "An army of principles will penetrate where an army of soldiers cannot; it will succeed where diplomatic management would fail: it is neither the Rhine, the Channel, nor the Ocean that can arrest its progress: it will march on the horizon of the world, and it will conquer."

Paine's proposal of ten and fifteen pound donations was not very radical even for its own time, but it was too advanced for the Directory. It had no effect beyond establishing the author as economically a middle-of-the-road figure with a definite plan. Politically he remained an extreme democrat. The preface had contained a dangerously bold appeal for the reestablishment of universal suffrage.

Though Paine would never endorse the undemocratic franchise under the Directory, he could not help giving the Directory his support. It was after all the nearest possible approximation to his revolutionary ideal, for socialistic Jacobinism and the infinitely more odious old régime were the only other choices. Paine endorsed the religious program of the Directors and the social implications of that program. The Directors believed in the formal separation of Church and State and in a variety of counterbalancing

282

religious sects. Since the Roman Catholic Church, affiliated with the Pope, the Pretender, and the aristocratic émigrés, was strong and dangerous to the Republic, the Directors tried to weaken or if possible to destroy it. They encouraged a civic religion, the Decadal Cult, consisting of a series of national festivals and the substitution of the tenth day on the revolutionary calendar for the Christian Sabbath. The philosophic Director, La Révellière-Lépeaux, welcomed the efforts of the publisher Chemin in the winter of 1796-97 to organize a Society of Theophilanthropists for non-sectarian worship of God and the cultivation of moral sentiments. Secret governmental funds paid for the simple altars, pulpits, and decorative placards bearing moral aphorisms, which marked the Theophilanthropist sections of the common churches. At their meetings the Theophilanthropists began by invoking the Father of Nature and searching their consciences in a Quaker-like silence. Then they listened to speeches, sang hymns about the seasons, paid tribute to eminently great and good men such as Socrates, St. Vincent de Paul, Rousseau, and Washington. Leading French intellectuals—Dupont de Nemours, Bernardin de Saint-Pierre, Marie-Joseph Chénier, the painter David, and others—attended the services, and Dr. Walker translated the *Manuel des Théophilanthropes* into English. Paine delivered a discourse to the Society asserting the existence of God. He would have liked to see a deistic society strong in its negations as well as its affirmations and he could hardly be at ease while Washington was being eulogized, but he recognized in Theophilanthropy the seed out of which the natural religion of the future might grow.

On the religious issue revolved the French political struggle of 1797. The Directory and the two legislative Councils had hitherto worked in harmony to consolidate a bourgeois republic. After the suppression of the Babouvist conspiracy in 1796, the Republic was threatened from the opposite end by the partizans of the old régime. English money and the royalist press, exploiting the popular discontent, were instrumental in the election of 1797 in bringing a clerical-royalist majority into the Councils, pitted against the bourgeois Directors. On the 12th of June, in the newly constituted Council of Five Hundred, Camille Jordan delivered a grandiloquently pathetic plea for a return of some of its old privileges to the Catholic Church. Ostensibly in the name of religious freedom this church-and-king politician entreated that the people be allowed "to follow the religion of their hearts in peace, to choose their ministers at will, and to rest in the bosom of their most sacred customs," one of which was the "innocent pleasure" of hearing the church bells again.

In his impassioned *Letter to Camille Jordan* Paine denounces the hollow chatter about the comforts of religion. "It is a want of feeling," he says, "to talk of priests and bells whilst so many infants are perishing in the hospitals, and aged and infirm poor in the streets, from the want of necessaries. The abundance that France produces is sufficient for every want, if rightly applied; but priests and bells, like articles of luxury, ought to be the least articles of consideration," and "One good schoolmaster is of more use than a hundred priests." Not the return of the priests, "the patrons of debauchery and domestic infidelity," but the improvement of social conditions ought to be the aim of the Councils. "Let France," he pleads, "exhibit to the world the glorious example of expelling ignorance and misery together."

Though Jordan could not make the church bells ring,

284

his faction won the repeal of laws against refractory priests and there was even some discussion about requiring no declaration of loyalty from the priesthood. Royalist agents of counter-revolution streamed back over the borders of France to incite new attacks on the Constitution and the Republic, while the Directors, having no veto power over legislation, issued proclamation after proclamation against the royalist menace. The royalists dominated the legislative Councils and the Club de Clichy and counted on the support of the royalist-minded Directors Barthélemy and Carnot; the republicans were organized around the Constitutional Club and three of the Directors—Barras, Reubel, and La Révellière-Lépeaux.

The conflict between revolution and counter-revolution came to a head on the 4th of September (the 18th of Fructidor). Although the Councils had been unsuccessful in seeking to oust three Ministers favorable to the Directory, they had decreed the closing of the Constitutional Club, and the Club had complied. But a Directorial army more than 12,000 strong had been bivouacked on the outskirts of Paris. On the 3rd of September the Councils decreed the mobilization of the National Guard preliminary to decrees contemplated for the next day impeaching the three republican Directors, declaring martial law, and ordering the Directorial army to retire. The republican Directors beat the Councils to the game. During the night the troops entered the city and occupied strategic points. In the morning they shot a few cannon-balls into the air. The legislative guard beginning to cheer for the Directory, the Councils had to admit a bloodless defeat. The Directory nullified the election of nearly two hundred councilors and ordered the deportation of fifty royalist leaders, includ-

285

ing Barthélemy and Carnot. The *coup d'état* of the 18th of Fructidor destroyed the royalist party.

Paine had opposed the Constitution of 1795 for its bourgeois exclusiveness, which in a heated moment he had declared to signify the dismal end of the Revolution. But, when the Republic so constituted was in danger, like other democratic theorists and even the remaining Babouvists, he stood by it against the Bourbons and their aristocratic and clerical cohorts. He had been an active member of the short-lived Constitutional Club. In his pamphlet *The Eighteenth Fructidor* he fitted into the fabric of his democratic dream this "extraordinary measure, not warranted by established constitutional rules, and justifiable only on the supreme law of absolute necessity." Yet even in this defense he insists on his old objection. "The only defect in the Constitution is that of having narrowed the right of suffrage; and it is in a great measure due to this narrowing the right, that the last elections have not generally been good."

The Directory, with the staunch republicans Merlin and François in place of Carnot and Barthélemy, was now at the height of its power. It renewed the legislation against émigrés and refractory priests and gave fresh encouragement to the Decadal Cult and Theophilanthropy. In October, 1797, the treaty of Campo-Formio awarded France control over Lombardy and Belgium. The triumphant and unified French Republic had only the British enemy to reckon with on the field of battle.

It was therefore a nation which dominated the continent of Europe that the Federalist rulers of the United States addressed for a stoppage of depredations on American commerce. A year had gone by since the end of Monroe's mission. After the recall of Monroe, Washington had appointed

Charles Cotesworth Pinckney ambassador to France. Pinckney was an extreme Federalist, fully as obnoxious to the Directory as Hamilton or Jay. It would have been sheer vexation and a waste of time to negotiate with him. Paine wrote to Foreign Minister Delacroix a memorandum recommending that Pinckney should not be formally received until his recess appointment had been confirmed by the Senate; but the angry Directors refused to receive Pinckney at all. They recalled their own ambassador to America, poured out their compliments and regrets on Monroe, and ordered Pinckney to leave the country. The news of the American elections of 1796 aggravated French bitterness. The campaign had been waged mainly on the issue of foreign policy, and the victory of Adams over Jefferson sanctioned and perpetuated the pro-British course of Washington.

An irreconcilable spirit ruled in Philadelphia as well as in Paris. The two republics were drifting towards a war which would have been disgraceful to both and from the viewpoint of their relative strength in the winter of 1797-98 calamitous for America. In this dangerous situation the American friends of the French Republic labored to iron out the differences and keep the peace. In America Jefferson opposed the warlike tendencies of the administration and in Paris Paine with the assistance of Joel Barlow and Fulwar Skipwith, former American Consul General, tried to placate the bellicose Directory.

In October, 1797, Charles Cotesworth Pinckney returned to Paris, accompanied by the two other American Commissioners, John Marshall and Elbridge Gerry. The reappointment of Pinckney had not been welcome in France, nor the appointment of Marshall, an outstanding champion of the

Jay Treaty; but the presence of the Republican Gerry offered a slight hope of an amicable solution. In the background of the negotiations, in the early stage, stood the figure of Thomas Paine, American citizen and confidant of the Directory, as peacemaker. France had just achieved internal unification and foreign victory, and French passion ran high against Adams's denunciation of the Directorial compliments to Monroe and insults to Pinckney. It was not a propitious moment for the Americans to demand freedom for neutral commerce and payment for previous depredations. The new Foreign Minister, the scheming Talleyrand, put the Americans off and the Directors evinced no desire to see them. In a few days an American by the name of Church, seeking out Gerry, came upon Marshall alone. On the authority of Thomas Paine, Church revealed that the Directors were planning regulations for neutral commerce which would be extremely advantageous to the United States, but that by undue haste the Commissioners might ruin everything. That night they received a letter from Paine himself in similar spirit, with some sharp criticism of the American Government. The Commissioners, agreeing that Paine spoke for the Directory, were divided on how to proceed. Marshall urged a haughty coldness to Paine, while Gerry favored more discussion with him. Pinckney siding with Marshall, the Commissioners refused to deal with their own fellow-citizen; but they did listen to the shady intriguers known to history as Mr. X., Mr. Y. and Mr. Z., who spoke in the name of Talleyrand. The French leaders, flushed with success, contemptuous and impatient, unfortunately mixed the grievances of the French people with personal greed in trying to drive an impossible bargain. Through his emissaries Talleyrand demanded a public loan and "something for the pocket" of the Directors and the Ministry before the consideration of American claims. The secret shakedown might have been arranged—was not America paying tribute to the Barbary pirates?—but the public loan would have been an act of war against Great Britain which the Federalist administration would not dream of committing. The conferences ended in March, 1798, in a burst of anger from both sides. Marshall and Pinckney left Paris. Gerry stayed on, for Talleyrand had warned him that France would immediately declare war if he left with his colleagues.

When the scandalous nature of the XYZ Affair became known in America, the war fever of the Hamiltonian faction swept over the nation with a stirring slogan, "Millions for defense, but not one cent for tribute!" President Adams recalled Gerry and was huzzahed throughout the land for his declaration that he would "never send another minister to France without assurances that he will be received, respected, and honored as the representative of a great, free, powerful, and independent nation." Republican members of Congress equally with the Federalists voted to abrogate the existing treaties with France. Washington came out of his retirement to organize and lead an American army. Merchantmen were armed, warships were ordered to seize French vessels preying on American commerce. Battles occurred in the coastal waters. France and America were at war without a formal declaration.

Still the American friends of the French Revolution and the international cause of democracy fought against war. They desperately appealed to France for a change of heart. In the summer of 1798 a Philadelphia Quaker, Dr. George Logan, appointed himself an ambassador of peace from the

American democrats to the French Republic. He arrived in Paris in August, bearing a letter of introduction from Vice President Jefferson attesting to his "good morals, irreproachable conduct, and true civism." According to Bonneville's paper, *Le Bien Informé,* for the 24th of August, it was Citizen Thomas Paine who introduced Logan to the French Government and obtained for him a generous welcome. The French press applauded Logan as a real peace envoy, Talleyrand received him cordially, Director Merlin honored him with a lavish banquet. Logan returned to America to publicize his impression that France was genuinely interested in negotiating for peace.

Talleyrand was now aware that he had overshot the mark in his corrupt dealing with the Commissioners. The French fleet had just suffered a crushing defeat at the hands of Nelson in the Battle of the Nile. British vessels manned by American sailors might sweep the French altogether from the seas. Talleyrand therefore stimulated friendly conversations at The Hague between Pichon, the French Secretary of Legation, and Vans Murray, the American ambassador. "After all," the wily Foreign Minister wrote Pichon on the 28th of August in a letter destined for the eyes of Murray, "distrust alone has done the whole. The Government of the United States has thought that France wanted to revolutionize it. France has thought that the Government of the United States wanted to throw itself into the arms of England." Knowing Paine's ill repute with the Federalist administration, Talleyrand coolly denied the truth of the item in *Le Bien Informé* and said that Dr. Logan met Paine only once and "found him so prejudiced against the United States, and so opinionative, with respect to an influence he neither possesses among them nor us, that he abstained from conversing any more with him." For his diplomatic purpose Talleyrand conveniently forgot that he had written Paine a few months before thanking him for his "valuable light," and that Paine and Barlow were in close association with the Director La Révellière-Lépeaux. In October Barlow wrote a letter to Washington, stating that the dispute was "simply and literally, *a misunderstanding*," and that "The balance of inclination as well as of interest, on both sides, is in favor of peace." Forwarding this letter to President Adams, Washington remarked that obviously Barlow spoke for a pacific-minded Directory.

If war could be avoided, Adams would avoid it, even if in so doing he might seem to favor the Republican party fed by the "spissitude of the black liquor" from Thomas Paine. To his eternal credit, to the amazement of the nation and wild fury of the Hamiltonians, Adams sent to the Senate on the 18th of February, 1799, the nomination of Vans Murray as minister to France. The war bubble had burst.

Paine, who had striven to bring the two republics together in unity, did not strut upon the stage of public life. He spent most of the time in his room at the work-bench, enjoying the work-play of all sorts of mechanical experiments. He constructed an improved crane. He invented a machine for planing boards into the shape of wheels, and Robert Fulton made a drawing of it. He experimented with gunpowder as a substitute for steam in turning the wheels of industry. And he returned to his great scientific love, the arch-bridge, his "pontifical works." First he made a delicate model in pasteboard, five feet in span and five inches high from the cords. Then he molded blocks of lead into another model of the same proportions. Late one night, removing the scaffold, he tested the work by repeated banging with a hammer. Elated at seeing the model hold firm, he could not keep the miracle or joy to himself. He ran down to the Bonnevilles and almost dragged them out of bed. "Come and look," he cried; "it bears all my blows and stands like a rock!" The Bonnevilles had to go up with him and stand in respectful admiration before the bridge while he sang its glories. "Nothing in the world," he exulted, "is so fine as my bridge,"—"except," he quickly added, his eyes resting on Madame Bonneville, "a woman!" At any hour of day or night the Rue du Théâtre Français might suddenly reverberate with fire-cracker explosions or the hammer's bang-bang from the workshop of the wonderful American.

So, under the tutelage of the Directory, Citizen Paine lived and labored—a builder of bridges, peace, democracy, security, political and spiritual freedom for all men.

But he was no match for Napoleon Bonaparte.

CHAPTER XXIII

The First Consul and the Last Republican

THE record of Napoleon Bonaparte reads almost like a page out of *The Rights of Man* illustrating the seizure of power by brigandage. The Corsican adventurer mutilated the revolutionary ideal and destroyed the prestige of the revolutionary theorists. Though Napoleon could not wipe out the solid social benefits arising from the abolition of the aristocratic order, he succeeded in completely overriding the great revolutionary principle of self-government by the people. He lavished upon France glory, land, markets —and multitudinous death on the battlefield. Democracy was crushed for more than a generation; and its most renowned apostle, thrown into the discard by the sequence of events, had to look elsewhere for a haven and a rostrum.

The young Napoleon built up a glamorous repute in serving the Directory which he came to destroy. As commander of the Parisian guard in 1795 he routed a royalist putsch against the new Directorial government. It was a division of his army which accomplished the coup of the 18th of Fructidor, and his extraordinary triumphs in the Italian campaign produced the advantageous peace of Campo-Formio. But already, in 1797, the twenty-eight-year-old hero aspired to the purple splendor of Alexander and Charlemagne. "Do you suppose that I gain victories to increase the glory of the lawyers of the Directory?" he snapped to his confidants that summer. "The nation wants a chieftain covered with glory, and cares nothing for theories of government, fine words, or dreams of idealists." On his return to Paris in the winter, affecting a modest aversion for the plaudits and honors of the grateful Republic, he put on the plain clothes and quiet manners of a civilian. At the celebration by the Directory the Foreign Minister Talleyrand, who had hitched his wagon to the rising star, praised the victorious general for simple and studious habits and civic devotion. Napoleon responded that throughout Europe the era of dominance by religion, feudalism, and monarchy was yielding everywhere to the era of self-government. He intimated, however, that France was not yet established on "the best organic laws." The inference was plain for whoever cared to make it—that the Republic might apply for these laws to the speaker himself, a genius equally in the arts of war and peace.

The Hero of Italy made overtures to the philosophic "dreamers" whom he secretly despised. On visiting Paine he gushed profuse compliments to the great republican author. He declared that he slept with a copy of *The Rights of Man* under his pillow and that Paine deserved a statue of gold in every city in the world. Nothing would please him better, he said, than to be honored with Paine's correspondence and advice.

Paine acknowledged the gesture as a tribute to his integrity and soon acted accordingly. The Directors had conceived the project of sending an army under Napoleon to invade the only remaining enemy, the "giant corsair" England. As one who knew England and the English terrain, Paine was invited to attend a discussion by the military council. There Napoleon, eager to sustain his glory, advocated the invasion with hysterical enthusiasm. The engineers hesitated. They feared the English fleet, they remarked that there was no Bonny Prince Charles, around whom to foment a popular movement against George III. "General," said D'Arçon, "the earth is our own, but not the sea. We must recruit our fleets, before we can hope to make any impression on England, and even then, the enterprize would be fraught with perdition, unless we could raise a diversion among the people." Napoleon shot back, "That is the very point I mean; here is Citizen Paine, who will tell you that the whole English nation, except the royal family, and the Hanoverians who have been created peers of the realm and absorb the greatest part of the land property, are ardently burning for fraternization." Paine refused to take the hint. It did not agree with his view at all; he had learned to respect the domestic strength of Pitt's government. "It is now several years since I have been in England," he said, "and therefore I can only judge of it by what I knew when I was there. I think the people are very disaffected, but I am sorry to add that, if the expedition should escape the fleet, I think the army would be cut in pieces. The only way to kill England is to annihilate her commerce." Napoleon asked how long it would take to do that. Paine replied that everything depended on peace—a revolting idea to a military adventurer not yet prepared to seize power. Napoleon never spoke to Paine again.

The invasion of England was not yet abandoned. The Directors sent Napoleon to reconnoiter the coast and they began the building of a thousand gunboats. On the 28th of January, in spite of his misgivings, Paine contributed a hundred livres for the invasion to the Council of Five Hundred. "There will be no lasting peace for France, nor for the world," he declared in the accompanying note, "until the tyranny and corruption of the English government be abolished, and England, like Italy, become a sister republic." Paine supported the project because he had become a part of it. He submitted a plan of attack to Director La Révellière-Lépeaux and he accompanied the expedition to Belgium, from where the descent was to be made. An English spy reported to his government in utter seriousness that the French planned to execute the King, most of the royal family, and a goodly number of ministers, nobles, clergymen, and bankers, and deport the rest of those groups; and that the Directory scheduled for England was "Paine, Tooke, Sharpe, Thelwall, Lansdown." But the whole scheme of invasion came to nothing when Napoleon suddenly decided that it was impracticable at that time.

Napoleon had merely exchanged one adventure for another. He represented to the Directors that an expedition through the Mediterranean to the East would threaten the British Empire in India, thereby dividing the British fleet and simplifying a future invasion of England. On the 19th of May, with a grand army of 40,000 men on 400 transports, he set sail from Toulon to rival the exploits of Alexander while the Directory shifted for itself against an aristocratic Europe itching to resume the continental war.

During the year and a half in which Napoleon was posing before the Pyramids and wrestling with the British navy and Syrian and Turkish armies, the French Republic lost the international prestige of Campo-Formio and the domestic unification of the 18th of Fructidor. The second Coalition of aristocratic governments tore Italy out of French hands and menaced the French hegemony in Switzerland and along the Rhine frontier. The left republicans accused the Directors of corruption and responsibility for the de-

feats, and, winning popular support and threatening outlawry and death, they forced the resignations of Treilhard,
Merlin, and La Révellière-Lépeaux. A Jacobin spirit was
reasserting itself to save the Republic.

On the 9th of October, 1799, having deserted his army in
Egypt, Napoleon landed in southern France and proceeded
to Paris in a continuous pageant of glorification. Again posing as a modest civilian, he frequented the company of scientists and philosophers—Monge, Berthollet, Chaptal, Caba-
nis, Laplace, and others—who marveled at the intellectual
interests and civic talents of the young warrior. But he
played no tricks on Paine. At the banquet given to the
Generals of the Republic, as Napoleon was walking by
Paine, the general fixed his wild gray eyes full upon the
republican author and sneered in a loud aside to General
Lannes, "The English are all alike in every country,—they
are all rascals."

Another intellectual, Paine's old adversary the Abbé
Sieyès, who had come out of hiding after the Reign of
Terror and had worked himself into membership in the
Directory, saw in Napoleon a military instrument for the
realization of his long-cherished dream to strengthen the
executive power. The two conspirators won over the Director Ducos, intimidated the other Directors, and on the 18th
of Brumaire (November 9, 1799) caused the removal of the
legislative Councils from the Jacobin-infested Paris to St.
Cloud. On the next day Napoleon and his battalion dispersed the Councils. The Directory was dead, and the nation found herself willy-nilly under the government of three
provisional Consuls, Napoleon, Sieyès, and Ducos. In a
month the new rulers offered France the Constitution of
the Consulate, Napoleon's alterations on the brain-child of

Sieyès. Universal suffrage, the great original political objective of the Revolution, was restored and obliterated at the same time, the people being permitted not to elect but to nominate. The First Consul, Napoleon, would make the appointments and govern the country for the next ten years. The Corsican adventurer was on top.

Paine did not like the coup of Brumaire. He wrote no pamphlet extolling it. He could not incorporate into his theory of free government a Constitution that sanctioned one-man dictatorship. But he had grown used to living in hope, and he hoped that the Napoleonic despotism was a passing phase. After all, the Republic still existed.

While the First Consul returned to the congenial theater of war, Citizen Paine exerted his own talents to strengthen the international position of the French Republic, still the beacon-light for republicans the world over. Once more he tried to win America to the side of France. In the spring of 1800 the American Commissioners Oliver Ellsworth and William Davie joined their colleague Vans Murray in Paris to resume the American claims against French interference with neutral commerce. The American Commissioners did not return the visits of Skipwith and Barlow, and they let it be known that they did not wish the company of Paine. That was of course enough to attract him, and he promptly called on Ellsworth to argue the French side of the controversy. Ellsworth, who was also Chief Justice of the Supreme Court, sat stiff and uncomfortable as if listening to a cantankerous attorney in a trial. "I mean not," said Paine, "to press you with any questions, or to engage you in any conversation upon the business you are come upon, but I will nevertheless candidly say that I know not what expectations the Government or the people of America may have of your mission, or what expectations you may have yourselves, but I believe you will find you can do but little. The treaty with England lies at the threshold of all your business. The American Government never did two more foolish things than when it signed that treaty and recalled Mr. Monroe, who was the only man could do them any service." The Commissioners did not return Paine's visit.

Paine overstressed the French case. Talleyrand, who had quit the service of the Directory only to return to power as Napoleon's Foreign Minister, was ready to compromise with the strait-laced Americans whom he had almost incited to war in the disgraceful XYZ Affair. After much protracted jockeying, it was finally agreed by the Convention of 1800 that France should quit seizing American ships engaged in neutral commerce and that America should abandon her claims for previous depredations.

Talleyrand's concession to America was part of a large naval scheme in which Paine played an important rôle. The maritime commerce of the neutral nations of the North was suffering under the interference of the British fleet, and Napoleon sought to encourage their opposition to the strong arm of his deadliest enemy. By flattery and petty concessions the First Consul prevailed upon the half-mad Paul of Russia to abandon the Coalition and to rally Denmark, Sweden, and Prussia into a compact of neutrals aimed against Great Britain. In the summer of 1800 Paine drew up a *Pacte Maritime* as a constitution of neutrality providing that neutral ships should have free access to the ports of any belligerent nation at the consent of that nation, and that rules pertaining to contraband should be promulgated and enforced by the neutral powers themselves. Barlow and Skipwith circulated Bonneville's translation of the *Pacte* among the neutral envoys in Paris, and the Russian general Spring-norten took several copies to the Czar. Napoleon spun his grandiose rhetoric about "sacred principles" and "the common cause of all Continental Powers," declaring that France would not treat for peace until "the Russian, Danish, Swedish, American, and Prussian flags shall be respected on the sea as the armies of these Powers are on land, and until England shall have acknowledged that the sea belongs to all nations." Paine's program called for resistance by economic boycotts. The Armed Neutrality of the North, however, not only placed embargoes on British vessels but met force with force and challenged British supremacy in the Baltic. America did not join, and the British victory at Copenhagen and the assassination of Paul put an end to the Armed Neutrality in June, 1801.

It was becoming increasingly apparent to Paine that Napoleon's France afforded no home for an irreconcilable democrat. In the summer of 1800, when the First Consul returned from his Austrian victories, he seized on the flimsiest pretexts to rid himself of republican opponents, executing them by scores and deporting them by hundreds. Paine was not in the favor of the First Consul and he would not seek it. Rather than the Palace of the Tuileries, he preferred the society of Irish and Polish revolutionists in the back rooms of greasy taverns in the working-class faubourgs. But these few staunch republicans with their following even smaller than the Babouvists could not fight Napoleon. Already in October, even in the midst of his efforts for the Maritime Compact, Paine wrote to Jefferson: "If any American frigate should come to France, and the direction of it fall to you, I will be glad you would give me the opportunity of returning."

While Democracy was passing into a long eclipse in Europe, it blazed in a new American splendor with the election of Thomas Jefferson to the Presidency in 1800. The American people repudiated the Adams administration, whose infamous Alien and Sedition Acts had attempted to make political opposition a criminal offense. The discredited Federalists wrung their hands at the imminence of mob rule under President Jefferson; the Republicans acclaimed the victory as a new Declaration of Independence and Jefferson spoke of it as the Revolution of 1800. In the spring of 1801 the Republican Congressman Dawson, coming to Paris for the final ratification of the treaty made with the Commissioners, bore a letter from Jefferson urging Paine to return with Dawson on the frigate *Maryland*. "I am in hopes," wrote the President, "you will find us returned generally to sentiments worthy of former times. In these it will be your glory to have steadily labored, and with as much effect as any man living. That you may long live to continue your useful labors and to reap the reward in the thankfulness of nations, is my sincere prayer." On the 9th of June, gladly returning the compliment, Paine declared, "I congratulate America on your election. There has been no circumstance with respect to America since the times of her revolution that excited so much attention and expectation in France, England, Ireland, and Scotland as the pending election for President of the United States, nor any of which the event has given more general joy." But since the Federalist papers were railing at the President for what could be pictured as sending a national ship to France, especially for the convenience of the demon of infidelity, Paine decided not to add fuel to their fires. He refused the return passage, though he needed a national ship or a miracle to get by the British cruisers which would regard the outlawed author of *The Rights of Man* as one of the richest prizes of the war.

Meanwhile, Napoleon was perfecting his despotism. The First Consul crowned his military conquests by sinuous diplomacy and advantageous treaties with all the hostile nations, including the Treaty of Amiens with England on the 25th of March, 1802, which made peace universal. The Pacificator of Europe turned to consolidate his power at home in a few swift strokes. He suppressed the rationalistic worship of the Theophilanthropists and won to his support a "sacred gendarmerie" by the Concordat with the Pope, arranging for payment by the state to Catholic priests and for the preponderance of the Catholic religion, church bells and all. He organized the Legion of Honor, a neo-aristocratic order for distinguished military and civic service to the Consulate. He obtained his life tenure in the Consulate. Napoleon was Emperor in all but name—a detail which he would attend to in due season. Adapting themselves to circumstances, the republican theorists who were not in prison or exile accepted his ribbons and occupied the seats in his mock-Senate. Almost alone, Paine remained articulate and true to the ideals of the Revolution. The greatest dreamer of them all was fully awake, dismayed, bitter, and irreconcilable in the presence of the new Caesarism. Not only in the intimate circle but even to random visitors he poured out his violent indignation at the dismal collapse of his ideals for a liberated human race.

Among the foreigners who flocked to Paris during the Peace of Amiens was the Englishman Henry Redhead Yorke. He had been a member of the British club which formed about Deputy Paine in Paris in the winter of 1792-93 and he had later as a radical agitator in England been

302

thrown into prison for two years; but, having experienced
a change of heart, he was now a partizan of the established
British system. However, since Yorke had lost no personal
admiration for his old leader, the lengthy Letter XLIII in
his *Letters from France* is probably in its essentials a true
sketch of Paine in 1802.

After considerable search—so quickly and so much had
Paine's importance dwindled—Yorke arrived at his dwelling-
place. "A jolly-looking woman," Madame Bonneville, having ascertained that the stranger's motives were friendly,
led him into Paine's little room. It was an unprepossessing
den, the chimney-hearth a heap of refuse, three shelves piled
high with pasteboard correspondence boxes, two large trunks
and various iron contraptions lying about, and opposite the
fireplace a board stacked with pamphlets and journals. Paine
came in, wearing a long flannel gown. "Time seemed to
have made dreadful ravages over his whole frame, and a
settled melancholy was visible on his countenance." Recog-
nizing the voice but not the identity of his guest, Paine frequently put his hand in puzzlement to his forehead while
Yorke, not giving his name, related some of the circumstances of their previous association. Suddenly Paine remembered. His face brightened, he pressed Yorke by the hand,
a tear stole down his cheek.

They had a genial rambling conversation or monologue,
Yorke touching off the sluices of Paine's thoughts on a
variety of subjects. Paine said that France was not a country
for an honest man to live in; that, after shedding blood
enough for liberty, the French had proved their ignorance
of the principles of free government. Surprised at Paine's
despondence, Yorke replied that something might yet be
done for the Republic. "Republic!" Paine exclaimed, "do

you call this a Republic? Why, they are worse off than the slaves at Constantinople; for there, they expect to be bashaws in heaven, by submitting to be slaves below, but here, they believe neither in heaven nor hell, and yet are slaves by choice. I know of no Republic in the world, except America, which is the only country for such men as you and I. It is my intention to get away from this place as soon as possible, and I hope to be off in autumn; you are a young man, and may see better times, but I have done with Europe, and its slavish politics." He gave Yorke two copies of Jefferson's Inaugural Address, which he had had printed by way of contrast with Napoleon. The thought of his friend Jefferson in the Presidency put an amusing idea in Paine's head. "It would be a curious circumstance," he laughed, "if I should hereafter be sent as Secretary of Legation to the English court, which outlawed me. What a hubbub it would create at the King's levee, to see Tom Paine presented by the American ambassador! All the bishops and women would faint away; the women would suppose I came to ravish them, and bishops to ravish their tythes"—a sarcasm ribald and angry, a true picture of Paine's standing with respectable society in his native land. But no, he would most likely never return to Europe. He would dispose of his American property, live on the interest, and amuse himself with mechanics and the writing of memoirs.

During another visit Yorke remarked that *The Age of Reason* had lost Paine the good opinion of many of his English advocates. That started Paine blazing away at the Christian religion. Passionately he affirmed that he would never have published that book if he had not thought it calculated to "inspire mankind with a more exalted idea of the Supreme Architect of the Universe, and to put an end to villainous impostures." In support of this opinion he was ready to lay down his life. "The Bishop of Landaff may roast me in Smithfield, if he likes, but human torture cannot shake my conviction." Yorke protested that the Bishop's book was a tolerant Apology. "Aye," replied Paine, "it is an Apology, indeed, for priestcraft; but parsons will meddle and make mischief; they always hurt their own cause, and make things worse than they were before; if he had said nothing, the church would have lost nothing; but I have another rod in pickle for *Mr. Bishop,*" and, reaching down a copy of the Bishop's *Apology,* he read a few passages and his own marginal comments for a projected reply. Finally, cooling a bit, he admitted the liberality of the Bishop and regretted that a similar temper was not always maintained in intellectual controversies.

One evening, at the request of an Englishwoman who was curious to meet the famous pamphleteer, Yorke invited Paine to dinner. Since the woman was a devout Roman Catholic and "felt tenderly" about religion, Yorke begged Paine beforehand not to touch upon religious matters and Paine good-humoredly consented. For more than four hours, the champagne enhancing sociability, Paine captivated his audience with comments and anecdotes on things American —the Indians, the Revolution, Washington, Franklin—and men and manners generally. But at a chance remark from one of the company about *The Age of Reason* he broke out on religion. Turning to Mrs. Yorke, he declared that the least inspection of the stars proved Moses to be a liar. The unhappy host Yorke tried to change the subject by attacking Paine's political theories, and, that failing, he asked for a song. Paine sang one of his own composition and immediately swung from astronomy to other arguments against the Christian system. "Every time he took breath," Yorke ruefully records, "he gained fresh strength, and on he went, with inconceivable rapidity, until the ladies gradually stole unobserved from the room, and left another gentleman and myself to contest, or rather to leave him master of the field of battle." Yorke reproached Paine for forgetting his promise and wounding the opinions of the ladies. "Oh!" said Paine, "they'll come again. What a pity it is that people should be so prejudiced!"

The Peace of Amiens having cleared the seas of hostile cruisers, there was no further necessity for staying in a France that gave no outlet for the energies of a democratic pamphleteer and sickened the democratic heart. Paine put his things in order and prepared to depart for America.

Thomas Rickman, his English friend and future biographer, came to Paris to say good-by. Together the two traveled to Havre de Grâce. Rickman has left no record of Paine's mood and thoughts at this time. The silence is eloquent of the utter desolation of spirit with which, after fifteen tremendous years of struggle for the democratic ideal, Paine at last, vanquished by Napoleon, turned his back on despotic Europe. September 1, 1802, the packet carried him away towards America.

As the packet faded out of sight beyond the quiet waters, the good-hearted Rickman, profoundly moved, wrote a few sentimental verses begging the waves to be smooth and gentle and to waft the wayfarer to the "blessing of freedom and friendship" among "the happy and free" on "LIBERTY's shore." But it was not Paine's destiny to find peace. He had a tempestuous voyage, and some of his "happy and free" fellow-citizens gave their old patriot a cruel homecoming because he did not worship at their altars.

CHAPTER XXIV

A Prophet in His Own Country

AFTER sixty days on the ocean Paine landed at Baltimore on the 30th of October, 1802, and a few days later he went on to Washington. Paine's blunt forthrightness had frequently embarrassed Jefferson and would do so again; but Jefferson, loving Paine as a kindred elder soul, welcomed him into the President's House. In that new city, with its cluster of boarding-houses and shops in the shadow of the Capitol a mile eastward from the President's House, the homecomer Paine stood out like a nine days' wonder. Republicans and Federalists watched, listened, tried to appraise him. "Years have made more impression on his body than his mind," wrote one sympathetic observer (in the Philadelphia *Aurora*). "He bends a little forward, carries one hand in the other when he walks. He dresses plain like a farmer, and appears cleanly and comfortable in his person, unless in the article of snuff which he uses in profusion. His address is unaffected and unceremonious. He neither shuns nor courts observation. At table he enjoys what is good with the appetite of temperance and vigor, and puts to shame his calumniators by the moderation with which he partakes of the common beverage of the boarders. His conversation is uncommonly interesting, he is gay, humorous, and full of anecdote—his memory preserves its full capacity, and his mind its irresistible and I may say its obstinate determination to pursue whatever object it embraces."

The Federalists did not paint Paine in such colors. He was the outstanding champion not only of increasingly popular republicanism but of increasingly unpopular deism, and they saw in him a convenient bogey—"famous throughout Europe and America, for his hatred to all government, human and divine"—with which to frighten good people away from the lure of Thomas Jefferson. Largely because of their malicious legends, deliberately concocted for political purposes, it is hard to know the real truth about Paine's old age. Long before he landed, they had assailed him as "the scavenger of faction," "that lying, drunken, brutal infidel," "whose abominable habits render him an object as offensive to the senses as his crimes make him abhorrent to the moral sentiments of mankind." Now that he was back in America, they found new epithets for him—"loathsome reptile," "demi-human arch-beast," "an object of disgust, of abhorrence, of absolute loathing to every decent man except the President of the United States."

Paine had come home from the revolutions of Europe with a yearning to lead at last a quiet life. But it was not in his nature to ignore the scurrilities and the factional animus behind them. He plunged into the fight in a series of *Letters to the Citizens of the United States*. "After an absence of almost fifteen years," he proclaimed in *Letter I*, "I am again returned to the country in whose dangers I bore my share, and to whose greatness I contributed my part." With high-spirited contempt he flung back the abuse of the Federalists. "In every part of the Union, this faction is in the agonies of death, and in proportion as its fate approaches, gnashes its teeth and struggles. My arrival has struck it as with an hydrophobia, it is like the sight of water to canine madness." In *Letter II* he riddled the claims of the Federalists to the credit of being the sole advocates of a national government and reminded the nation that he himself, a Republican, had made some of the first proposals towards that objective. The Federalists, he contended, always believed in monarchy and hereditaryship, and as far back as 1776 John Adams's head was "as full of kings, queens, and knaves, as a pack of cards. But John has lost deal." A political tug-of-war grew out of these letters. The Federalists added up the number of times Paine had used the pronoun I and they railed at the "flagrant and billingsgate attack, while seated at the elbow of the President, upon the hoary-headed and venerable Adams." The Republicans, shooting sarcasms at "the satellites of King George and King John in America," burlesqued the typical Federalist tone: "Fire!—age of reason! look what a long nose he has got! he drank all the brandy in Baltimore in nine days!" The nation rocked with Tom Paine.

Warming to the fight, in *Letter III* Paine laid ungentle hands upon two institutions which the Federalists considered their special and most precious property—the memory of George Washington, who had died in 1799, and the Christian religion. There was sorrow as well as bitterness in his reproach of the commander-in-chief whose military mistakes he had minimized in the *Crisis* papers in order to preserve the unity of American forces in the Revolution. "He accepted as a present (though he was already rich) a hundred thousand acres in America, and left me to occupy six foot of earth in France." Yet Providence, said Paine, has been kind, and in spite of many dangers and the chorus of "Crucify him, crucify him" has protected and nurtured the deist, bringing him in safety and health to the Promised

Land. Maybe Providence is herself an infidel, Paine whimsically suggests.

Now the Republican politicians took alarm at Paine. He was not playing their game at all. George Washington had already become a haloed national figure, his birthday celebrated by Republicans and Federalists alike; and even the lightest banter at the Christian dogma would not be tolerated in America. "Paine's third letter gives me considerable uneasiness," William Duane, editor of *The Aurora,* wrote to Jefferson on the 27th of November. "He has in fact commenced the subject of *The Age of Reason* in it." Being then in Washington, Duane called on Paine and begged him to quit preaching deism. He warned Paine that a continuance of such arguments would turn even the Republicans against him, would invalidate his political writings, would destroy his fame. Paine refused to hear him out. In 1776, he told Duane, he had been warned that Independence and Republicanism were dangerous words—but he had used them. And nothing would stop him now from exercising the right to express his religious views. It was a characteristic decision. "In taking up any public matter," he declared in *Letter IV,* "I have never made it a consideration, and never will, whether it be popular or unpopular; but whether it be *right* or *wrong*. The right will always become the popular, if it has courage to show itself, and the shortest way is always a straight line. I despise expedients." When the aged Samuel Adams gently reproved his "defense of infidelity," Paine replied in a courteous public letter, firm and serenely philosophic in reasserting his religious system and its integral principles, intellectual freedom and universal philanthropy. What is this thing called Infidelity? "If I do not believe as you believe, it proves that you do not believe as I believe, and this is all that it proves." The true religion is the religion of practical benevolence, and we have to answer for our theological opinions not to our fellow-men but to the Creator. "The key of heaven," he concluded, "is not in the keeping of any sect, nor ought the road to it be obstructed by any. Our relation to each other in this World is as Men, and the Man who is a friend to Man and to his rights, let his religious opinions be what they may, is a good citizen, to whom I can give, as I ought to do, and as every other ought, the right hand of fellowship, and to none with more hearty good-will, my dear friend, than to you." Humane, liberal sentiments— and practically political suicide in the United States of 1802.

Thomas Jefferson the philosopher agreed with these sentiments, but Thomas Jefferson the politician could not publicly profess them. The open deism of his friend Paine disturbed the President and forced him into conciliatory gestures to religious orthodoxy. Federalist members of Congress snickered at the spectacle of President Jefferson, suddenly converted, riding horseback through the rain-splashed swamps from the President's House to the Capitol in order to attend religious services. After a while Jefferson ceased his invitations to Paine. Quick to sense a slight, Paine wrote reproaching the President for "shyness." Jefferson rose promptly to the occasion. He had been busy, he protested, not "shy," and had "openly maintained in conversation the duty of showing our respect to you and of defying federal calumny in this as in other cases, by doing what is right." Calling again at the President's House, Paine was received with the old cordiality. "The defamer of Washington, and the vile blasphemer of his God, is still the table companion of our Chief Magistrate," groaned *The Connecticut Courant* on the 9th of February. Yes, and he would always be welcome while Thomas Jefferson was the Chief Magistrate.

In the spring of 1803 Paine returned to Bordentown. His old friend Kirkbride, flouting that sleepy Federalist village, took Paine into his house. John Hall, the assistant of Paine's first bridge-building days, visited him. "He was well and appeared jollyer than I had ever known him," Hall noted in his diary. "He is full of whims and schemes and mechanical inventions, and is to build a place or shop to carry them into execution, and wants my help." From Bordentown Paine wrote steadily for the newspapers, offering his bridge ideas free to the nation and time and again laying the lash on the Federalists. In his seventh *Letter to the Citizens of the United States,* in order to silence Federalist misinterpretation, he published the much-discussed letter from Jefferson inviting him to America. The Federalists immediately seized upon the wish, "That you may long live to continue your useful labours," and pestered the President with sneering inquiries about these "useful labours." Still Jefferson stuck by Paine. In August long letters passed between Monticello and Bordentown concerning the chief problem of the hour, the extent and future government of the Louisiana Purchase. The indefatigable sixty-six-year-old Paine beheld in this vast new acquisition another field in which to spread the gospel of freedom. "I have half a disposition to visit the Western World next spring and go on to New Orleans," he wrote to Senator Breckenridge. "They are a new people and unacquainted with the principles of representative government and I think I could do some good among them." Meanwhile, in leisure hours over a nip of brandy in Deborah Applegate's inn he was ready for all comers to converse and argue on politics and religion.

In the remote village with his old neighbors Paine was personally on safe ground. When he ventured out, he was liable to the barbarities of religious fanaticism fostered by political hate. In March of 1803 on a trip to New York he got his first strong taste of pious blood-lust in America. At Trenton, two stage-drivers refused him a seat. "I'll be damned if he shall go in my stage," said one, and the other agreed, "My stage and horses were once struck by lightning, and I don't want them to suffer again." A gang of young Federalist hoodlums gathered at the stage-depot, jeered and catcalled, beat the rogue's march on a drum. Paine took it all calmly; persecution had no terrors for him. How simple, he must have thought, to fight the tyrants of the body; how hard, how lonely, to challenge the insidious tyrants of the mind. He got out of Trenton somehow and reached New York, where the Republicans in power gave him a great banquet at the City Hotel and hostile fanatics did not dare to strike openly. Less eventful was the visit to Philadelphia, where on the 29th of May Paine sat down with more than sixty diners at the Franklin Hotel in the room which had been Franklin's library, rich in memories. At both the New York and Philadelphia celebrations Paine was eulogized as the fearless writer of *Common Sense* and *The Rights of Man*. That he was also the fearless writer of *The Age of Reason* was quietly ignored.

When, after the excitement of homecoming had waned, Paine looked about him for the bread and butter of his last years, he saw a discouraging prospect. He had figured vaguely that his Bordentown and New Rochelle properties were more than enough to assure him simple comfort. Now he discovered that his Bordentown house was worth very little and the tenant was not accustomed to paying rent regularly; and that the New Rochelle tenant, having kept the place in order, did not feel indebted to him at all. Since Paine had never bothered or thought it necessary to get a title-deed for his New Rochelle farm, he could not readily dispose of it in whole or part. Furthermore, in the summer of 1803, Madame Bonneville, accepting his general invitation to the family, came out with her children as Paine's guest; Bonneville himself was under police surveillance as a radical agitator and was not permitted to leave France. So it happened through an expansive impulse that Paine was encumbered with a French woman who could not speak English and three boys, the oldest only fourteen—a new and oppressive responsibility to one who had grown used to living unto himself. The last six years of his life were destined to be an unravelable tangle of personal economic difficulties; and his super-normal public spirit functioned both as an escape from and as an increasing aggravation of those difficulties.

As a means of easing his financial anxieties, Paine intended to spend the winter of 1803-04 in cutting wood on his New Rochelle farm for the New York market. But while staying in New York he was stricken with the gout, and during his convalescence, he had a severe fall on the ice in the garden. The wood-cutting had to be abandoned. Personal anxieties, however, were pushed out of mind by the engrossing political situation at home and abroad. The American election campaign was in progress, and in Europe the Napoleonic Wars were again raging. Realizing that his open advocacy might be a liability for Jefferson rather than an asset, Paine did not participate in the campaign except to endorse the administration indirectly in newspaper articles and in two important pamphlets.

The first pamphlet concerned the European struggle. As between George III and Napoleon, Paine did not long hesitate. In spite of his repugnance for Napoleon, he believed that the best ultimate interests of mankind were connected with the triumph of French arms; for he sensed the tremendous reaction that would follow a victory by the Coalition. He even imagined that the invasion of England, which Napoleon was again projecting with eloquent promises to liberate the English people, might usher in the glorious birthday of English freedom which he had heralded in *The Rights of Man*. Too sick from his fall on the ice to hold a pen, he dictated *To the People of England*. Why should the English people, he asked, support their tyrants, their government of mystery and show, in futile combat with Napoleon? It is better to avert the horrors of the Napoleonic invasion by setting up a free government on the American model, for "We see America flourishing in peace, cultivating friendship with all nations, and reducing her public debt and taxes." But Napoleon suddenly abandoned the project, and Paine's advice and lurid warnings lost their pointedness.

The second pamphlet dealt with the Louisiana situation. The French merchants and planters of Louisiana had drawn up a memorial hotly contending that the autocratic régime fastened upon them by the American Government was a violation of American ideals; it was no less a democrat than Thomas Paine who gave them the sufficient answer in *To the French Inhabitants of Louisiana*. The people of Louisiana may rely upon the democratic President Jefferson, "who is not only not a man of intrigue but who possesses that honest pride of principle that cannot be intrigued with, and which keeps intriguers at a distance." The memorialists, unaware of the irony, had asked for the "right" to import slaves. "Dare you put up a petition to Heaven for such a power," cried Paine, always the consistent advocate of Negro freedom, "without fearing to be struck from the earth by its justice? Why, then, do you ask it of man against man?"

In New York Paine joined in the courageous efforts of Elihu Palmer and John Foster to develop a Deistic Society. He attended their meetings in rented hotel rooms and helped to dispense the gospel of reason and philanthropy to small audiences of working-men and shopkeepers. To Palmer's short-lived monthly magazine, *The Prospect,* Paine contributed several deistic articles and a jibe at the Connecticut blue laws, which "make a labour of rest." Thus Paine and his associates nurtured a feeble movement for humane and rational religion in America, which limped into a later day to merge with new and more critical opponents of literal Christianity.

The New York atmosphere was as congenial as Paine could expect in America. The fuming of religious bigots and political malcontents was impotent here. Republicans big and little, including Mayor DeWitt Clinton, honored him and enjoyed his company in strolls on bustling Broadway or under the poplar trees in Battery Park. Paine knew these fellow-Republicans too well to attempt converting them to unpopular deism. One evening at a dinner given by Dr. Nicholas Romayne, the most distinguished physician in the city, the journalist-politician John Pintard tried to tease Paine into a religious discussion. "I have read and re-read your *Age of Reason,*" said Pintard, "and my doubts which I before entertained of the truth of revelation have been removed by your logic. Yes, sir, your very arguments against Christianity have convinced me of its truth." "Well, then," answered Paine, with a sarcastic gleam, "I may return to my couch tonight with the consolation that I have made at least *one* Christian."

Many other Americans—not the majority, but a large and vociferous element—were not disposed to joke over the social board with the notorious man who trod upon their idols. They hated and despised Paine as the political and spiritual Antichrist; and the pugnacious-tongued old man often played into their hands. Here is a typical incident, narrated by a clergyman's son, Beal Lewis, in a letter to his father. Young Lewis was on the stage-coach for New York which stopped early one November morning in 1804 at the post office in New Rochelle. The driver was asked whether he had room for another passenger. "Yes," he said, and turning his head into the coach whispered excitedly, "Tom Paine, as I am a sinner." Everybody within strained forward to catch a glimpse of "this *imp* of the *old fellow* with his big *iron claws.*" They saw an old man, wearing "an old threadbare surtout, a small wool hat, a very greasy pair of nankeen smallclothes, and a pair of woolen stockings—and, to give a finish to his dress, a pair of dirty old shoes slipshod, as we say, about his heels." Paine climbed up on the front seat with the driver. When they paused for breakfast at a tavern in East Chester, Paine immediately began washing his shoes in a wash-bowl on the piazza. One of the travelers, a Dr. Bell, asked Paine why he washed his shoes on such a cold morning, and everybody laughed and felt superior at Paine's answer, but Lewis does not give that answer. Maybe Paine was experimenting to improve on a scientific notion of his friend, Thomas Jefferson, who washed his feet every time he washed his hands in order to avoid colds. At breakfast, the American Revolution being

317

the topic, Paine discoursed about his own experiences and about various mistakes in generalship. When it dawned upon Lewis that the sacrosanct Washington was under attack, his blood throbbed and surged furiously within him. In fact, the young patriot felt almost equal to knocking the old defamer to the floor. Luckily the impulse passed. They returned to the coach and, after Paine found himself a minority of one in defense of President Jefferson, they rode along quietly for a while. Soon the other travelers began talking with loud approbation about various eulogies on the leader of Federalism, Alexander Hamilton, who had fallen a few months before in the duel with Burr. True to form, Paine turned and stuck his head into the coach to blurt out that the tributes to Hamilton were "rank nonsense," and that other writers gave an opposite impression of Hamilton's character. Lewis, taking the long-awaited cue, sat up straight and shouted that those writers could not injure Hamilton's reputation any more than Thomas Paine could destroy Washington's character "by writing letters filled with falsehoods." While the coach rattled with applause at this outburst, the old man spoke up, "Let me tell you I am that Thomas Paine." "Well, Sir," answered Lewis, "if the garment fits you, you are welcome to wear it." And a Mr. Clark—"who all the time seemed anxious to close in with him"—chimed in, "Mr. Lewis has expressed the opinion of every honest man from Maine to Georgia," and launched into a fifteen-minute tirade at the old fellow on the front seat. The author of *Common Sense* fell into a complete silence, and so the coach rolled into New York.

The overwhelming endorsement of Jefferson in the election of 1804 seemed to promise a cessation of partizan strife and a period of national peace and unity. In the serene after-

318

election days Paine made plans to settle permanently in New Rochelle. "As every thing of public affairs is now on a good ground," he wrote to Jefferson in January, "I shall do as I did after the War, remain a quiet spectator and attend now to my own affairs." On his three-hundred-acre farm amid green fields and placid horizons he would enjoy the retired life. Though not strong enough to engage in mechanical experiments, he could at least bring together his past writings, which he might conscientiously publish at a profit. Here, too, he would solve the Madame Bonneville problem. That lady, after having incurred expenses in Bordentown which annoyed the man who was trying to provide an inheritance for her children, had quit the dull village and come to New York, taking a room in the same boardinghouse where Paine stayed. Irritated by her inconsiderateness and concerned lest a false idea should spread about their relationship, Paine had refused to pay her board bill of thirty-five dollars, had been sued, had won the suit, and had then paid the bill. With the repentant Madame Bonneville as housekeeper and with George Derrick as caretaker, Paine moved in the late fall of 1804 to the farm, for which he now had a clear title-deed. He sold off a section for about $4,000. Having such an embarrassment of riches, he planned an addition to the house with a new kind of arched roof and a healthful open-air room, about which he corresponded with his amateur architect friend in the President's House.

In the same letter to President Jefferson in which he avowed his intention to become "a quiet spectator," his irrepressible public spirit roved imperiously over a wide gamut of topics, attacking religious bigotry, denouncing the slave trade and the British impressment of American sea-

319

men, urging American mediation in the blood-soaked troubles between San Domingo and France, recommending the gradual democratization of Louisiana and the encouragement of free immigrants instead of the extension of slavery, explaining the Pennsylvania system of redemption servants, discussing the relative aptitudes for colonization possessed by Germans, Scotch, Irish, and English, and sighing for the vigor of youth so that he might personally conduct settlers from Europe. This looks like a prologue to action, not an epilogue. And from his village retreat he wrote for the New York Republican papers new attacks on the Federalists, whose political system he described with caustic genius in *Letter VIII To the Citizens of the United States* as "similar to atheism with respect to religion, a *nominal nothing* without principles." There was ferment and unrest in the mind of Mr. Paine of New Rochelle.

And, alas, there was ferment and unrest in his household. Before the winter of 1804-05 had set in, the caretaker Derrick proved wasteful and inefficient and Paine discharged him. On Christmas Eve, as Paine was reading in his ground-floor study, some one crept up to the house and fired at him. The shot went through the window-sill and shattered the glass, but did not hurt Paine. Derrick was arrested and released on bond. No trial took place; perhaps the case against Derrick was weak, or perhaps, after the excitement subsided, Paine pitied him.

To maintain the extensive farm in good order was too great a task for a sixty-eight-year-old man who had never shown talent for anything but political and intellectual revolutions. Madame Bonneville was less than no help. New Rochelle bored her, Paine lived in a world of his own, she had expected something better from the illustrious writer than the job of housekeeper. In the summer of 1805 she returned in a huff to New York with her son Benjamin. "Mrs. Bonneville was an encumbrance upon me all the while she was here," Paine grumbled in a letter to his New York friend, John Fellows, in July, "for she would not do anything, not even make an apple dumplin for her own children." With her gone, maybe now he would have peace. "I am master of an empty house, or nearly so," he continued in the same letter, describing his rickety establishment. "I have six chairs, and a table, a straw-bed, a feather-bed, and a bag of straw for Thomas, a tea kettle, an iron pot, an iron baking pan, a frying pan, a grid-iron, cups, saucers, plates and dishes, knives and forks, two candlesticks and a pair of snuffers. I have a pair of fine oxen and an ox-cart, a good horse, a chair, and a one-horse cart, a cow, and a sow and nine pigs. When you come you must take such fare as you meet with, for I live upon tea, milk, fruit-pies, plain dumplins, and a piece of meat when I get it; but I live with that retirement and quiet that suit me." Sometimes he escaped the confusion and clutter of his estate by visiting or boarding with his neighbors, the Deans and the Bayeauxs. Frequently he sat in front of Mr. Pelton's general store, handing out cakes and candies to the children of the village, whom he loved with the large tenderness of a childless man; and they gathered about him with spontaneous affection.

There was another escape, sure and satisfying—high politics. Paine watched with great hopefulness the most stirring political development of 1805, the spontaneous mass movements throughout the States to democratize the State governments in the spirit of the Jeffersonian administration. The most spectacular battle was being waged in Pennsylvania, where under shelter of the State Constitution of 1790 an arbitrary régime had been imposed upon the people by life-tenure judges in connivance with the reactionary Governor McKean and an aristocratic Senate. The Pennsylvania radicals aimed to restore the Constitution of 1776, which provided for a single-house legislature and a governor without veto power. To this democratic movement the New Rochelle recluse, who had been one of the chief inspirers of the Constitution of 1776, contributed a vigorous fillip in June with a brief pamphlet, *To the Citizens of Pennsylvania on the Proposal for Calling a Convention*. But in the election of 1805, the Pennsylvania radicals and their proposal were defeated, Governor McKean nosing out the insurgent Simon Snyder.

From that electioneering document in the most energetic and heated Pennsylvania campaign in fifteen years, Paine could have drawn a considerable sum of money which few would have begrudged him. As usual, however, he gave it gratis. Duane published the pamphlet serially in *The Aurora* and separately at a very low price, "as Mr. Paine reserves no copyright." This was phenomenal generosity coming from a man increasingly distressed by financial anxieties.

Early in 1806 Paine accepted the invitation of William Carver, whom he had known many years before in Lewes, and moved to the home of that blacksmith-veterinarian on Cedar Street in New York. He brought with him a manuscript, *The Cause of Yellow Fever*, which traced that recurrent plague of eighteenth- and early nineteenth-century America to the filthy accumulations in the earth embankment of the wharves and recommended the construction of wharves on stone arches; its publication was favorably received by physicians and for once Jefferson enjoyed the luxury of praising an essay by Paine without fear of political consequences.

Living alone or boarding with the New Rochelle neighbors had not been good for the old man. He was in poor health, a condition which was not improved by his stay with the Carvers. One evening in July, as he was going up to bed, Paine was stricken with an apoplectic fit, fell down the stairs, and lay for a few moments unconscious. For nearly three weeks afterwards he was unable to get in or out of bed without being carried in a blanket by two persons. Mrs. Elihu Palmer, whose free-thinking husband had died a few months before, took a room with the Carvers and nursed Paine back to health.

Even in convalescence Paine would not indulge himself in pondering on his own condition. World affairs were too exciting, too much in need of great ideas and persuasions. Europe was ablaze from end to end with the Napoleonic Wars. After abandoning the invasion of England, Napoleon bowed to British naval supremacy in the encounter at Trafalgar in October, 1805; but he dominated the continent, knocking down by might of arms one age-encrusted monarchy after another, new-fashioning the social structure by the elimination of privileges, stirring vaguely remembered hopes in the hearts of democratic reformers if they could shut their eyes to his colossal despotism. Paine wished Napoleon success in a war to the finish with the Coalition headed by His Majesty's Government, the arch-enemy of all the ideals of the Revolution. In his conversation with John Melish, the English traveler who visited him in August of 1806, Paine endorsed the French side and declared that a peaceful settlement between England and France was impossible even though the implacable

323

Pitt was dead. "The war," he said, "must inevitably go on till the Government of England falls; for it is radically and systematically wrong, and altogether incompatible with the present state of society." Melish countered that a Whig administration was now in power and would probably repair all the mischief done by the Tories. Paine shook his head. He knew the English Government well, he said, and he was convinced that no man or set of men could ever be able to reform it; the system was wrong and would never be set right without a revolution, which was as certain as fate and at no great distance in time.

In the autumn of 1806 Paine went out to New Rochelle to vote. The election inspectors—Tories in the Revolution and Federalists under the Republic—had done some investigating in Paine's history. They informed him at the polling booth that the circumstances attending his imprisonment in the Luxembourg proved that he was not an American citizen. Paine protested vehemently, until he was threatened with arrest. After returning to New York, he wrote grievous letters to Vice President George Clinton, Secretary of State Madison, and others about this generation to whom the struggles of the Revolution meant nothing or less than nothing, and he tried to collect documents and testimonials to challenge the decision of the inspectors. But he never obtained a court verdict of citizenship. The ironic fact must be recorded that the great American advocate of an enlarged franchise everywhere was left without a vote in his own country.

From this experience Paine recoiled morbidly suspicious, tensely on guard against fresh insults and impositions—a mood in which ordinary living-together is extremely difficult. At the advice of a physician he moved from the Car vers' and became a guest of the celebrated artist, John Wesley Jarvis, on Church Street. Characteristically he had made no arrangement with Carver as to terms before entering his household. Carver had been so insistent in his invitation that Paine, always grateful for signs of friendship and respect, assumed there would be no charges. He put Carver down in his will and freely made purchases out of his own funds for the common stores of the family. Then suddenly, when living with Jarvis, Paine received a bill from Carver for one hundred and fifty dollars, including his own board and that of his nurse, Mrs. Palmer. To the touchy old man the bill itself seemed a shocking betrayal of friendship, and the amount exorbitant. He took Carver out of his will and hard words passed between the two before the charge was finally paid.

With the bon-vivant Jarvis Paine could have lived pleasantly enough, writing for the newspapers on political questions and reserving his religious views for friendly conversation since no journals would publish them. But the harpies of orthodoxy were flapping their wings over him. One afternoon, while Paine was taking his usual after-dinner nap, a very old woman came seeking him. Jarvis was about to send her away, but she was so old and wanted to see Paine so "very particularly" that Jarvis took her into the bedroom and woke Paine up. Paine rose on one elbow, and, glaring at the intruder, asked, "What do you want?" "Is your name Paine?" "Yes." "Well, then," she said, "I come from Almighty God to tell you, that if you do not repent of your sins, and believe in our blessed Saviour Jesus Christ, you will be damned, and—" "Poh, poh," he interrupted, "it is not true. You were not sent with any such impertinent message. Jarvis, make her go away. Pshaw, he

325

would not send such a foolish, ugly old woman as you about with his messages. Go away. Go back. Shut the door." The old woman raised both hands in horror and walked out in a speechless trance at this hard lesson in rational religion.

In the spring of 1807, as a reaffirmation of deism and a final test of religious belief in America, he selected a section of either his reply to the Bishop of Llandaff or Part Three of *The Age of Reason,* both of which he had brought in manuscript from Paris, and published it at his own expense as *Examination of the Prophecies.* The *Examination* takes up one reputed prophecy of Christ after another and demonstrates it to be either grossly inapplicable, or too generalized, or deliberately distorted, or in itself a record of past happenings rather than "a wild-goose chase into futurity." Throughout the pamphlet eloquently recurs the plea for intellectual adulthood and independence—"Ah, reader, put thy trust in thy creator, and thou wilt be safe; but if thou trustest to the book called the scriptures thou trustest to the rotten staff of fable and falsehood," "Man, in a state of groveling superstition from which he has not courage to rise, loses the energy of his mental powers," "HE THAT BELIEVES IN THE STORY OF CHRIST IS AN INFIDEL TO GOD." Anti-Christianity, however, was not and could not be made popular in America, and the clergy had ceased the custom of advertising it by rushing to the press or the pulpit with diatribes against Paine. The sale of the *Examination* was very slight.

If, as a missionary of natural religion, Paine cut no figure in American life in 1806-07, as a political journalist he stood forth in a final sunset glory. The European conflict had become the chief American problem. Both France and England wrought havoc with American commerce; but the American grievance against England was infinitely the greater, for England issued the first decrees against neutral trade, enforced them by the most powerful navy in the world, and yanked real and alleged deserters from His Majesty's Fleet off the decks of American merchant vessels. When Napoleon struck back in the fall of 1806 by declaring a blockade of England, the bulk of Americans, though averse to the Napoleonic despotism, hailed him as the God-appointed avenger on the arch-tyrant of the seas. Paine went with the stream of American interest, coinciding with his own fixed and primary hatred of the English government. "Bonaparte has done exactly what I would have done myself, with respect I mean to the present war, had I been in his place, which thank God I am not," he wrote in Cheetham's *American Citizen* on the 16th of December, 1806. "The opposers of Bonaparte," he continued, "say he is a usurper. The case is that all the kings in Europe are usurpers, and as to hereditary government it is a succession of usurpers."

Events in 1807 widened the breach between England and America, making the Napoleonic despotism continuously less odious in American eyes. Late in June the British frigate *Leopard* on a search for deserters fired three broadsides into the American frigate *Chesapeake;* three of the crew were killed and eighteen wounded. At news of this assault on the American flag the cry for war was shouted throughout the and with such furious unanimity as the independent republic had never known, not even in the XYZ Affair. "I say, 'Down with England,'" exclaimed the normally pacific-minded President Jefferson, "and as for what Bonaparte is then to do to us, let us trust to the chapter of accidents."

"Will There Be War?" asked Paine on the 15th of August in a series of articles in the New York *Public Advertiser*. England, he answered, will not declare war as long as she is permitted "at her own discretion, to search, capture, and condemn our vessels, control our commerce, impress our seamen, and fire upon and plunder our national ships." The question comes down to this: "Shall we make war on the English Government, as the English Government has made upon us; or shall we submit, as we have done, and that with long forbearance, to the evil of having war made upon us without reprisals?" Jefferson, however, his passion waning swifter than it had risen, hoped to avoid war even in the midst of war; he put his faith at this juncture in restrictions on British imports, in the spirit of Paine's Maritime Compact of 1800.

In carrying on the discussion in the newspapers Paine got into a rancorous controversy not of his own seeking with a man destined to vent his inhuman vindictiveness over Paine's dead body. Paine had transferred his contributions from Cheetham's *American Citizen* to a new Republican paper, the *Public Advertiser,* because he had been frequently irritated by Cheetham's revisions and alterations of his "testimonies" and because he suspected Cheetham of pro-British sympathies. Cheetham was in fact an unscrupulous and irresponsible adventurer with a newspaper, shifting his political allegiance from faction to faction as rapidly as the seasons, and in his short journalistic career sitting at least ten times in the defendant's chair in trials for slander and libel. In the summer of 1807 Paine suggested that the New York harbor might be protected by gunboats and a chain of narrow beams like the *chevaux de frise* in the American Revolution. Cheetham ridiculed the suggestion, advocated soli block obstructions, and with perfect irrelevance launched into a sweeping attack on Paine's conduct in the days of 1776; *Common Sense,* he declared with the gusto of an honest man catching a thief, copied Locke "idea for idea" and Paine did all his fighting with his pen "in a safe retreat." These nonsensical charges pierced the old man in a vulnerable spot, pride in his revolutionary career. He angrily replied that he had never read Locke and that Locke had not written for the American situation, that he had borne his share of dangers in the times that tried men's souls, and —after saying all this—that he would not degrade himself in order to engage in debate with the "ugly-tempered" Cheetham. Soon, however, they were at each other again, with President Jefferson an involuntary factor in the wrangle. On the 9th of October Jefferson wrote Paine a gloomy letter about the darkening national prospect. "All the little circumstances coming to our knowledge," he said, "are unfavorable to our wishes for peace." Paine mentioned Jefferson's view to some of his friends. When Cheetham got wind of this, he forthwith denounced Paine's assertion as the "drunken belchings" of "old pestilence." "Paine has told a lie," said Cheetham, denying that Jefferson had written such a letter. Paine demanded an apology and, when Cheetham contemptuously refused, Paine announced that he would bring "the unprincipled bully" to trial.

In December the Embargo Act, that ultimate measure of peaceable coercion, forbade the departure of all ships to foreign ports until the freedom of neutral commerce should be respected. For a brief season discussion and public excitement dropped off. Paine's thoughts were thrown back upon himself and he laid aside his resolution to prosecute Cheetham as he began to ponder moodily about money and fame. He was not facing immediate destitution, for he owned, besides an indeterminate small bank account, insurance stock worth about $1,500, and after his death Madame Bonneville sold only a part of the New Rochelle farm for nearly $4,000. But he was now a paying boarder at Mr. Hitt's in Broome Street, without a livelihood, with dwindling resources, with poor health, and with his pledge to the Bonneville children haunting him. And in the old age that yearns for an honorable close to life, the tired hero brooded on his lost franchise, on Cheetham's insults, on the apparent indifference of the Republic whose banner he had borne in the glamorous Revolution.

On the 21st of January, 1808, he sent a memorial to Congress requesting compensation for his work in the Laurens mission to France in 1781. In his heated imagination he gave himself nearly the entire credit for that venture from beginning to end; and, though definitely disclaiming any desire to be paid for his writings and other labors for the Revolution, he piled them helter-skelter into the memorial. "All the civilized world know," he said, "I have been of great service to the United States, and have generously given away talent that would have made me a fortune." This memorial was published in the newspapers; and while Republicans here and there drank toasts to the author of *Common Sense*—"He opened our eyes to our interests, may ingratitude never shut them upon his services"—his enemies made merry over the man who had lambasted pensioned writers and wanted to become one himself. In rising mortification and dismay Paine watched the days and weeks go by with no word from a Congress which perversely did not consider his petition the most pressing national business. On the 14th of February he wrote to the committee explaining that previous grants from Congress did not refer to the Laurens mission. On the 28th he insisted on a definite answer. On the 7th of March he asked with feeble bitterness whether the members of the committee were "of younger standing than 'the times that tried men's souls,'" and, losing the last shred of patience at the "unmanly policy" of burying his memorial, declared, "After so many years of service my heart grows cold towards America." This pathetic outcry should at least have shamed Congress into action; but Congress would not be hastened. The heartsick old man felt spurned and humiliated before the world by the official representatives of his own people.

Yet even with such rankling provocation Paine could not alienate himself from America. He could not by a mere act of the will put a period to his insatiable absorption in the great concerns of his fellow-men, an absorption that saved him time and again from protracted worry over personal difficulties—and made those difficulties inevitable. On the 8th of July, living shabbily in a tawdry lodging house on Partition Street, he picked up his pen to inquire of President Jefferson what he had done about the memorial. After a surprisingly brief and temperate inquiry Paine hurried on "from this disagreeable affair to what I like much better—public affairs." Since England was losing revenue as a result of the Embargo, he suggested that the British Ministry would probably "be glad to tread back their steps, if they could do it without too much exposing their ignorance and obstinacy" and that the mediation of America might achieve the rescinding of both British and French objectionable decrees. In this letter, perhaps the last one extant by Paine, the words were indistinctly shaped and the paper profusely blot-stained by a trembling pen, but the mind was as clear and sharp as ever and the ending characteristic and loyal, "Yours in friendship." On the 17th Jefferson, disregarding his recent embarrassment in the Paine-Cheetham newspaper rumpus, replied. He could not substantiate Paine's memorial, he regretted, because he had been occupied in Virginia during most of the Revolution. "Your ideas expressed in the latter part of your letter are undoubtedly correct," he said, and closed with "salutations and assurances of great esteem and respect." So Paine and Jefferson—"the two mad Toms"—exchanged thoughts for the last time.

In the summer of 1808 Paine moved into the home of Mr. Ryder on Herring Street in Greenwich Village, which consisted of a few straggly houses in the wild country a mile or two north of the city proper. The drama of life and high enterprise was closing. After August he wrote no more articles on current issues. But his interest in them did not abate; he took in and read the newspapers and when ill had them read to him, and he dominated political conversations with his visitors over the social glass of rum and water. On religion he had developed a proud reserve towards strangers, especially towards Christian missionaries. To them he would say, "My opinions are before the world, and all have had an opportunity to refute them if they can; I believe them unanswerable truths, and that I have done great service to mankind by boldly putting them forth; I do not wish to argue upon the subject; I have labored disinterestedly in the cause of truth." When he had no visitors, he would sit quietly reading in his room on the first floor, his left arm crooked on the table to support his chin and his right arm resting on the book or newspaper before him. Nearby was a decanter of rum or brandy, out of which he poured a drink now and then. The house was situated between streets named Columbia and Reason, and the ailing man may have mused in solitary moments in the dead silence on what, between the two, he had won after all of life's struggle.

On the 1st of February, 1809, more than a year after Paine had presented his petition, the Committee of Claims recommended that it be rejected. In strict legality the Committee could do nothing else, for Paine's connection with the Laurens mission had been unofficial, he had presented no substantiating papers, and John Laurens, the only man whose word might bear weight, had been dead more than twenty-five years. The report was, however, a crushing blow to an old patriot who considered himself above strict legality and who felt that his days were numbered. There was balm in Congressman Matthew Lyon's denunciation of the Committee for its pettifogging treatment of "the man to whom this nation is indebted for its independence more than to any living being," and in the constant filial devotion of the *Public Advertiser,* which placed Paine "in the foremost rank of the patriots and sages of our time."

Yet these things, if they comforted, could not heal. Paine was breaking up. His heart was weakening, his appetite gone, he could not move without assistance. At the ministrations of the Ryder family he was exhibiting the pathetic irritability of the hopelessly sick. Madame Bonneville, now a French tutor in New York, having made her peace with Paine, came out to see him twice a week. It did not seem enough. "I am here all alone," he complained to her, "for all these people are nothing to me, day after day, week after week, month after month, and you don't come to see me." In May, sacrificing herself to him for once, she took a house

333

in the neighborhood and he was carried into it in an arm-chair. Here he lay down and resigned himself to the end which he knew was not far off.

But Paine was not permitted to die decently. What he had feared came to pass. When the news of his impending death spread to the city, pious fanatics gloatingly picked up the cross to bring it to the great unbeliever in Greenwich Village. They invaded the room where he lay coughing, retching, and groaning in dropsical torment, and set to wrestling with him for his soul. A Methodist clergyman declared with uplifted hands that unless he repented of his unbelief he would be damned. Sick as he was, Paine rose angrily in bed to say that if he had the strength he would put the impertinent intruder forcibly out of the room. Two Presbyterian clergymen came, and one of them intoned to the suffering patient, "You have now a full view of death, you cannot live long, and whosoever does not believe in Jesus Christ will assuredly be damned." "Let me have none of your popish stuff," Paine shouted. "Get away with you. Good morning, good morning." When they finally left, he begged Mrs. Hedden, the housekeeper, "Don't let 'em come here again, they trouble me." The faithful Pres-byterians returned to the siege and Mrs. Hedden, a pious woman herself, refused them admittance, saying that if God did not change his mind, no human power could. Paine kept his wits almost to the very end. Hearing the voice of his physician, Dr. Romayne, he roused himself to speak. " 'Tis you, Doctor. What news?" "Mr. such an one [Madame Bonneville, who tells the story, did not catch the name] is gone to France on such business." "He will do nothing there," said Paine. "Your belly diminishes," said the Doc-tor. "And yours augments," Paine replied to the enormously corpulent Romayne. On the 7th of June, the night before his death, Madame Bonneville bent over to ask whether he was satisfied with the treatment in her house. "Oh, yes," he mumbled, and went off into delirious incoherence. Perhaps he was babbling of the Republic of the World, of the grand old times that tried men's souls, of Jehovah and Moses and Robespierre, of cruel men and their cruel God, and of the unco guid who crowed over him on the brink of the eternal. He lapsed into a coma, and in the morning he was dead.

Paine had hoped, with the sentimentality of the dying, that he might be buried in the Quaker cemetery with the simple rites of that fellowship in which he had been born and of which he had always spoken kindly; but the Quakers refused him. To the other Christian sects he would not apply. On the day after his death Madame Bonneville conducted the funeral. Before the coffin was lifted into the carriage, she put a rose upon the bosom of the dead man. With hardly a coachful of mourners, including, it is said, a Quaker and two Negroes, the cortege moved to the interment at New Rochelle. There, on an open and uncultivated corner of his farm, which Paine had himself selected, the coffin was lowered into the ground. The few spectators standing speechless by, Madame Bonneville put her son Benjamin at one side of the grave and she stood at the other, and as the dirt fell heavy on the coffin she cried, "Oh! Mr. Paine! My son stands here as testimony of the gratitude of America, and I, for France!" A week later, according to the instructions in his will, she set up a headstone bearing the inscription with which the dead American appealed through the ages to the grateful memory of his fellow-citizens: "Thomas Paine, Author of Common Sense, died the eighth of June, 1809, aged 72 years."

Four months later James Cheetham's *Life of Paine* was published. It is the chief source book for all those who hate Paine's principles and prefer in defiance of the most elementary justice to think the worst of him. In disgrace with the Republicans, the envenomed Cheetham had turned to a task for which in common decency he was the most unsuited person on the face of the planet—a biography of the man with whom he had lately exchanged words of blazing hatred. For an American public, the "biographer" somewhat restrained himself in dealing with Paine's career in the American Revolution; in other matters he laid on the calumnies with a large and free hand. He did not glut his malice by labeling Paine "a robustious anarchist," "a hypocrite," "a base trembling slave," "an enormous sinner," and finally "a little old man, broken down by intemperance, and utterly disregardful of personal cleanliness"—vicious falsehoods masquerading as historic record. He also called Paine Madame Bonneville's "paramour" and said that of the Bonneville children *"Thomas* has the features, countenance, and temper of Paine." The dead man could not defend himself, but Madame Bonneville could; she haled Cheetham into court on a charge to which he was habituated—slander. Jarvis, Mrs. Ryder, Mrs. Dean, Pelton, Foster, and others gave the lie to Cheetham in court and even Carver disappointed him. The jury found Cheetham guilty, but Judge Hoffman assessed a fine of only $150 including costs because the slanderous book "tended to serve the cause of religion."

In the grave there was no peace or dignity for what was left of Thomas Paine. Curiosity-seekers tore away branches of the cypresses and weeping willows which Madame Bonneville had planted, and they even hacked off bits of the tombstone to decorate their mantelpieces. In 1819 William Cobbett, formerly a vilifier and now an enthusiast, committed the final atrocity, digging up the defenseless bones and shipping them to England. He planned to exhibit the relics in monster pageants throughout the chief industrial towns, thereby to effect the reformation of Church and State; but the Government refused to permit such spectacles. The bones passed from one obscure place to another, and so out of sight of history.

"As to his bones," wrote Moncure Daniel Conway, that great pioneer of Paine study, "no man knows the place of their rest to this day. His principles rest not. His thoughts, untraceable like his dust, are blown about the world which he held in his heart."

Paine was born into a momentous period of human history, when whole peoples threw off the bondage of the aristocratic order and took up arms for freedom. Of the fundamental dreams and the revolutionary logic of the millions he became the most eloquent, most sustained, most disinterested voice. The triumphs and the defeats of the Revolution are pictured in the long trajectory of his public life, and the spirit of the Revolution lives in his writings. The warfare between aristocracy and democracy continued far into the nineteenth century, and was complicated and finally overshadowed by the growth of new forms of oppression which looked for their justification to the ideals of the great revolutionary epoch. The Edmund Burkes of the twentieth century speak in the phrases of Thomas Paine. But he was not of them. He dedicated himself to the vision of a world of free men, free in body, free in mind; and the

337

definition of freedom changes with the changing tyrannies. The career of Thomas Paine therefore cannot be regarded as a story that is told. It will stand on the mountains of history, an inspiration and a challenge as long as any form of slavery shackles the human race.